PENRIC'S PROGRESS

BOOKS by LOIS McMASTER BUJOLD

The Vorkosigan Saga
Shards of Honor • Barrayar
The Warrior's Apprentice • The Vor Game
Cetaganda • Borders of Infinity
Brothers in Arms • Mirror Dance
Memory • Komarr
A Civil Campaign • Diplomatic Immunity
Captain Vorpatril's Alliance • Cryoburn
Gentleman Jole and the Red Queen

Falling Free • Ethan of Athos

Omnibus Editions
Miles, Mystery & Mayhem • Miles, Mutants & Microbes

World of the Five Gods
The Curse of Chalion • Paladin of Souls
The Hallowed Hunt
Penric's Progress • Penric's Travels (forthcoming)

The Sharing Knife Tetralogy
Volume 1: Beguilement • Volume 2: Legacy
Volume 3: Passage • Volume 4: Horizon

The Spirit Ring

ALSO AVAILABLE FROM BAEN BOOKS
The Vorkosigan Companion,
edited by Lillian Stewart Carl and John Helfers

To purchase Baen titles in e-book form, please go to www.baen.com.

PENRIC'S PROGRESS

by

LOIS McMASTER BUJOLD

PENRIC'S PROGRESS

Introduction copyright © 2020 by Lois McMaster Bujold, "Penric's Demon"
copyright © 2015 by Lois McMaster Bujold, "Penric and the Shaman"
copyright © 2016 by Lois McMaster Bujold, "Penric's Fox" copyright © 2017
by Lois McMaster Bujold

A Baen Books Original

Baen Publishing Enterprises
P.O. Box 1403
Riverdale, NY 10471
www.baen.com

ISBN: 978-1-9821-2429-8

Cover art by Dan dos Santos

First printing, January 2020

Distributed by Simon & Schuster
1230 Avenue of the Americas
New York, NY 10020

Library of Congress Cataloging-in-Publication Data

Names: Bujold, Lois McMaster, author.
Title: Penric's progress / by Lois McMaster Bujold.
Description: Riverdale, NY : Baen Books, [2020] | Series: World of five
  gods
Identifiers: LCCN 2019040449 | ISBN 9781982124298 (hardcover)
Subjects: GSAFD: Fantasy fiction.
Classification: LCC PS3552.U397 P46 2020 | DDC 813/.54--dc23
LC record available at https://lccn.loc.gov/2019040449

Printed in the United States of America

10 9 8 7 6 5 4 3 2 1

CONTENTS

INTRODUCTION

THE FIRST THING new readers who have picked up *Penric's Progress* need to know is that it doesn't require them to have read any other of its series-sibling books, or indeed any other Bujold work, before diving in. The book itself will teach you how to read it.

The Penric & Desdemona novellas were written to be stand-alones, fresh entry points for a still-growing fantasy series that has come to be dubbed *The World of the Five Gods*. The present collection of three tales (all previously appearing separately, but only as e-editions or limited deluxe hardcovers) starts with "Penric's Demon," Penric kin Jurald's very first adventure as written, as published, and in his internal chronology, so pretty inescapably first.

For a quick overview of all my stories and how they relate to one another, I've provided a reading-order guide at the end of this volume. For this novella collection, the chronological arranging has been done for you.

So from my point of view, the ideal reader should now put down this introduction and turn to the start of the actual story, spoiler-free. Come back later; these words will wait, and the leisurely chat that follows will make more sense in context.

❖ ❖ ❖

My books, and my series, tend to grow organically, rather than being bolted to some grand over-arching plan. I have to write my way into a story in order to find out what happens, and along that road find opportunities for invention and surprise that could never have occurred on day and page one. I can't create in a vacuum, of course. Research reading and viewing (in the broadest sense) plus the general pool of my life experiences come first. From that, story notions will begin to coalesce in my mind and link up with each other, working toward some critical mass, but nothing happens until I glimpse and then grasp characters that interest me; in seed form, to be sure, but with their genetics set. It is also possible for me to begin with settings, plots, or themes, and lay in the other elements as needed, but mostly my characters generate their worlds.

Characters can't grow in a vacuum either, but must be created by their actions as they move through their tales. So setting, character, and plot are all tightly interlinked in a connected circle. When that wheel starts rolling, story happens. For a novel I will typically produce maybe fifty pages of hand-written notes on all aspects of the proposed piece, until Scene One come glimmering up out of the fog. Once gripped, the first link of the chain begins to pull up the rest into view scene-by-scene, each completed section both constraining and changing the possibilities for the next, in a sort of continuous-flow creative process.

As far as settings go, and risking the hazards of revealing how sausages are made, I often use real places and historical events much the way working artists use reference photos when arranging their compositions; not because I am trying to draw a portrait of the model, but as a quick way to get proportions and perspectives right for a coming overlay pursuing quite another purpose. Readers who try to process the result as portraiture—either as historical fiction with the serial numbers filed off, or as historical critique—are using inappropriate viewing protocols for this style of composition. Attempts to draw exact one-to-one correspondences between my impressionist fiction and history thus naturally tend to go awry. Granted, spot-the-references can be a fun game, especially if it leads to more reading.

One of the side-effects of my methods is that I tend to resist naming my series—coming up with book titles is hard enough—until well into them. This results in the fans naming them for me. "The Vorkosiverse" is not what I would have titled the science fiction series centering around the planet Barrayar, nor even "The Miles Vorkosigan Stories." I might have picked something to do with its wider space-setting of the wormhole nexus, but "wormhole" is kind of an ugly word, so I dragged my feet. Thirty-something years in, I've still never given the set of, by accretion, seventeen books and a few stray novellas a name, but it says "The Vorkosigan Saga" on my first Hugo award for best series, so I guess that's official now.

My more recent fantasy work was similarly slow to grow its series title. First, it was just one book, *The Curse of Chalion*, written, and published by HarperCollins, around the turn of the millennium. It spawned a sequel, the way books do, taking up some unfinished business with a key minor character who quickly grew into a major one with her own themes in *Paladin of Souls*. From its setting and the needs of marketing, this was dubbed "The Chalion Series."

By this time, I was thinking about a series connected not by continuing action, but by a thematic pattern or template of one book for each of my world's five gods, a grand over-arching plan at last. (Turns out that trick never works, at least not for me, but I had *intentions*.) Inspired and informed by my history research reading, I went off in a different direction with the third book, back almost three hundred years in time and over to another realm, god-of-focus, local system of magics, and new cast of characters for what became *The Hallowed Hunt*. This took aback a lot of readers who plunged into it expecting a standard series development of their favorites from the first two books. So the third "Chalion" book had nothing to do with the country of Chalion, which created a conundrum. The fans started dubbing it "the 5GU" for the five-gods universe, which sounded like some kind of computer part to me.

Then the series and the grand-plan notion foundered on my general disinclination to write books for the two remaining gods, and I turned instead to what became the tetralogy *The Sharing Knife*, which also permitted me to explore yet another series structure, the one-tale-in-multiple-volumes. That one was named early and officially. And after that I returned to some unfinished business with the Vorkosigan saga, which eventually turned into three more books and one trailing novella.

The last novel, which eventually became *Gentleman Jole and the Red Queen*, had stalled out in the middle due to a combination of life issues—house moves and major surgery are both very distracting, it turns out—and the stubborn refusal of the material to be dragged into any kind of expected action-adventure genre template. Some writers talk about characters running away with their story. Mine go on sit-down strikes. We were at loggerheads for a long time, as I could neither abandon the project midway nor, apparently, write anything else till it was finished. I finally said rude words to myself, and wrote it as it wanted to be. Much better.

I had by that time reached retirement age—not that writers stop until tackled to the ground; I have a theory that writing fiction is actually a dissociative disorder—so, having no one else to do it, I discharged myself from the working army. I decided to re-compose my career ala carte, taking only the parts I enjoyed onto my plate and leaving the stressful bits on the table. (The first thing to go was travel and public speaking. This entailed learning to say "No" to nice people who like me, which is not easy. Keeping tax records alas continues to death and beyond.)

Having had good experiences by this time with e-book reprints of my older material, I was also keenly interested in what would happen if I tried an original piece as an indie e-pub. I also wanted to write something *shorter*. I also hankered for the fun of writing about a really powerful magician of some sort.

And I had also had recent experience with the beneficial results of tossing out rigid templates. If the plan of five novels was *preventing* me from writing more in the world of Chalion, it obviously was not serving me anymore, nor my readers.

All these alsos came together in the somewhat unexpected person of Penric.

My first inner vision was of an older Penric. Not wishing to make extra work for myself, because, semi-retired!, though mostly because there were a lot of implications about magic hinted at but left under-explored in the prior Chalion books, I settled him into that fictional universe, where he immediately put down roots. With that choice, a great many aspects of his magic and how it could work—and, importantly for drama, be constrained—slotted right in.

This also gave occasion to rename the series to something having a wider scope, so, taking direction from the fans, it became "The World of the Five Gods." A little unwieldy, but flexible and informative, so I think it will stick henceforth. It's now engraved on my second Hugo for best series, so is set in, if not stone, metal.

I immediately knew I wanted to fit Penric's possibilities into novellas. It was a form familiar from my youthful reading, not only from magazines, but from the old Ace Doubles, which used to present two novellas, each too short for a proper paperback, glued back-to-back to make up market weight, and also from several much-beloved fix-up collections. These latter models included John Brunner's *The Traveller in Black*, Roger Zelazny's *Lord of Light*, and Fritz Leiber's tales of Fafhrd and the Gray Mouser, not to mention a lot of Sherlock Holmes, among many others. By this early imprinting, I associated novellas with grand adventure, but *wait*, there's *more . . .* all kinds of story-aspects that novellas, swift and light on their feet, can take on.

I actually wrote my very first novella, "The Borders of Infinity," back in 1986 for a Baen invitational anthology called *Free Lancers*, which introduced me to the pleasures and advantages of the form from the writer's side. I'd already captured ideas for that Miles story in penciled notes, but they'd just sat fallow, obviously failing to be novel-length. Here was a chance to write the tale at exactly the length it wanted to be. Without subplots, it had the exhilaration of speeding down a freeway with no exits: one subject, tight scope, less getting mired in the middle.

The arrival of e-books as a publishing medium blew open the market for the length and likewise for subject matter, formerly constricted to a very few paper magazine slots with limited editorial needs. E-novellas gave Penric a place to go, and their ala carte publication offered great flexibility for series content, sequence, setting, production—everything. Like trading a straitjacket for wings.

Various disconnected scenes from my sorcerer's possible future life sloshed around in my imagination for a while, while I focused in on some more directed research reading. I eventually decided to wind him back and begin him at his beginning, when he first contracted his magic as a naïve and earnest young man.

In the world of the five gods, magical powers are not inborn but obtained, by—among other methods—acquiring a chaos demon, an invisible bodiless entity stemming ultimately from the fifth god, known as the Bastard in His holy family. This led me to the need to make up the character of the demon, which, in this system, opened up a huge range of possibilities, since demons, all beginning as identical blobs of escaped chaos, learn their diverse personalities from the succession of sorcerers they symbiotically inhabit over, potentially, many lives. This also, to my vast amusement, gave me the chance to combine the fetching young male protagonist beloved by the market with the cranky older woman so familiar from the inside of my own head.

But the reader can better learn all about what came of that beginning just as I did, by starting at page one and going on.

Ta, L.

July 2019

PENRIC'S
PROGRESS

PENRIC'S DEMON

PENRIC'S DEMON

THE MORNING LIGHT sloped across the meadows, breathing pale green into the interlaced branches of the woods beyond, picking out shy pink and white blossoms here and there among the new leaves. The spring air hung soft with promise. Penric's mother, before she had gone off in the wagon with his sisters to oversee the final preparations, had turned her face to the cool blue sky and declared it a perfect day for a betrothal; surely the gods were smiling upon the House of Jurald at last! Penric had refrained from pointing out that the learned divines taught that the gods did not control the weather, and been rewarded for this filial forbearance with a sharp maternal injunction to hurry up, finish dressing, and follow! This was no time to be dragging his feet!

Penric stared glumly between his horse's bobbing ears and reflected that it would have been an even better day to go fishing. Not the most exciting pastime, but it was the one thing he'd ever found to do that made people stop *talking* at him. He tried to imagine the muddy, winding road going somewhere less familiar than Greenwell Town. He supposed it actually did, if you followed it far enough. As his elder brother Drovo had done? Not a happy thought.

He frowned down at the brown sleeves of his jacket, laced with orange and gold-colored thread betraying a brassy tarnish. Even for this, he was still wearing hand-me-downs. The fine suit had been new when Drovo had first worn it at age thirteen for his oath to the militant Son's Order as a page-dedicat; not just as customary for his sex and age and rank, but true to his boisterous heart, Penric fancied. Drovo had outgrown the garb too swiftly for it to become much frayed or patched. Pulled out of a storage chest reeking of camphor, it had been fitted to the nineteen-year-old Penric merely by stealing a little fabric from the shoulders to lengthen the legs of the trousers. He tried to encourage himself with the thought that at least he wasn't wearing hand-me-downs from his *sisters*, except that he was fairly sure the linen shirt, shabby and soft, under the jacket had once been a blouson.

Well, Drovo wouldn't be outgrowing any more clothes now.

His death last year in Adria, of a camp fever before he'd even had a chance to help lose his mercenary company's first battle, had been the second mortal disaster to befall the family in four years. The first had been the death of their father, of a swift infection in the jaw following a neglected abscess of a tooth. They'd all missed the jovial Lord of Jurald, if not, perhaps, his drinking and gambling. Penric's eldest brother Lord Rolsch had seemed a soberer hand on the helm, if only he hadn't been such a gull for every pious beggar, whether in rags or Temple robes, to come down the pike. And if the Lords of Jurald hadn't ruled over a local peasantry whose main pastimes seemed to be archery, poaching, and tax evasion. So Drovo had taken his oath-money from the company recruiter, spent it in equipping himself, and gone off to the wars beyond the mountains, cheerily promising to come back rich with spoils to repair the family fortunes.

At least his fate had cured the clan of urging Penric to do the same . . .

Not that he'd ever been tempted. One rowdy Drovo had been enough to make Pen's youth a misery; camp life with a whole company of like-minded bruisers was a nightmare in prospect. And that was before one even got to the grim battles.

"Pick up the pace, Little Pen," his groom, Gans, advised him in the familiar terms of his childhood. "I shouldn't like to hear it if I deliver you late."

"Nor I," Pen sighed agreement, and they kicked their horses into a trot.

Pen tried to drag his thoughts into a sunnier mode, matching the morning. The bed of the daughter of a rich cheese merchant certainly made a more attractive arena in which to try to better his lot than the battlegrounds of the north. Preita was as nice and round as the purse she came with. He wondered if she understood what a hollowed-out lordly title her family was buying for her. The three times they'd been allowed to meet, strictly chaperoned, she had seemed a trifle dubious about it all, if tolerably pleased in turn with Pen's appearance. Shyness, or shrewdness? Pen's sister-in-law Lady Jurald had found and fostered the match, through some connection with Preita's mother. Well, presumably the girl's parents understood what they were purchasing. It would be up to Pen to make sure she did not regret the bargain.

How hard could husbanding be? *Don't drink, don't gamble, don't bring hunting dogs to the table. Don't be terrified of tooth-drawers. Don't be stupid about money. Don't go for a soldier. No hitting girls.* He wasn't drawn to violate any of these prohibitions. Assuming older sisters weren't classified as girls. Maybe make that, No hitting girls *first.*

Perhaps, once he had secured his bride and her dowry, he might persuade her to move somewhere farther down the road? Pen imagined a cottage by a lake, with no servants he had not hired himself. But Preita seemed quite devoted to her own family. And neither half of the couple was likely to enjoy more than a modest allowance before Pen reached his majority. Until then, the purse strings would remain in Rolsch's hands. Who was unlikely to be persuaded, while there was still room at Jurald Court, to part with unnecessary expenses for housing not under his fraternal eye. And Pen was fairly sure Preita hadn't thought she was signing up for life in a cottage. Which would probably be given to damp, anyway.

Do your best, Pen told himself firmly as they turned onto the main road to Greenwell, and then, his head coming up, *What's this?*

An odd collection of horses and figures was halted on the verge.

A man with a badge pinning jaunty blue-and-white feathers on his hat, marking him as of the Daughter's Order, held four restive horses. The weapons of a Temple guardsman hung at his belt. A second guardsman and a woman in a superior sort of servant's garb knelt by a figure laid out supine on a spread cloak. Had a rider in the party been thrown? Pen pulled his horse to a halt.

"Is someone hurt here?" he called. The supine figure, he saw at closer range, was a slight, elderly woman, gray-haired and gray-faced, in a muddle of robes of no particular colors. "Do you need help?"

The second guardsman rose and turned eagerly to him. "Young sir! Do you know how far it is to the next town, and do they have physicians of the Mother there?"

"Yes, Greenwell; not five miles up the road you're on," said Pen, pointing. "The Mother's Order keeps a hospice there."

The guardsman took the reins of three of their mounts from his fellow, and clapped him on the shoulder. "Go; ride for help. Get a litter—better, a wagon." The man nodded and sprang to his saddle, wheeled, and smacked his heels to his horse's flanks. It galloped off in a spray of dirt clods.

Pen dismounted and handed his own reins up to Gans, who stared at the scene in doubt. The middle-aged woman took in Pen's neat, pious brown suit, and seemed to grow less wary. "Divine Ruchia has taken suddenly ill on the road," she said, gesturing to the older woman, who lay breathing in short gasps. "She was struck by a great pain in her chest, and fell."

"Oh, I was taken ill long before that," the old woman commented between huffs. "I lingered too long in Darthaca . . . *Told* the fools to bring the ceremony to me."

Torn between curiosity, concern, and a reflection that if he'd left for town earlier as he'd been charged, he could have avoided all this, Pen lowered himself to the old woman's side. Cautiously, he felt her forehead, as his mother had used to do for him; her skin seemed clammy, not feverish. He had not the first notion of what to do for her, but it seemed wrong to just remount and ride away, for all that Gans was now glaring in tight-lipped worry.

"I am Lord Penric of kin Jurald, barons in this valley," he told her, gesturing back to the road they'd come from. He wasn't sure what to say next. She seemed most in authority here, but surely least able to command, in her current distressed state. Her cloak slipped off her shoulder, revealing Temple braids pinned there marking a divine—not in the green and gold of the Mother of Summer, as he would have expected, or perhaps the blue and white of the Daughter of Spring, but the white, cream, and silver of the Bastard, the fifth god, master of all disasters out of season. He gulped, swallowing his surprise.

She wheezed a short laugh and stirred, lifting a claw-like hand to his face. "Pretty boy. There's a better last sight than scowling Marda. Gift of sorts. But those colors don't suit you, you know."

He raised his head to the servant woman who, as he'd knelt, had retreated. "Is she delirious?"

The servant shook her head. "Can't tell, can I? She's been

spouting things no one else understands since I was assigned to ride with her."

The old woman's lips twitched back. "Really?" she said. She did not seem to be addressing Marda. Or Penric. "*That* will throw the fools into a tizzy." She fought for another breath. "Illogical to wish to see it, I suppose."

Increasingly frightened, and feeling quite stupid and helpless, Pen tried: "Let me serve you in your need, Learned."

She stared intently up at him for two more disrupted breaths, then wheezed, "Accepted."

She's dying. Cold, slick, not like the fevered heat and stink of his father's deathbed, but the advancing pallor was unmistakable. He wanted nothing so much as to run away, but her hand, falling back from his face, found his and gripped it weakly. He wasn't enough something—cowardly, brave?—to shake it off. Both the servant and the guardsman, he saw out of the corner of his eye, were hastily backing away. *What?*

"Lord Bastard," she breathed. "Y'r doorway *hurts.* 'D think y' could arrange things better f'yr servants . . . "

If all he could do was hold her hand, Pen decided in desperation, well, that was what he would do. His grip tightened.

For a moment, her brown eyes seemed to flash with a deep violet light. Then, between one breath and . . . none, her eyes went dull and still.

No one was looking back at him now.

He heard a confusion of women's voices babbling in half-a-dozen languages, most of which he didn't recognize, crying out in terror and pain. His head, throbbing with tension, seemed to explode in a thick, tangled net of lightning, all white.

Then all black.

Strange dreams scattered as Penric woke to a fierce headache, a raging thirst, and a desperate need to piss. He was in a bed in a small chamber, high up under the eaves judging by the slope of the whitewashed ceiling. He wore only his shirt and trews. As he stirred and groaned, an unfamiliar face appeared over him. Pen was not quite reassured to see the man wore the green tunic of a dedicat of the Mother's Order. A few minutes of bustle followed as the man helped him to a chamber pot, then drew him back from the window where Pen tried to put his head out. By his glimpse of the street and the sky, he was in Greenwell Town, probably at the Mother's hospice. Still morning, so maybe he wasn't so *very* laggard? At the dedicat's urging Pen reeled back into the bed and negotiated for a cup of water, which left him with only the headache and a vast confusion.

"How did I come here? I was on the road. Did I faint? Where is my suit?" He'd better not have lost or ruined the suit. Not to mention his good boots, also missing. "There was this sick old woman—a divine—"

"I will fetch Learned Lurenz," the dedicat told him. "Don't move!"

The man hurried out. Muffled voices sounded from the hallway, then steps thumping away. Pen spotted his suit, folded neatly atop a chest, with his boots beside it, which relieved him of one worry. He squeezed his eyes open and shut, and sat up to help himself to another cup of water. He was trying to decide if he could stagger across the room to retrieve his clothes when footsteps tapped once more, and he hurriedly tucked himself back under the sheets as instructed.

Without knocking, there entered tall, skinny Learned Lurenz, the Greenwell Town Temple's chief divine; reassuringly recognizable, alarmingly tense. He bent over Pen as if about to feel his forehead, but then drew back his hand. "Which are you?" he demanded of Pen.

Pen blinked, starting to wonder if he had fallen not ill, but into some bard's tale. "Learned Lurenz, you know me! Penric kin Jurald— you taught me arithmetic and geography—you used to pop me on the head with your stick for inattention." Hard enough to sting, too. That had been a decade ago, before the divine had been promoted to his present position. Lurenz was a long-time devotee of the Father of Winter, though as senior divine he supervised all five holy houses now. The growing city was angling for an archdivineship to be established here, Rolsch had said; Pen supposed Lurenz hoped for the promotion.

"Ah." Lurenz let out a sigh of relief, straightening up. "We are not too late, then."

"I'd better not be! Mother and Rolsch will be peeved, I can tell you. No idea what poor Preita will think, either. Where is Gans?"

"Lord Penric," said Learned Lurenz in his stern voice, as if about to ask Pen to recite the major rivers of Darthaca, "what do you remember of yesterday?"

Pen squeezed his eyes shut and open again. They still throbbed. "Yesterday? There was nothing special about yesterday, except for Mother and my sister fussing about the fit of that stupid suit. They wouldn't let me go riding."

They stared at each other in a moment of mutual incomprehension. Then Lurenz muttered "Ah!" again, and continued, "On the road. You were riding into town with Gans, and you came upon the party of Learned Ruchia . . . ? She was lying ill on the ground?"

"Oh! That poor old woman, yes. Did she really die?"

"I'm afraid so." Lurenz signed himself, touching forehead, lips, navel, groin, and spreading his hand briefly over heart, Daughter-Bastard-Mother-Father-Son, tally of the five gods. "We brought her body to lie in the Bastard's orphanage here, awaiting burial, and some resolution to this tangle."

"What tangle?" asked Pen, getting a sinking feeling in his stomach to add to his headache.

"Lord Pen"—the nickname was oddly steadying—maybe he wasn't in *too* much trouble yet?—"tell me everything you remember about your encounter with Learned Ruchia, and how you came to, ah, swoon. Every detail." Lurenz pulled up a stool to the bedside and sat, suggesting that he did not mean Pen to stint on the tale.

Pen described the events, together with what everyone had said as exactly as he could recall, strange as it had been, in case it was important—he didn't have to cast his mind back very far, after all. He hesitated before mentioning the violet light and the babbling voices, because it made it sound as if he'd been seeing things, but finally put them in, too. "But what did she mean by saying *Accepted*? Not that you expect someone who's busy dying to make a lot of sense, but she sounded pretty definite. And, really, I don't like to say it, but her servants didn't seem very loyal. Or"—a horrible new thought—"had she some contagion?" He rubbed the hand that had gripped hers surreptitiously on the sheet.

"A contagion to be sure, but not a disease," sighed Lurenz, sitting up from his intent crouch. He frowned at Pen in a very unsettling fashion. "Did you realize she was a Temple sorceress?"

"What?" Pen gaped.

"A very senior one, I am given to understand, bearing a demon of great power. She was on her way to her Order's main house in

Martensbridge, to make some report, and seek aid in her illness for, for handling the creature. Or handing it on, in the event of her death. The Bastard's people have some rituals to control this procedure, with which I am, ah, not familiar. Not exactly my god."

The sinking feeling was turning into a stone. "I've never met a sorcerer before." A choking arose in his throat, and without his volition his mouth added, "Well, now you are one, blue-eyed boy!" The tart cadences of the dying divine seemed to echo in the words; then the choking feeling slid back, as if the effort had exhausted it. He clapped his hand over his mouth and stared at Lurenz in terror. "I didn't say that!"

Lurenz had jerked back, glaring. "You had better not be trying on some jape, boy!"

Pen shook his head violently, suddenly afraid to speak.

Low voices from the hallway rose in sharp argument. The door banged open, and Pen's mother barged through, yanking her arm from the grip of one of the Temple guards Pen had met on the road. Lord Rolsch, following, held up a stern hand that daunted the man from trying to grab her again. Learned Lurenz rose and quelled the altercation by motioning the guardsman back, shaking his head in a mix of negation and assurance.

"You've awoken! Thank the gods!" The senior Lady Jurald rushed to the bedside and seemed about to fling herself on Pen, but then, to his relief, stopped short. She clutched the sleeve of Lurenz's robe, instead, tugging it in her urgency. "What has happened to him? Can you tell yet?"

Rolsch detached her from the divine and restrained her, but after a worried glance down at Pen, turned a face almost as anxious as hers upon Lurenz. They both seemed startlingly changed from this morning's ceremonial tidiness, though still in the same best clothes. Lady Jurald's face was puffy, her eyes red-rimmed, her hair awry with random wisps escaping from her braids. Rolsch looked exhausted, too, his face . . . unshaven?

This isn't this morning anymore, Pen realized at last. *This is tomorrow . . . today . . . oh gods.* Had he slept the sun around . . . ?

Lurenz, not a man to shirk a painful duty, captured Lady Jurald's fluttering hands and straightened up into his most grave and fatherly pose. "I am so sorry, Lady Jurald." His nod took in Rolsch as well. "It is just as we feared. Your son has been possessed by, or it seems rather, *of*, a demon of the white god. It revealed itself to me plain a moment ago."

Rolsch flinched; Pen's mother gasped, "Lady of Summer help us! Can nothing be done?"

Pen, now sitting up against the headboard, stared down at his body in alarm. A demon of the Bastard, inside him? *Where* inside him . . . ?

Lurenz moistened his lips. "It is not as bad as it could be. The demon does not appear to be ascendant—it has not yet seized control of his body for itself. I am told that such a wrenching transference disrupts or weakens it for some time, before it becomes established in or, or accustomed to, its new abode. If Lord Penric is firm of will, and obeys, ah, all his holy instructions, there may yet be a way to save him."

"They go into people," Rolsch tried; "There ought to be a way for them to go out." He undercut this tentative optimism by adding, "Besides the person dying, of course."

Another nod from Lurenz, altogether too casual in Pen's opinion. "As the unfortunate Learned Ruchia did. Which is how Lord Penric came to be in this predicament."

"Oh, Pen, why ever did you . . . ?" his mother flung at him.

"I . . . I didn't . . . " Pen's hands waved. "I thought the old lady was sick!" Which had been, well, not *wrong*. "I was just trying to help!" He shut his mouth abruptly, but no strange force rose in his throat to add a sharp comment.

"Oh, *Pen*," moaned his mother; Rolsch rolled his eyes in general exasperation.

Lurenz cut short what promised to be a lengthy round of recriminations. "Be that as it may, the harm is done, and there is no way to undo it here in Greenwell Town. I have discussed this possibility with Learned Ruchia's escort. The late divine's fleshly husk must necessarily be buried here, but her escort is obliged to carry her possessions on to her destination, that her Order may dispose of them howsoever she willed. That mandate must include, I have suggested"—forcefully, his tone implied—"her greatest treasure, her demon."

What did Lurenz mean by *a way to save him*? Just about to vent objections to being talked over when he was *right here*, Pen registered the drift of this, and eased back, alert. Transporting the demon must perforce mean transporting Pen to . . . somewhere beyond Greenwell Town, anyway. Freitten, even?

"The Temple guards have agreed to escort Lord Penric to the head house of the Bastard's Order in Martensbridge, where, I trust, they will have the scholars to . . . to decide what properly to do."

"Oh," said Lady Jurald, in a dubious tone.

Rolsch frowned. "Who shall pay for this journey? This seems a Temple matter . . . "

Lurenz took the hint, if not cheerily. "The Temple will undertake to gift him with the rest of Divine Ruchia's travel allowance, and the use of its remounts and hostels along the road. After he reaches Martensbridge . . . that must be for her Order to decide."

"Hm," said Rolsch. It had been Rolsch, last year, who had forbade Pen's scheme to go to the university lately founded in Freitten, on the grounds that the family could not afford it, and then stifled Pen's protests by dragging him in mind-numbing detail through all his baronial accounts to prove it. It had been quite disheartening to find his brother not selfish, but truthful. While not Freitten, Martensbridge was *even farther* from Greenwell.

Tentatively, Pen cleared his throat. It still seemed his own . . . "What about the betrothal?"

A grim silence greeted this.

Rolsch finally said, heavily, "Well, it didn't happen yesterday."

His mother put in, "But dear Preita's kin were kind enough to feed us anyway, as we waited here to see if . . . for you to wake up. So at least the food hasn't gone to waste."

"So much cheese . . . " muttered Rolsch.

Pen was beginning to get the picture of all that must have happened while he'd been lying here like a warmish sort of corpse in this bed, and it wasn't merry. His body brought back in a wagon alongside that of a dead woman, Mother and Rolsch somehow found—*Gans, of course*—the celebration broken up just as it began, his anxious kin, quite obviously, up all night . . . "How is Preita . . . taking it?"

"She grew quite horrified, when we saw your body," said Rolsch.

"Her mother has her in charge now," said Lady Jurald.

"Someone should send to her, and tell her I'm all right," said Pen, dismayed at this.

The silence following this lay a little too long.

Lady Jurald sighed. She was not a woman to shirk a painful duty either, or she could not have stayed married to their father all those years. "I had better go to her myself. There is a great deal to explain. And discuss."

Pen wanted to ask if becoming a sorcerer made a man more, or less, attractive as a husband, but he had an uneasy feeling that he could guess. Cravenly, he let his mother go off without any messages from himself, necessarily under Rolsch's escort though she plainly didn't want to leave Pen alone.

"Is there anything else you need right now, Lord Penric?" Learned Lurenz inquired, also preparing to take his leave.

"I'm quite hungry," Pen realized. And no wonder, if he hadn't eaten since yesterday's breakfast. "May I go down to the refectory?"

"I'll have a dedicat bring you a meal on a tray," the divine promised him.

"But I'm really not hurt." Pen rolled his shoulders and stretched his legs, beginning to feel more at home in his body again, as though recovering from a bout of fever. "I can get dressed and go down. No need to trouble anyone."

"No, please stay in this room, Lord Penric," said Lurenz more firmly. "At least for now."

He let himself out, the door closing as he paused to speak with the Temple guardsman still standing before it. Despite being safe in the Mother's hospice, the man bore all his weapons that he had carried on the road. What in the world did he think he needed to guard against in here . . . ?

Oh.

The hunger pangs in Pen's belly seemed to congeal, and he huddled down in his sheets.

After Pen ate, and a dedicat came to take his tray away, Pen dared to poke his head out into the hallway. The big Temple guard he had seen earlier was gone, replaced by an even bigger fellow in the uniform of the Greenwell Town watch. He looked less like a candidate for the mercenary recruiters than a veteran back from the wars, hard and grim.

"Where did the fellow go who came with . . . " Pen wasn't sure what to call her, *dead sorceress* seeming disrespectful though definitive. "With the late Learned Ruchia?"

"The dead sorceress?" said the watchman. "They both went off to witness her funeral, so they pulled me in to stand their post."

"Should—should I not attend?"

"I was told you are to stay in this room. Lord Penric. Please?" He looked down at Pen and offered an apprehensive smile that took Pen utterly aback.

Helplessly, Pen returned the smile, in the same false measure. "Of course," he murmured, and retreated.

There being no more comfortable seat in the little chamber than the stool, Pen went back to bed, to sit up hugging his knees and trying to remember everything he'd ever learned about sorcerers and their demons. It seemed meager.

He was fairly sure real ones weren't much like the ones in children's tales. They did not call castles to sprout out of the ground like mushrooms for passing lost heroes, or enchant princesses to hundred-year sleeps, or, or . . . Pen was not sure about *poison princes*, but it seemed to him unlikely to call upon a sorcerer for something an apothecary could do better. Pen's life so far had been sadly free of heroes, princesses, or princes, in any case.

He was not, upon reflection, at all sure what the real ones did for a living, either when subjected to Temple disciplines, or gone renegade. The common saying was that a man became a sorcerer upon acquiring a demon much as a man became a rider upon acquiring a horse, with the implication that the inept horseman was riding for a fall. But what made a good horseman?

Demons were supposed to begin as formless, mindless elementals, fragments escaped or leaked into the world from the Bastard's Hell, a place of chaotic dissolution. Pen had a dim mental picture of something like a ball of white wool shot with a prickle of sparks. All that demons possessed of speech or knowledge or personhood was taken from their successive masters, though whether *copied* or *stolen*, Pen was unclear. It had seemed a distinction without a difference if they only left with their prizes when their masters died, except . . . maybe not, if the ripped-up souls could not then go on to their god. He was growing uncomfortably sorry he had dozed or doodled through so many of those droning theology lectures in school.

Tales *not* from the nursery told of demons becoming ascendant within their masters, taking the body for some wild ride while the mind of the man was trapped as a helpless witness within. The demons were careless of injury, disease, or death, since they could jump from their worn-out mount to another like a courier riding relay. And the corrosion of such unchanneled chaos ate away at the sorcerer's soul.

Except it seemed Learned Ruchia's soul was expected to go to her god as usual, so maybe that varied as well? Or was it something about the mysterious Temple disciplines that made the difference? Pen had not the first idea what they might be. Was anyone going to think to tell him?

Did the hospice library have any books on the subject, and would they let Pen read them if he asked? But the Mother's house seemed more likely to harbor tomes on anatomy and medicines than on the doings of her second Son and his demonic pets.

As night fell, his fretting was relieved by the return of Gans, bearing a load of Pen's clothes and gear from home and a pair of saddlebags to pack them in. The load exceeded the capacity of the bags, yet certain necessities seemed to be missing.

"Did my brother not send me a sword?" The armory at Jurald Court could surely spare one.

The graying groom cleared his throat. "He gave it to me. Instead, I guess. I'm charged to go along with you on the road to Martensbridge, look after you and all." Gans did not look best pleased with this proffered adventure. "We're to leave tomorrow at dawn."

"Oh!" said Pen, startled. "So soon?"

"Soonest begun, soonest done," Gans intoned. His goal, clearly, was the *done*. Gans had always been a man of settled routines.

Pen set about extracting a view of yesterday's events as Gans had witnessed them, but his laconic account did not add much to what Pen had already imagined, except for a strong sense leaking through that Gans considered it unjust of Pen to encounter such a disaster on Gans's watch. But his new task, it seemed, was not a punishment; the Temple guards had requested his witness in Martensbridge of the events he had seen.

"I don't know why," he grumbled. "Seems to me a scribe could write it down on half a page, and save me the saddle sores."

Gans took himself off to sleep elsewhere in the old mansion gifted to the Mother's Order and converted to its present charitable purpose—Pen guessed his own quarantined chamber had once been some servant's quarters. He turned to the problem of packing his bags. Someone back at Jurald Court had apparently just grabbed all the clothing he owned. The brown suit went on the impractical pile to be returned there in the morning, along with the most threadbare of his unloved hand-me-downs. How long was he to be gone? Where was he going, exactly? What would he need there?

He wondered if packing for the university would have been anything like this. 'Sorcerer' had certainly not been on Pen's former list of scholarly ambitions, but then, neither had 'theologian,' 'divine,' 'physician,' 'teacher,' 'lawyer,' or any other high trade taught there—yet another reason for Rolsch's dubiousness about it all. The Bastard's Order must have a separate seminary of some sort . . . ?

Pen washed in the basin and put himself to bed, there to lie awake too long trying to sense the alien spirit now parasitizing his body. Did demons manifest as a stomach ache? He was still wondering when he finally drifted off.

Penric carried his saddlebags down to the entry hall in the morning gloom to find a send-off he hadn't expected in the form of Preita herself, in all her pretty roundness, escorted by a frowning brother and sister.

"Preita!" He went to her, only to have her flinch back, if with a tremulous smile.

"Hullo, Pen." They stared uncertainly at each other. "I hear you're going away."

"Only to Martensbridge. Not to the ends of the world." He swallowed, and got out, "Are we still to be betrothed?"

Regretfully, she shook her head. "Do you even know when you will return?"

"Er . . . no." Two days ago, he'd known everything about his future. Today, he knew nothing. He was not sure this change was an improvement.

"So—so you can see how difficult that would be. For me."

"Uh, yes, to be sure."

Her hands started to reach out, but then retreated behind her back and consoled each other there. "I am so sorry. But surely you see any girl must be quite afraid to marry a man who could set her on fire with a word!"

He'd dreamed of setting her alight with kisses. "Any man could set a girl on fire with a *torch*, but he'd have to be deranged!"

This won only an uneasy shrug. "I brought you something. For the road, you know."

She motioned to her brother, who handed over a large sack that proved, when Pen opened it, to contain a huge wheel of cheese. "Thank you," Pen managed. He glanced at his bulging saddlebags, and ruthlessly turned to hand it on to the impatiently waiting Gans. "Here. Find a place to pack this. Somehow."

Gans shot him a beleaguered look, but carried it out.

Preita gave him a jerky nod, but ventured no closer; apparently, he was not to get even one soft farewell hug to see him off. "Good luck, Pen. I will pray that all goes well with you."

"And I, you."

The two Temple guardsmen stood outside, holding the saddled horses. The late sorceress's gear was packed aboard a sturdy cob, where Gans was securing the sack of cheese. Another mount awaited Pen.

He made for it, but paused at a call; it seemed he had one more painful farewell to endure. His mother and Rolsch hurried up as Preita and her siblings hurried away, exchanging awkward nods in passing. His kin looked less harried and exhausted than yesterday, but still unhappy.

"Pen," said Rolsch, gravely. "The five gods protect you on your road." He thrust out a small bag of coin, which Pen, surprised, took.

"Wear it around your neck," his mother told him anxiously. "I hear those cutpurses in the cities can have away with a purse off a man's belt and he never feels a tug."

The cord had been lengthened for such prudence; dutifully, Pen obeyed, sneaking a peek within before tucking the soft leather into his shirt. More copper than silver, and no gold, but it made him not quite entirely a beggar at the Temple's table.

Pen steeled himself to endure the embarrassment of a tearful maternal embrace, but, though Lady Jurald started forward, she stopped much like Preita. She raised her hand in a farewell wave, instead, as though he were turning out of sight and not standing a pace away.

"Be more *careful*, Pen!" she begged, her voice breaking. She turned back to Rolsch.

"Yes, Mama," Pen sighed.

He went to his horse. Gans offered him no leg up, not that Pen had any problem lifting his wiry body into a saddle. As he did so, he had the quelling realization that not one person had touched him since whoever had carried him up and dumped him into that bed day before yesterday.

The senior guardsman motioned them forward, and the party rode off up the cobbled main street beneath the whitewash and half-timbering of the houses lining it. No flowers yet brightened their window boxes, in the chill of early spring. Pen turned in his saddle to wave one last time, but his mother and Rolsch were entering the hostel and did not see.

Pen cleared his throat and asked the senior guardsman, whose name was Trinker, "Did the Learned Ruchia's funeral go all right, yesterday afternoon? They didn't let me attend."

"Oh, aye. Taken up by her god, all right, signed by that white dove and all."

"I see." Pen hesitated. "Can we please stop where she is buried? Just for a moment."

Trinker grunted but could not gainsay this pious request, so nodded.

The graveyard where the Temple-sworn were buried lay beyond the walls, on the road out of town; they turned aside, and Trinker escorted Pen to the new mound, as yet unmarked, while Gans and Wilrom waited atop their horses.

Nothing much to see, now, in the dawn damp; nothing much to feel, though Pen extended all his exacerbated senses. He bowed his head and offered a silent prayer, the wording haltingly remembered from services for his father, and that other brother who had died when Pen was little, and some aged servants. The grave returned no answer, but something inside him seemed to ease, as if pacified.

He mounted again, and Trinker urged them into a trot as they crossed the covered wooden bridge over the river and the town fell behind.

The bright sunshine of the past two days, like a misplaced breath of summer, was gone, replaced by a more usual misty damp, which would likely turn to a chill drizzle before the morning was out. The high mountains to the north hid their white heads in the clouds, which lay like a gray lid over the wide uplands of Pen's country. The road followed the river downstream, into what passed in these parts for flatter lands—or at least the valleys widened and the hills shrank. Pen wondered how soon they would catch a glimpse of the Raven Range, that other long stone hedge on the opposite side of the plateau, which divided the Cantons from the great realm of the Weald to the south.

The Temple guards kept them mostly to a trot, walking up the hills, a rhythm designed to eat the most miles in the least time. It was not the breakneck pace of a courier, but it did assume a change of horses being available, which they took at a noon halt at a Temple way-station. They passed farm carts, pack mules, cows, sheep, and country folk in small villages. Once, carefully, they rode around a company of marching pike men, recruits on their way to being exported to other lords' wars. *Like Drovo*, Pen thought. He wondered how many would ever march home. Better it seemed to export cheese or cloth, but it was true that fortunes were made in the military trade. Though seldom by the soldiers, any more than by the cheeses.

While ascending the hills, Pen coaxed their guards to talk a little. He was surprised to learn that they were not Divine Ruchia's own retainers, but had been assigned to her at the border town of Liest, when she'd crossed out of Darthaca on her way to Martensbridge; likewise the woman servant Marda. Gans was indignant to learn that Marda had been allowed to give a deposition and then head for home. Trinker and Wilrom were quite apprehensive about what their seniors would say when it was learned that they had lost their charge on the road, helpless though they had been to prevent it. They had come prepared to fight bad men, not bad hearts. As for the fumbling of her valuable demon into the chance-encountered younger brother of a minor valley lord . . . no one seemed to be looking forward to explaining that.

At dusk, with forty miles of muddy road behind them, they halted at a modest town that boasted a house of the Daughter's Order, which took them in. Penric was again shown to a room by himself. A smiling dedicat brought him hot water and food, and he smiled back in gratitude, but she did not linger. A check outside his door found a local guardsman standing sentry. Pen said a hesitant hello and retreated, too tired to mind.

His room was as small as the one at the hospice, but better furnished; chairs with embroidered cushions, a table with a mirror and stool clearly meant for lady guests, something a house of the Daughter of Spring was more likely to host. Pen took advantage by sitting down with his comb, undoing his queue, and attacking the day's accumulated snarls, which his fine, pale blond hair was prone to.

When he glanced up at the mirror, his mouth said, "Yes, let's get another look at you."

Pen froze. Was the demon awake again? His jaw clamped shut; his throat tightened.

How did the thing perceive the world, anyway? Did it share his vision, his hearing? His thoughts? Did it have to take turns looking out, as with his voice, or was it always there, like a bird perched on his shoulder?

He breathed, unlocked his muscles. Said, "Would you like to speak?" And waited.

"Want to look," said the demon through his mouth. "We want to see what we've bought." Its speech was fairly clear, its accent the cultured Wealdean of the lands around Martensbridge, as Ruchia's had been.

Pen had not spent much time in front of mirrors since he'd grown big and fast enough to evade older sisters bent on using him as a large doll. His own features, in the glass, suddenly grew strange to him. But his vision did not go black; it seemed the two of them shared his eyes together.

His face, as lean as his body, had good bones, he'd been told. His fair skin was redeemed from its youth by what he hoped was a reasonably assertive nose. Long lashes framed what Mama had fondly called lake-blue eyes. In Pen's experience lakes were more often gray, green, blinding white with snow, or black glass if frozen on a cold, still night. But on a rare bright summer day lakes could be that color, he supposed.

Nobody else had been talking to him; nobody else had been telling him *anything*. Had he been missing a chance? He exhaled, relaxed his throat, tried to soften the set of his tired, tense shoulders. To make himself open. "Can you answer questions?"

A snort. "If they're not too witless."

"I can't guarantee that."

The *Hmm* from his throat answering this did not seem hostile, at least.

Pen began in the simplest way he could think of. "What's your name?"

A surprised pause. "My riders call me Demon."

"That's like calling your horse Horse, or me Boy. Or Man," he hastily revised this. "Even a horse gets a name."

"How would *we* get a name—Boy?"

"I . . . suppose most names are given. By people's parents. By creatures' owners. Sometimes they are inherited."

A long silence followed this. Whatever the entity had been expecting from him, it evidently hadn't been this.

His mouth said, hesitantly, "I suppose we could be *Ruchia*."

Another voice objected, "But what about *Helvia*? Or *Amberein*?"

Yet another voice said something in a language Pen didn't even recognize, though the cadences seemed to tease his understanding; he thought *Umelan* might have been another name. More unknown words spouted from his mouth, three voices, four; he lost track till it all ended in an inarticulate growl and a weird squeal.

"How many are you?" asked Pen, startled. "How many . . . generations?" How many riders had this old demon attached itself to, and copied—or stolen—life from?

"You expect *us* to do arithmetic?"

Pen's brows went up. "Yes," he decided.

"There will be a price. He doesn't know about the price." That accent was . . . Darthacan?

"Ruchia has lately paid," said Ruchia's voice. "That reserve will be long, drawing down."

A surly pause. "Twelve," said a voice.

"Only if we count the lioness and the mare," muttered another. "Must we?"

"So . . . so are you twelve persons, or one?" Pen asked.

"Yes," said the Ruchia-voice. "Both. At once."

"Like, um, like a town council?"

". . . We suppose." The voice was not impressed.

"Are—were—you all, er, ladies?"

"It is customary," said a voice. Though another added, "*She* was no lady!"

Customary, Pen gathered, for a demon to be handed on to another rider of the same sex. But not, obviously, theologically required, or he wouldn't be in this fix. *Dear gods. Have I just acquired a council of twelve invisible older sisters?* Ten, he supposed, if he didn't count the mare and the, what, *lioness*? Did either of *them* have names in their animal tongues to argue about?

"I think you had better have one name," said Pen. "Though if I want to speak to, to a particular layer of you, that one could have—inherit— her old rider's name, I suppose." *Twelve?* He would sort them out somehow.

"Hmm." A most dubious noise, of uncertain origin.

"I have two names," he offered. "Penric, which is my particular name, and Jurald, which is my kin name. The name for all of you could be like your kin name."

Pen hoped no one was listening to this—all in his voice, ultimately—through the walls. No wonder Marda had believed the sorceress's utterances incomprehensible. He thought to add, "Did you speak to Learned Ruchia in this fashion?"

"In time," said the Ruchia-voice, "we had silent speech."

How much time did that take? Pen wondered. And if it went on long enough, might a man no longer know which voice was his own? He shuddered, but wrenched his mind back to the moment. "You ought to have a name for when I mean all of you, as one. Not Demon. Something nicer than what I'd call a dog, for the five gods' sakes. How if I pick something? Make it a present."

The silence this time was so long, he wondered if the creature had gone back to sleep, or into hiding, or whatever it did when he could not feel or hear it. "In twelve long lives," it said quietly at last, "no one has ever offered us a present."

"Well, that's not . . . not an easy thing. I mean, you don't exactly have a body, so how could anybody give you any material gift? But a name is a thing of the air, of the mind and the spirit, so a fellow could give it to a spirit, right?" He felt he was making headway, here. And because betrothal had been lately on his mind, he tossed in, at a hazard, "A courting gift."

He had the sense of an explosive *Huff!* but no sound came with it. Had he thrown a creature of chaos into confusion? That seemed only fair, considering what it was doing to *him*.

But then the ambiguous voice said, cautiously, "What do you offer? Penric of Jurald."

He hadn't actually got that far in his thinking yet. He choked in panic. Steadied himself. Reached for inspiration, and caught it. "Desdemona," he said, suddenly certain. "I read it in a book of tales from Saone, when I was a boy, and thought it sounded very fine. She was a princess."

A faint, flattered exhalation through his nose.

"Amusing," said the Ruchia-voice. It seemed to be the dominant one; was that because it was freshest? Or had the late divine held the creature longest? Or what?

Another long silence; Pen yawned in exhaustion. Were they taking a vote in there? Had he started a civil war in his own gut? That could be bad. He was about to take it all back, when the ambiguous voice said, "*Accepted.*"

"Desdemona it is, then!" he said, relieved. He wondered if it would shorten to *Des*, when they grew to know each other better. Like *Pen*. That could be all right.

"We thank you for your gift of the spirit. Pretty Penric . . . " The voice fell away in a weary whisper, and Pen guessed the uprooted creature was spent for the night.

As was he. He staggered dizzily to bed.

The next morning's ride brought them early to the big Crow River at the foot of the Raven Range, where they turned downstream on the main east-west road that followed it. The Ravens, once the mist cleared enough to unveil them, and before the afternoon rains closed in, were greener and less lofty than the fierce icy peaks in whose shadow Pen had grown up, but formidably rugged still. The road crossed the swelling river twice, once over a wooden span and once over a stone bridge with graceful arches, both with tolls collected by the villages that served them. With the spring melt, the Crow ran too high for upstream traffic, but rafts of logs or cargo packed in barrels still made their way down on the spate. Pen thought the nimble raft men must be brave to dare the cold waters, and beguiled an hour imagining himself one of their company.

More than local traffic kept the road a busy one; merchants' pack trains, small parties of pilgrims, and enclosed wagons were added to the usual farm carts, cows, pigs, and sheep. Three times they passed or were passed by galloping couriers, from towns or the Temple; the latter waved cheerily in return for Pen's guards' salutes. *Courier*, now there was an honorable task a lean, light man might undertake . . . though by the end of that second day's ride, Pen's backside was questioning this ambition.

Nightfall brought them to a town at the confluence with the River Linnet, not fifteen miles from their destination and under its territorial jurisdiction. Although it was probably not possible to get lost following the Linnet's valley upstream to where it drained the big lake at Martensbridge, Trinker ruled that they dare not risk arriving after the town gates closed, and instead found them impromptu, but free, lodging at the local Lady-school.

The Lady-school, dedicated to the Daughter of Spring, was not unlike the one in Greenwell that Pen had attended in his youth, being a couple of rooms on the ground floor of the house where the teachers lodged. It was not appointed for pilgrims like the big chapterhouse of the Daughter's Order last night—where Pen had been able to sell his cheese to the refectory for a substantial addition to his pocket money—but a private bedchamber was cleared for him nonetheless. Pen did not think this was because he was the most honored guest.

As a prisoner, he had been well treated, but his status was plain. He checked the tiny window, four floors up over the street. If his captors imagined it would hold him, they had reckoned without his slight build or his years spent climbing, either up trees out of reach of Drovo, or in the mountains hunting. He could skin out of their grip in a moment, but—where would he go?

This was like waiting for the physician, that time he'd broken his arm. Uncomfortable, but there was nothing he could do to hurry events. Except, it seemed, continue on to the mysteries of Martensbridge.

He lay down and attempted sleep, only to become aware, after a few minutes, that he was sharing the narrow cot with a family of fleas. He flicked, rubbed, turned again. *Or maybe a festival of fleas.* Would they celebrate all night? He muttered an imprecation as one bit his calf, beginning the banquet.

"Would you like some help with that?" said Desdemona, amusement lacing her voice.

Pen clapped his hand over his mouth. "Quieter!" he whispered, alarmed. "Wilrom is sleeping right outside the door. He'll hear." And think . . . what?

Desdemona obligingly whispered, "We can destroy fleas, you know."

Pen hadn't. "Is it permitted?"

"Not only permitted, but encouraged. We must have done in armies of them, over the years. Vermin are not considered theologically protected, even by the Bastard whose creatures they are. And it is a magic that runs safely downhill, from order to disorder."

"Less disorder for my bed, surely."

"But great disorder for the fleas," Desdemona whispered back. Pen's lips grinned, not by his volition. "The sharpest fall of all, from life to death."

That last comment was unsettling, but so were the fleas. "Go ahead," whispered Pen, and lay still, straining to sense whatever was going to happen.

A pulse of heat, a slight flush through his body. Its direction was vague, though it seemed more down from his back, into the mattress, than up from his chest toward the ceiling.

"Twenty-six fleas, two ticks, three beetles, and nine lice," said Desdemona with a satisfied sigh, like a woman consuming a sweet custard. "And a multitude of moth eggs in the wool stuffing."

As the first magic he had ever worked, this lacked glamor. "I thought you didn't do arithmetic?" said Pen.

"Huh." Pen wasn't sure if her huff was peeved or pleased. "You pay attention, do you?"

"I'm . . . presently spurred to."

"Are you," she breathed.

His bedding might be depopulated, but he was still not alone. It also occurred to him, belatedly, that he didn't know whether demons could *lie*. Did they always speak truth to their riders, or could they trick them? Could they cut the cloth of fact to fit their goals, leaving out essential information to reverse its effect? Desdemona was the one . . . person, he decided for simplicity he would think of her as a person, he could not ask. Or rather, he could ask, she might answer, but it wouldn't help.

Instead, he inquired, "Before Ruchia, were you a, that is, *with* a Temple sorceress as well?"

"Helvia was a physician-surgeon," said the Helvia-voice—he might as well start thinking of her as Helvia—in the reassuringly local accent of Liest. "High in the Mother's Order."

"And I, Amberein, before her," said the thick Darthacan accent. "In the Temple school in Saone."

"I thought you said . . . physicians heal, sorcerers destroy?" said Pen, puzzled anew. "How can you be both?"

"We can do uphill magic as well, but it is very costly," said Desdemona.

"Some healing is done by destroying," said Amberein. "Stones of the bladder. Reduction of cysts or tumors. Amputations. Many subtler things."

"Worms," sighed Helvia. "You would not believe how many people suffer from worms. Not to mention fleas, lice, and other infestations." It took a breath, and added, "Which was why, when Helvia's time ran out, we did not jump to the young physician they had prepared, but to Ruchia. We were so tired of worms. Hah!"

Before Pen could ask what Ruchia had done to make her so preferable, another voice interjected a comment in a language he did not know. "Who was that?"

"Aulia of Brajar," put in Desdemona. "Good Temple-woman. She spoke no Wealdean, only Ibran, though in time you will come to understand her. Before her, Umelan the Roknari."

"Roknari!" said Pen, startled. "I thought the Quadrene heretics abjure the Bastard. How came she by a demon in the Archipelago?"

"It's a long tale, which I'm sure she will tell you—in tedious detail—when you gain her tongue," soothed Desdemona.

I, gain her tongue? It seemed to Pen that she had gained his, for she used it to make what sounded like a tart rejoinder.

"Can you give me a short tale?" asked Pen.

"She was born in the Archipelago, taken as a slave in a war raid, bought for a servant by Mira, a famous courtesan in the lagoon city of Adria, who possessed us at the time. Mira was untrained, but clever; we'd found in her our best rider yet. When Mira died, we jumped to Umelan, who ran away back home only to find the ill fate meted out to sorcerers on those islands."

Pen's imagination, briefly stuck on the *courtesan* part, raced to catch up. "Which is what?" Not that he had any intention of going to *those* lands.

"Sometimes they are burned alive, but often, they are taken out to sea and put overboard with a cushion that slowly fills with water and sinks. By the time the sorcerer drowns, the boat will have got far enough away that the demon will have nowhere to jump but to the fishes."

Both he and Desdemona shuddered at this picture, Pen fancied, if perhaps for different reasons.

Pen's mouth emitted a spate in that strange language, the words unknown to him but the tone of grievance very clear. Umelan adding her views?

"After her executioners rowed off, but before she was quite drowned, she was spotted by a passing galley from Brajar. The rescue was not much better than the capture, but we were set ashore alive in Brajar and, at a loss for any other course, went supplicant to a house of the Bastard's Order. It was . . . good, there." A slight pause, and she added, "For the first time, we were *understood*."

Pen counted up on his fingers. Not the whole tally even yet. "And before, uh, Mira of Adria?"

"Rogaska, a serving-woman in the court of the Duke of Orbas. He made a gift of her to Mira. Before her, Vasia of Patos in Cedonia, our first rider who could read and write—a widow, then something of a courtesan as well, after the manner of that city. Which was how she came to die in luxury at the court of Orbas. Roundaboutly."

Pen blinked. Cedonia? That seemed a country of fable to him, a place for tales to be set far enough away that none could gainsay their wonders. Also said to be warm. He was impressed. And envious. This creature had seen places and peoples that Pen could scarcely dream of.

"Before her, Litikone, a goodwife of the Cedonian northern provinces; before her, Sugane, a village woman in the mountains. She slew the aging lioness when it attacked her goats, all by herself with a rusty spear. She was a proper rider, despite her ignorance! Before that, the wild mare of the hills, that the lioness killed and ate, and before that . . . we know not. Perhaps the white god."

"Do you, did you, er . . . " Pen was not sure how to put it. "Did you *experience* all these deaths?"

The voice was dry as dust. "Up to a point."

But not any balancing births. Not that he remembered his own, either.

As long as he hosted this entity, Pen realized, he need never lack for bedtime stories, though he might lack for the ability to sleep, after.

But not tonight. Helplessly, he yawned, settling back in his warm and flea-less bedding. His voice whispered on for a while in unknown words, like a mountain rivulet, as he drifted off.

Pen woke aroused, rolled over sleepily, and reached for himself. The room seemed warm and dim and safe and quiet.

His hand had barely touched its target when his mouth commented, "Ooh, I've not felt it from *this* angle before. This should be interesting."

Pen's hand froze.

"Don't stop on our account," said Desdemona. "Physicians, remember?"

"Yes, don't be shy. I've seen a thousand of 'em."

"Speak for yourself!"

"Well, *I've* certainly diapered them a thousand times."

Pen had no idea what the next comment was, and it might just have been the language, but it certainly *sounded* obscene.

He rolled from the bed and dressed as fast as possible. He couldn't be out on the road soon enough.

The Linnet ran green and swift in the spring melt, and surprisingly wide. A few merchants' boats dared the flood. The road coursed alongside it, with more pack trains going upstream than down. Its valley was hedged by what were, by Pen's standards, low hills. As they passed the third broken fortification glowering down from these modest crags, he was moved to ask, "What happened to the castles?"

Wilrom and Gans shrugged, but Trinker, craning his neck, said, "Martensbridge did, I heard. Some local lords had taken to robbing merchants outright, though they'd started by calling it tolls. The guilds of the city combined with the princess-archdivine's troops to destroy the nests that they couldn't buy out, and made the road safe for all from the lake to the Crow. And all the tolls go to Martensbridge, now."

Not, Pen reflected sadly, a method of gain Jurald Court might have mimicked; the roads in its reach were more likely to hold herds of cows than rich caravans.

Villages clustered around weirs and mills and, once, a wooden bridge. Then they rounded a curve in the valley and Martensbridge came into view. Pen stared, fascinated.

The place was easily ten times the size of Greenwell. The river bisected it, twice crossed by stone bridges and once by one of timber; buildings of stone as well as wood rose up the slopes, packed behind its walls. Trinker stood in his stirrups, and guessed that the substantial edifice crowning one hill might be the palace of the famous princess-archdivine, and heart, therefore, of his Order in this region. Beyond the city, the wide vista of lake opened out to the north, bordered with farms and fields and vineyards on the lower slopes, dark woods on the steeps. Covered merchants' boats and open fishing skiffs dotted the ruffled surface. Then more hills, and then, dreamlike on the far horizon, a line of familiar white peaks, briefly making a bow from the curtain of the clouds.

It was not possible to get lost in Greenwell. After they had made their way through the south gate, they discovered that this was not the case for Martensbridge. They rode up and down several streets, all of them paved with cobbles, while Pen gaped at the high houses, the well-dressed men and women, the bright markets, stately merchants and hurrying servants, fine fountains in squares crowded with laundresses, elegant or clever wrought-iron signs for artisans' shops and guildhalls, windows of stained glass with *pictures*. Trinker referred again to the scrap of paper holding his directions, looking hot and frustrated.

"Turn left here," said Pen suddenly, when Trinker made to lead them right. Pen had no idea where the certainty in his voice came from, but everyone followed. "Right here," he said at the next street. "And up," at the next intersection. "And here we are."

Pen sat in his saddle and peered at the stone building, crowded in a row along the steep street with its neighbors. Though narrow, it stood some five floors tall, looking like a lesser guildhall of some sort. It boasted no stained glass. The only marker was a discreet wooden sign over the door showing two hands painted white, loosely closed, one thumb pointing up and the other down. The thumb was the sign and signifier of the Bastard, the one finger on the hand that touched all the others. Aside from that, the place did not look in the least temple-like. Trinker cast Pen a disquieted look, dismounted, and knocked on the door.

It was answered by a porter wearing a tabard with the same two-hand design stitched on it, otherwise in common dress. His glance took in the official badge of the Daughter's Order and blue-and-white feathers on Trinker's hat. "Yes, sir?"

Trinker cleared his throat, awkwardly. "We are the escort of the Learned Ruchia, ridden from Liest. We were told that someone awaited her in this house. We need to see him."

The porter looked over their party. "Where is the divine?"

"That's what we need to see somebody about."

The porter's brow wrinkled. "Wait here, sir. If you please." The door closed again.

Pen had to give Trinker credit, he stood his ground, back straight, and did not suggest they *all* run off. Half of why Pen had not made his escape through his window last night had been the reflection that it would be a cruel trick to play on his guards, who were only carrying out their duties and who had done him no harm. The other half was pure curiosity over what the Bastard's Order here was supposed to *do* for him in his predicament, for surely he wouldn't have been sent all this way unless there was something?

He wondered if the gruesome Roknari ploy with the cushion would work out on that lake. Probably, and swiftly, given the spring chill of the water. He tried to stop thinking.

In a few minutes, the door opened again, the porter escorting an anxious-looking man of middle years, height, and girth, his neatly trimmed beard and hair a graying brown. He wore an ordinary townsman's gown, belted and soberly hemmed at his knees, over trousers of some dark stuff. The unbleached wool of the tunic only hinted at his allegiance, but the divine's braid in white, cream and silver pinned to his shoulder made it plain. Easy to remove and pocket if he wished to walk about incognito, Pen wondered?

"I am Learned Tigney," he said, his glance summing the party. Gans was clearly a groom, the two Temple guards were easy to place; Penric less so, and the gaze caught on him for a moment before going back to Trinker, waiting to speak with his hat in his hands. "I'm told you have news of Learned Ruchia? We were expecting her anytime this week."

Trinker cleared his throat. "News, sir, but not good. Learned Ruchia was overtaken on the road with a seizure of the heart, some five miles short of Greenwell Town. She passed away before Wilrom"—he nodded at his comrade—"could return with help. The Temple of

Greenwell saw her buried there with her due rites—their white dove signed her for her god, all proper. Not knowing what else to do, and being more than halfway here already, we brought on all her clothes and cases, to give to those who should have them."

Tigney cast him a sharp look. "Not opened, I trust?"

"No, sir," said Trinker fervently. "She *was* a sorceress, after all. We didn't dare."

Tigney's posture of relief was short-lived; he tensed again. "But— what happened to her demon? Did it go to her god with her, then?"

"Uh, no." He nodded toward Pen.

Tigney's head whipped around. Pen offered a weak smile and a little wave of his fingers. "Here, sir. I'm afraid."

"Who . . . ?" Tigney gave him a long, pole-axed stare. "You had better come inside."

He told off the porter to take Ruchia's things to his chambers, which resulted in a bustle of unloading from the packsaddle into the hall, then sent him off with Gans and Wilrom to deliver the horses to some nearby mews that kept a place for Temple beasts.

"This way." He led Penric and Trinker up one flight to a small, well-lit room overlooking the street. Seeming a cross between a scholar's study and a counting house, it held a table cluttered with papers and writing tools, a scattering of chairs, and some jammed shelves. Pen eyed them and wondered why a divine of the Bastard should have twenty or so courier dispatch cases lined up.

Tigney scrubbed his hand through his beard and gestured them to sit. "And you are . . . ?" he continued to Pen.

"Penric kin Jurald of Jurald Court, near Greenwell Town, sir." He wondered if he was obliged to introduce Desdemona. "My eldest brother Rolsch is lord of that valley."

"How came you to—no. Begin at the beginning, or there will be no making head nor tail of things." He turned to Trinker, and efficiently extracted an account of his doings from the time he was assigned to escort the divine at Liest until the disaster at Greenwell. The party seemed to have traveled rather more slowly than with Pen.

"But why were you on that road at all?" asked Tigney, a plaintive note in his voice. "It's not the most direct route from Liest to Martensbridge."

Trinker shrugged. "I know, sir. The divine told us to go that way."

"Why?"

"She said she'd shuttled back and forth from Liest to Martensbridge on the main road three dozen times in her life, and wanted a change of scene."

"Did she say anything else about why she chose that course? Or was it just caprice? Any hint or strange comment?"

"No, sir . . . ?"

Tigney's lips twisted, taking this in, but then he blew out his breath and went on. "There was a woman servant, you say? But then why didn't—where is she?"

"Went back to Liest, sir. The Greenwell divine took her sworn deposition, first. Should it go to you?"

"Yes, for my sins."

Trinker pulled out this document and handed it across; Tigney unsealed and read it, his frown deepening, then set it aside with an unsatisfied sigh.

Pen ventured, "Learned, do you know of these things? Sorcerers, and demons and . . . things?"

Tigney began to speak, but then turned his head at a knock on the door. It proved to be Wilrom and Gans, delivered back. With all the witnesses present, the divine turned to their accounts of Ruchia's death, each offered with slightly different details but clearly congruent. Pen thought Gans's description of him "flopped over as gray and limp as a dead eel" was unduly blunt. Tigney collected Pen's own testimony last: final words, purple flashes, and mysterious voices dutifully not left out, even though it made everyone stare at him in alarm except his interrogator, who seemed to take them as a matter of course.

Tigney then asked an intent string of questions ascertaining that there was no way Pen or anyone else at Jurald Court could ever have met Ruchia before, or known about her in any way, before the chance meeting on the road. The divine compressed his lips and turned to Pen once more.

"Since you awoke from that long swoon, have you felt or experienced anything unusual? Anything at all."

"I had a very bad headache, but it wore off by the time we left Greenwell." *And no one will touch me, I have been summarily unbetrothed, and I have been made a prisoner even though I have committed no crime.* Best leave that out. Tigney was just beginning to relax when Pen added, "Also, night before last the demon woke up and began talking to me."

Tigney went still. "How?"

"Er . . . through my mouth?"

"Are you sure of this?"

Pen couldn't tell what to make of that question. Did Tigney suppose him to be delirious or hallucinating? Was that common among the newly bedemoned? "I know it wasn't me. I don't speak Ibran. Or Roknari, Adriac, or Cedonian. She was really chatty once she got started. Also argumentative." Ten women all stuck together, no wonder. Or their ghosts, disturbing thought. *Images of their ghosts* was scarcely better.

Tigney took this in, then rose and went to shout down the staircase for the porter, whose name was apparently Cosso. Or perhaps, *Cosso!* "See that these three men are fed," he ordered the fellow, shepherding Gans and the guards out. "Find a place in the house for Lord Penric's groom, tonight." He reassured the guards, "We'll send you two to lodge with your own Order at the palace temple, but don't leave before I have a chance to speak to you again."

He closed the door on them all, then turned and studied Pen. Pen looked hopefully back. At length he placed a hand on Pen's brow and intoned loudly, "Demon, speak!"

Silence. It went on until Pen stirred in discomfort. "I'm not stopping her," he offered. "She may sleep during the day. So far, she's only talked to me before bed." The only times he'd been alone?

Tigney scowled and deployed that commanding voice once more. "Speak!"

"Should I try?" said Pen brightly, growing nervous. He softened his tone. "Desdemona, could you please say something to Learned Tigney, here, so he doesn't think I've gone mad or, or that I'm lying? Please?"

After a long moment, his mouth said mulishly, "We don't see why we should. Cowardly demon-destroyer. Ruchia may have thought him diligent, but *we* always thought him a prig."

Pen's hands sprang to his flushing face as if to dam this alarming spate; he lowered them cautiously. "Sorry, sir. She seems to be a bit opinionated. Er . . . had you two met before?"

"I've known—knew"—he made a pained hand-wave at the

correction—"Ruchia these twenty years. Though only after she acquired her mount."

Pen said hesitantly, "I'm sorry for your loss. Were you friends, then?"

"Say *colleagues*. She had the training of me when I first contracted *my* demon."

"You're a sorcerer, too?" said Pen in surprise.

"I was. Not anymore."

Pen swallowed. "You didn't end it by dying."

"No. There is another way." The man could certainly put the *grim* in grimace. "Wasteful, but sometimes necessary."

Pen wanted to follow this up, but instead Tigney began asking him all about his childhood and youth at Jurald Court. It seemed to Pen to make a short and boring biography.

"Why did you stop on the road?" he asked at last.

"How could I not? The lady appeared to be in grave distress." Which had turned out to be all too true. "I wanted to help."

"You might have volunteered to ride for the town."

Pen blinked. "I didn't think of that. It all happened so fast. Wilrom was already galloping off by the time I dismounted to see what was going on."

Tigney rubbed his forehead, and muttered, "And so all is in disarray." He looked up and added, "We had expected to house Learned Ruchia at the palace temple, but I think you'd best stay here, for now. We'll find you a room." He went again to shout for Cosso; when the man arrived, he gave more orders as a master might. Was Tigney very senior, here? This was plainly a house for functionaries, for the practical business of the Temple, not for worship or prayer.

"What do you do in the Bastard's Order, sir?"

Tigney's brows rose. "Did you not know? I oversee all the Temple sorcerers of this region. Comings and goings, assignments and accounts. I'm a bailiff of sorcerers, if you like. And you know how much everyone loves bailiffs. Thankless task. But Bastard knows they do not organize *themselves*."

"Must I stay in my room?" Pen asked as he was ushered into the hallway.

Tigney snorted. "If the demon is already awake, it is probably pointless to try to hold you, but I *request* that you not depart the house without my leave. Please." That last seemed dragged out of him, but he did sound earnest.

Pen nodded. "Yes, sir." One building seemed enough of Martensbridge for the moment. He didn't think he could get lost in here.

"Thank you," said Tigney, and added to the porter, "Send the two Daughter's men to me again, then the servant Gans. And let Clee know that I will be needing him later, and not to go off."

Pen followed the man out.

The porter led Pen to the top floor, given over to a series of tiny rooms for servants or lesser dedicats. The chamber to which he was gestured did have a window, with a battered table shoved up to it, holding a basin, mismatched ewer, a few grubby towels, a shaving mirror, and someone's razor kit. It was flanked by two cots. There were other signs of occupation—pegs hung with clothing, a chest at the foot of one cot, boots scattered about, more possessions pushed under both beds. The second cot had been cleared, with Pen's saddlebags dumped atop. A supper would be served below-stairs for the house's denizens at dusk, Cosso told him before departing; Pen was pleased to be invited. Apparently, his exile from human contact was ended, if only for lack of space. He hoped the room's resident would not be too dismayed by his imposed guest. At least he wouldn't have to share a *bed* with a stranger, as sometimes happened in crowded inns.

Finding cold water still left in the ewer, Pen washed the road dirt from his hands and face, pulled a few things from his saddlebags for later, and sat on the edge of the cot, trying to overcome his disorientation.

"Desdemona? Are you there?" A stupid way to phrase it. Where, and how, would she go? "Are you awake?"

No answer. After few more minutes of sitting, bone-tired but not sleepy enough to nap, his mood shifted to frustration. Tigney had implied he had the run of the house, hadn't he? If no one else was going to show him how to go on, he'd just have to figure it out for himself. He rose to explore.

Nothing else on this floor but more servants' cells. The next floor down was mostly closed doors, if fewer of them; the one left open gave onto someone's bedchamber. Pen let only his glance stray within. The next floor down from that had more open doors, to workrooms like Tigney's, with people about, though what tasks they performed therein were not at all obvious to Pen. He poked his head into the large, quiet room that he gauged was above Tigney's, and stopped short.

It was the house's library, and Pen had never seen so many books and scrolls in one room in his life. Even the Greenwell Lady-school had only boasted one bookcase, the entire contents of which Pen had read up by his second year. There was no tradition of scholarship among his ancestors, either; Jurald Court had account books, records of hunts and harvests, a few books of tales shared around till the pages had worked loose, a couple of tomes of theology left to gather dust. Pen stepped within, marveling.

A pair of long writing tables stood endways to the two windows overlooking the street, sharing the light as fairly as possible. One was taken by a fellow who looked not much older than Pen—heartening— his head bent over his work, quill carefully scratching. His dark hair was cut soldier-fashion, as if to pad a helmet, though it showed no sign of a helmet ever having rested there. By the stack of cut and scored blank sheets to his left, the smaller stack of filled ones to his right, and the book propped open on a wooden stand in front of him, he was working as a copyist.

He glanced up at Pen and frowned, not welcoming interruption. Pen tried smiling, with a silent little wave to indicate his friendliness and harmlessness and general willingness to be greeted, but the man merely grunted and returned his eyes to his page-in-progress. Taking the rebuff in good part, Pen shifted his attention to the shelves.

One whole floor-to-ceiling case appeared to be theology, no surprise in this place. Another was devoted to chronicles, mostly of other times and realms; Pen's own land was more noted for producing cheese than history, he feared. Some ancient, fragile scrolls resided on a set of shelves all to themselves, with corded silk tassels hanging down holding slips of wood inked with titles for each, which he dared not touch. He was thrilled to spot a collection of what appeared to be books of tales, looking well-thumbed. Then a tall case of works in Darthacan, of which Pen had a grasp his Lady-school teachers had grudgingly pronounced adequate; a couple of shelves of works in unreadable Ibran; and then another entire shelf in the ancient tongue of Cedonia, with its exotic letters.

Pen had only seen fragments of the mysterious language before, on old coins or carved on the fallen temple ruins above the road to Greenwell, lone legacy in his hinterland of an empire that had, over a millennium ago, stretched two thousand miles from the warm Cedonian peninsula to the cold Darthacan coast. Scholars described it as fleetingly glorious, like some shooting star, but three hundred years of such ascendency did not seem so fleeting to Pen. In any case, after those swift generations it had fallen apart again, split and re-split among revolts and generals just as Great Audar's empire out of Darthaca was to do hundreds of years later, when his heirs failed.

Pen's hand went out to a work bound in waxed cloth, a modern copy and so not too daunting, with its title inked enigmatically on its spine in the beautiful letters. Wondering who had copied it out, he let it fall open in his hand just to see the calligraphy, as lovely as scrollwork or interlace and about as informative.

Instead, his eye picked out a paragraph: "In the sixth year of the reign of Emperor Letus dubbed The Engineer, for so he had served in his youth in the armies of his uncle, undermining the fortifications of his enemies, before the second plague made him heir, he caused to be built the first aqueduct of the city, nine miles from the springs of the Epalia, watering the gardens of his Empress and piped to new fountains throughout the town, for the health and pleasure of its inhabitants . . . "

Pen gasped and squeezed his eyes shut. After a few moments, he peeked again, very cautiously. Still the same elegant, alien lettering. But now they had become *words*, their meanings flowing into his mind as effortlessly as any Wealdean text.

"I can read this!" he whispered aloud in astonishment.

"Oh, good," said Desdemona. "We'd hoped you'd be a quick study."

"But I *can't* read this!"

"In time," she replied, "you will come to know most of what we know." A pause. "That runs both ways."

Pen snapped his jaw shut, trying to master his sudden unsteadiness. He could only think that he would have the better part of that exchange.

A bored voice remarked from behind him, "The librarian should be back soon, if you need help."

"Thank you," Pen managed, turning and smiling. "Just, um, talking to myself, here. Bad habit. I didn't mean to interrupt you."

The man shrugged, but did not return at once to his page.

"What are you working on?" asked Pen, nodding to the papers.

"Just a collection of tales." He ticked at the volume with his fingernail, dismissively. "Stupid stuff. The important books go to the senior dedicats."

"Still, I'd think you'd learn a lot, doing that. Do you ever make up the blocks of wood to print many copies? I've heard they do that in Martensbridge."

"Do I look like a woodcarver?" He wriggled his inky hand. "Though that work, and the pay for it, also goes to the seniors."

"You are a dedicat?" Pen hazarded. The scribe wore no braids or badges, just ordinary town dress of tunic and trousers. "Lay, or Temple-sworn?"

He stretched his shoulders and grimaced. "Sworn. I mean to make acolyte soon, if all the places don't go to those who brought richer dowries."

One of the several routes into the Bastard's Order, Pen had heard, was for the families of children born out of wedlock to dedicate them to the Temple, together with a portion for their keep. That is, if the families were well-off. Poor foundlings were left more anonymously, and cheaply, at the orphanages. Not liking to ask for clarification, lest this be a sore issue for the fellow, Pen said instead, "At least it's indoor work. Not like herding cows."

The man smiled sourly. "You a cowherd, country boy?"

"At need," Pen confessed. The scribe's tone made it sound a low task, rather than the occasional outdoor holiday Pen had found it, but then, it hadn't been Pen's daily portion without relief. "And haying," he added. "Everyone turns out for the harvest, high or low."

The hunting in the mountains had been a happier chore. He'd had good luck with wild sheep, often able to take one down with a single arrow, not to mention being most nimble at retrieving carcasses from awkward slopes and ledges, a task to which his servants had cheered him on with suspicious enthusiasm. It was the one activity that had reconciled Pen to the god naturally apportioned to his age and sex. The Son of Autumn's rule over comradeship-in-arms had less appeal, if Drovo and his friends had been anything to go by.

"Cowherds. Why?" the fellow muttered, and dipped his quill again, incurious of an answer.

An older woman entered, carrying a stack of books. An acolyte's looped braid hung on the shoulder of proper white Temple robes, and a pair of gold-rimmed spectacles swung by a ribbon around her neck. Martensbridge was noted for its glasswork; perhaps ordinary people could afford such rich aids here? Certainly this must be the librarian. She stopped and stared at Pen, more interested than hostile. "And who are you?"

He ducked his head. "Penric kin Jurald, ma'am. I'm a . . . visitor." Because that sounded better than *prisoner*. "Learned Tigney said I might go about the house."

Her brows rose in surprise at the divine's name. "Really."

Pen couldn't tell from her tone if she thought that good or bad, but he forged on. "I was wondering if you had any books on sorcery or demons. Practical ones," he added prudently, lest he be gifted with some thick tome in a high and soporific style. He didn't see how the subject *could* be made boring, but he'd read—well, tried to read—some theological works from Learned Lurenz's shelves, and didn't underestimate the determined drabness of Temple scholars.

She took a step back, her head coming up. "Such books are restricted to those of the rank of divine and above. I'm afraid, young man, you have not yet earned the braids for them."

"But you must have such books, yes?" *Somewhere.* He'd seen none in his survey of the shelves.

Her glance went to a tall wardrobe set against the far wall. "Locked up, certainly. Or they would quickly become the most stolen of our treasures."

Pen stared with fresh interest at the capacious cabinet, wondering how many books it might hold. "If a divine said it was all right, would it be all right?" Could, or would, Tigney give permission?

"Such authorizations are possible, yes, but there must be need. What do you imagine your need to be?" She smiled at him with the ironic air of a woman long experienced in resisting the blandishments of her juniors angling for forbidden treats. Well, he'd always been able to get around the Jurald Court cooks . . .

"Ah, you see, I lately contracted a demon of my own, from a Temple sorceress who died on the road at Greenwell. It was an accident, truly it was, but if Desdemona and I are going to be stuck with each other, I think I'd better know more about what I'm doing than I do. Which is almost nothing, so anything at all you could lend me would be a start." He smiled his most hopeful smile at her, trying for maximum sunniness. Trustworthiness, too; he should definitely try to look trustworthy.

Evidently he failed, for she took a hastier step backward, her hand going to her throat. She frowned at him for a long, long moment. "If that is a jape, young man, I will have your hide for binding leather. Wait here." She set down her armload of books on the table and hurried out again.

Pen's glance went again to the now-riveting cabinet, and he wondered if she could possibly mean that threat literally. A librarian of the demon-god, after all . . .

The quill had stopped scratching, and Pen turned to find the dedicat-scribe staring at him as if he'd sprouted antlers from his head. "How did *you* come by a demon?" he asked, astonished.

Getting practiced by now, Pen recited the short tale, summing the disaster in as few sentences as he could make sound coherent. Fairly coherent.

The scribe's wide eyes narrowed. "You know, none below the rank of divine are allowed to receive a Temple demon, and the gift of its sorcery. It's considered a high and rare accomplishment. Men compete just for a place in line, studying and preparing, then wait for *years*."

Pen scratched his head. "There must be other accidents, from time to time. I mean, you can't control the time or place of a person's death." Well . . . there was one sure way that sprang to Pen's mind, but he'd heard no rumors of the Temple doing *that*.

Lips compressed, the scribe just shook his head.

The librarian returned with Learned Tigney in tow. Pen brightened.

"Oh, sir! May I be permitted to read the books here?" He gestured to the locked cabinet. "You certainly can't say I don't have need."

Tigney sighed. "Lord Penric, I've only just begun to unpack the Learned Ruchia's cases. I've no idea yet what needs I am going to find in this tangle." He eyed Pen, who returned his best starving-boy look. The divine's expression did not so much soften, as grow shrewd. "But, while you wait, you might certainly have leave to read the books from the other shelves, here in this room when it is open. That would keep you occupied for a time, I should think."

And feet fastened in one place, too, Pen fancied was the unspoken cap to that. But Tigney hadn't, actually, said *No, never.* "Indeed, sir." He tried to project dutiful resignation, pending a rematch. He realized he still had the Cedonian chronicle in his hand, and lowered his voice, showing the book to Tigney.

"When I opened this book, I found I could *read* it. Is that . . . usual?"

Tigney's lips quirked up. "If you are a Cedonian, I suppose."

Pen mustered a feeble smile at the heavy humor. Better than anger or thunderous forbiddings, certainly. "But I'm not. I had not a word of it until, well, just now."

His witticism duly rewarded, Tigney granted Pen a short nod of reassurance. "Yes, it's usual. If any demon serves a master long enough, it will take up an imprint of its rider's mother tongue. And pass it along, in due course. Ruchia had half-a-dozen such languages at her command, all spoken as a native. Very useful to her, and to the Temple."

"Was she a great scholar, then?"

Tigney hesitated. "Not as such." He eyed Pen a moment more. "You were very quick to absorb it, though. It more often requires some weeks or months for such knowledge to, so to speak, leak through. But then, Ruchia's was an unusually old and powerful mount." He drew breath. "It is going to take me some time yet to sort through Ruchia's effects. I may want to speak to her old demon directly, as the most intimate, if not necessarily the most reliable, witness to her affairs. If you might hold yourself in readiness here for that, I should be most grateful."

"Certainly, sir," said Pen, deciding to take this half-victory while he could get it. "Although . . . I don't seem to *control* her speaking."

"You do; you just don't know it yet."

Pen bit back another bid for the cabinet. It wasn't as though he was going to be able to read all these books in a day anyway.

Tigney went on, "Or rather, if it controlled *you*, you would most certainly know it." He looked away, grimly, making Pen wonder again about the former sorcerer's somehow-discarded demon.

The divine turned to the shamelessly listening scribe, who had stopped even pretending to write. "Clee, when you are done with that page, come downstairs. I've some letters need copied before they go out."

"Yes, sir," said the scribe, with a dutiful wave of his quill, and went back to diligent scratching.

Tigney motioned the librarian after him; Pen glimpsed them making some low-voiced exchange out in the hall, punctuated by glances his way, after which Tigney departed and the librarian came back. She gave Pen a provisional sort of nod in passing, and took up her mysterious business at a desk in the corner.

Overwhelmed by his choices, Pen started to make for the shelf of tales, but instead went to sit at the second table and reopen the Cedonian chronicle, driven by a faint, irrational fear that his newfound skill might desert him as abruptly as it had arrived, and he'd better seize this chance while he could. A chronicle was as good as a tale, anyway, imperial courts seeming almost as fantastical as ogres' lairs. And he really wanted to find out more about the emperor who was an engineer, who had made fountains for his people. It seemed a strangely un-imperial task; weren't emperors supposed to go around conquering people? Which was how they became emperors, one presumed.

The scribe Clee finished his page, tidied his supplies on a shelf, and departed, with a sort of grunt-nod in Pen's direction; not exactly a friendly farewell, but politely acknowledging his existence. Pen returned a smile and head-duck, feeling like an envoy signing a truce to a skirmish he had not known was being fought. The librarian didn't leave until the light failed and Pen went down to seek supper. She locked the outer door carefully behind them both.

Supper, plain food but abundant, was served in a whitewashed cellar refectory with a long table. Not all of the dedicats and acolytes who worked here were fed here, Pen discovered, as some lived in lodgings nearby, or were married. Tigney wasn't present, but Clee was, and not-uncordially waved Pen to a seat on the bench next to him, where he was introduced merely as "a visitor." Pen, tired out and hungry, was content to listen, and not talk much; Clee turned off any questions that drew too near to the real matters that had brought Pen to Martensbridge. Mostly younger folk, the dedicats gossiped, exchanged comments about their work, which seemed to be mostly administrative, ate fast, and hurried off.

The servants had the next turn at the table; coming out, Pen met Gans coming in. The groom seemed contented enough to have nothing to do and all food provided for the next few days, but still asked, "When can we go home, Lord Penric?"

"I don't know yet," Pen admitted. "Learned Tigney seems to be the man to decide, after he goes through Learned Ruchia's effects." How hard could that task be? They had all fit on one packsaddle, and had been mostly women's clothes. *Well . . . except for the demon.* "I guess he's her executor, of sorts."

Gans accepted this with a glum grunt, and Pen followed Clee upstairs, where he discovered that it was the scribe's room he was sharing. He didn't seem as put-out to lose his privacy as Pen might have feared. The rule of the house was early to bed and rise at first light, so Pen, too, readied himself to lie down. Truly, this day felt a year long, so crowded with changes as it had been. Clee did not blow out their shared candle at once, but rather, asked a few leading questions about Pen's family as rustic lords of what Pen was beginning to realize must seem quite a minor mountain valley.

"Are you from this city?" Pen asked in turn. The scribe seemed sophisticated enough to be.

"I am now," said Clee. "I wasn't born here. I was born at Castle Martenden, about ten miles up the lakeshore. My brother is baron there."

"Oh, the same as Rolsch," said Pen, pleased to find some connection. "You are Dedicat Lord Clee, then?"

Clee grimaced. "I should say, my half-brother."

"Ah," said Pen. After an awkward moment, he offered, "I have a half-uncle, who farms near Greenwell. I like him. His wife is always very kind to me." *These things happen,* Pen hoped this implied. *Not a problem.*

Clee snorted. "Castle Martenden is not merely some fortified farmhouse. Kin Martenden have been great landholders in these parts for centuries."

Pen thought this an unjust description of Jurald Court. Or at least, it ought to be *large, sprawling fortified farmhouse.*

"My brother is at loggerheads with the city, which covets his lands and rents and rights," Clee went on. "The city fathers grow big in their own esteem. They've bought out a dozen minor lordships already that fell into their debt. *I* think the merchant guilds conspire to net the foolish that way."

Pen remembered the ruins on the road in, and thought the city's outlying district might have grown as much by force of arms as mercantile trickery. Although, he supposed, wealth must come first, before arms could be bought. Martensbridge was a royal free town, its charter making it unbeholden to any lords except the Hallow King of the Weald himself. It stood oddly balanced between its distant lord, and its treaties with its nearer neighbor cities with their more varied allegiances. Pen's impression was that Martensbridge felt itself a lot more free than royal, and recalled the joking prayer an acolyte had told him over dinner: *Five gods bless and keep the Hallow King—far from us!*

"What about the princess-archdivine?" Pen asked. "I've never met a princess. Or an archdivine, for that matter. I hope I might get a chance to see her before I go home. Is she very beautiful?"

Clee vented a laugh. "She's fifty."

Pen supposed princesses in tales always seemed to be young and lovely because when they grew older they became queens. The princess-archdivine's title was more political, and unrelated to her marital status. "I suppose even royal princesses can have callings."

Clee shrugged. "The archdivineship of Martensbridge has been a dumping ground for Wealdean royal spares for centuries. I'll give this one credit, though, she's powerfully shrewd. Besides managing Temple lands, she's fostered the silk makers here, which has brought even more coin to her hands, which has allowed her to buy yet more territory. No one knows what will happen when the city and the princess run out of other fodder, and have to start in eating each other."

With that ambiguous remark, Clee blew out the candle and rolled over. Pen, eyelids weighted with exhaustion, did not even attempt to talk to Desdemona.

For the next two days Pen sat in the library and read, trooped downstairs to eat, and smiled shyly at people who all seemed too busy to talk to him, save, sometimes, Clee, when taking a stretch from his scribal work. The locked cabinet was an itch at the corner of his eye.

Pen supposed even librarians had to go to the garderobe sometime, but this one never left the room unless there were other persons present; another copyist or two, or dedicats or acolytes reading and taking notes. None of the valuable books were allowed to be removed and read elsewhere save by divines of the highest ranks, of which there seemed to be three or four here besides Tigney, and even they received stern looks and admonitions along with their volumes.

Pen finished the fascinating Cedonian chronicle, and started another in Darthacan. He discovered his reading in that language had somehow become far more fluid and swift—he didn't have to stop and think through the sentences, and he seemed to know many more words than he'd ever learned in the Greenwell Lady-school. A slimmer chronicle in comfortable Wealdean supplied a short history of Martensbridge. The marsh hamlet at the outlet of the long lake had acquired its name when an earlier lord of kin Martenden had built the first stone bridge, the text asserted, convincingly enough. The improved roads had brought increasing wealth. Somewhat unfairly, Pen thought, kin Martenden had lost control of the growing town when their own overlord's family died out, and the greater territory fell to a prince of the Weald. The town had bought or won or bribed— on this, the chronicle was unclear, but it seemed to involve lending money to the right lords with hungry armies—its first royal charter soon thereafter, swept in under the cloak of the princess-archdivine, and never let to lapse thereafter. Glass- and silk-makers came down from the north over the high passes from Adria and Saone, metal-workers from Carpagamo, and settled in the new free town. Caravans arrived from as far away as the reduced modern descendant of the Cedonian Empire, ah! Pen wondered if he might meet such travelers in the marketplaces or counting houses, and test his new tongue.

The chronicle claimed that Great Audar had once resided here, and told a legend of a bargain he made with a helpful talking marten that somehow resulted in a blessing for the locality, and a more exciting source of its name. Pen had read of that legend appended to at least two other towns, one with a snake and one with a hawk, though both with Great Audar, which made him distrust the book's author just a little. Apart from the talking animals. While there were rumors about the Hallow King's strange, secretive cadre of royal shamans having some special understanding of the kin animals of their land, Darthacan

Audar had been the bitter enemy of the Old Weald and its forest magics in his long-ago day, so Pen didn't think this could be some oblique reference to those mysterious practices.

By the third day, although his mind was still wildly excited by the written riches in the room, Pen's eyes were burning, and his not-well-padded haunches were rethinking his calling as a scholar much as they had a career as a courier. Besides, for the first time this week it had stopped drizzling and the sun was out. Desperate for movement, he went down to see Tigney.

The divine's door was open; Pen leaned on the frame, cleared his throat, and ventured, "How goes it, sir? Is there anything I can do here? To help? Any task at all?"

"A task . . . ?" Tigney leaned back from his writing table and regarded Pen thoughtfully. "I suppose you are a mountaineer. Not used to being cooped up all day, I daresay."

"The library is very fine, but that's so, sir. Even in the winter, we hunted in the lower forests every week, or ran the trap lines."

"Hm." Tigney drummed his fingers on the scarred tabletop, then gestured to a neat stack of clothing folded on a chair. "Ruchia had no heirs of the body. Often in such cases a Temple sorcerer's possessions are willed to their successor along with their demon, but Ruchia left no directive with me. You cannot wear her clothes, but if you would like to run an errand, you could take them to the garment merchant on Elm Street, and turn them into money for the Order."

A modest task, but it would allow Pen to walk about the town. And, if he performed it well, Tigney might find other work for him. Being the errand boy of this house couldn't be worse than being the errand boy of Jurald Court. He'd never felt a calling before to serve the gods, but who knew? "Certainly! I'd be glad to."

While Tigney gave him more precise directions to Elm Street, Pen went to tie up the bundle. His hand hesitated.

"I think you do not want to sell this one, sir." It was an elaborate, embroidered skirt. Pen shook it out, puzzled. It seemed just a skirt, if heavy. Why had he said that?

Tigney's brows rose. "I thought I'd checked them all. Ah—was that you, who spoke just now?"

"Not sure, sir." Pen ran the long hem through his fingers, which found an unsewn slot. Poking within, he drew out a folded length of thin cloth. He shook it free to find it covered all over with fine writing, in none of the languages he recognized. *No, it is a cipher. What?*

Tigney held out his hand in demand; Pen delivered both skirt and cipher. "Ah!" said Tigney. "Cloth, not parchment. No wonder I felt nothing. Clever Ruchia!" He glanced up rather sharply at Pen. "Are there any more like this?"

"I . . . don't know."

Pen didn't feel there were, but Tigney ended up prodding through every hem and fold in the stack to be sure. He then sat up and read the message on the cloth, without referring to any cipher-book. Leaning back with a relieved sigh, he muttered, "Nothing too difficult, then. Thank His Whiteness. I think."

Pen swallowed. "Sir—was Learned Ruchia a *spy*?" That frail old woman?

Tigney waved a hand in vigorous negation. "Certainly not! A trusted agent of the Temple, yes, able to sail smoothly through some very troubled waters, I will give her that."

Pen took in this evasion. He was pretty sure it came out to a *yes*. Which made Tigney . . . her spymaster? Neither personage fit his mental image of either role. He smiled hesitantly and said nothing.

As Pen bundled up the cloth once more and made for the door, Tigney added kindly, "You can keep half of whatever you can sell them for."

"Thank you, sir!" Pen waved and left quickly, before Tigney could change his mind about either the errand or its reward, after the capricious manner of seniors.

Safely out of earshot on the steep street, Desdemona snappishly remarked, "Half! Tigney is a cheeseparing drudge. You should have had it all."

So, she hadn't been asleep. "I thought it very generous. He didn't *need* to offer me any. Also"—he grinned—"he forgot to tell me when I had to be back."

"Humph," said Desdemona, sounding amused. "Well, we do like a truant."

Pen took the long way to Elm Street, down to the river and along it past the old stone bridge to a market, still busy even though it was early afternoon. He stood a while and listened to a pair of musicians, one with a fiddle and the other with a skin drum, set up to amuse the crowd with silly or mournful songs, a hat at their feet upturned invitingly. Pen reflected that unlike all the other vendors here, they could not call back their merchandise if the bargain was bad, and fished a few precious coppers out of his thin purse for the hat before continuing down the quayside.

At a low point of the embankment wall, he set the clothing bundle down and leaned over, trying to see up the river to the lake. He might need a higher vantage. "Desdemona . . . is music a good gift of the spirit?"

"Oh, aye. We like a good song."

"What about knowledge? Reading?"

"That's good, too."

"Were you reading along with me, these past days? Over my shoulder, as it were?"

"Sometimes."

"Should I do that more?"

"To please me, do you mean?" She sounded disconcerted.

"Well . . . yes, I guess so."

A long silence, then: "Those things are all interesting, but it is the share of your *body* that is my daily gift, without which I could not maintain existence in this world. Or in any other. So gifts of the body are actually very acceptable."

"That would be . . . my body, right? Things done for my body?" said Pen, trying to work this out. Not that he could maintain his own existence in the world without it, either.

"Have you any other body? I don't."

"At present." Though the demon had shared a dozen other bodies before his. Would she share more, after . . . ? His memory reverted, unwilled, to the interrupted morning bed activities back at the Lady-school, and his face heated. However discomfited he had been, sooner or later his body was going to have its way about that, chatty audience or no. Not that he hadn't been willing to share that intimacy with Preita, in prospect. And this was different, how . . . ?

Desdemona drew a long breath. "Think of how a good rider maintains his favorite horse. Brushed and glossy and well-fed. Sound shoes. Carefully exercised and trained, and taken out for fast gallops. Ribbons braided in its mane, fine saddles and bridles to make a show, maybe trimmed with silver or colored glass beads. A steed to be proud of."

Wait, I thought I was supposed to be the rider . . . ? All these equine metaphors were growing befuddling.

"In short," said Desdemona briskly, "as we have never had an actual lord before, could you at least try to dress like one?"

Pen snorted, eyeing the sleeve of his countryman's smock. "I'm afraid this *is* how actual lords dress, when their purses are as flat as kin Jurald's." Also, the demon was beginning to sound disturbingly like his sisters again, which sat uncomfortably with the thoughts he'd been having just before she'd gone off about horses.

"Put another way—what you enjoy, we enjoy, for the most part."

Pen was startled by this. "Food? Drink?" Other pleasures of the flesh . . . ?

"Yes, indeed!"

"Wine-sickness?"

She said smugly, "Oh, the wine-sickness can be all yours."

"You . . . can evade my pain?" The implications of that were odd.

"We can withdraw from it to a degree, yes."

"Surely managing one's demon should be harder than managing a horse." Not that horses were easy, five gods knew. "I mean, those Temple disciplines and so on?" Everyone kept talking about the all-important Temple disciplines, but no one ever explained what they *were*.

"The hard things will come on their own. You need not go hunting them." She added after a reflective moment, "Though I pity the poor demon who gets stuck with a Temple ascetic. Hair shirts, really, what is the *point*?" She gave the impression of a faint, dramatic shudder, and Pen smiled despite himself. She added more tartly, "And it indicates a deep confusion of thinking to mistake one's own discomfort for a benefit to another."

Pen blinked, an old puzzle suddenly laid open to him, bare and plain. *Yes. That's it exactly.*

Feeling a need to digest this, he heaved the bundle of clothes back up. "Let's go find Elm Street."

He was quite out of his reckoning with Tigney's directions by now, but Desdemona, clearly, knew the town well. They arrived at their goal efficiently, without any doubling back.

The shop was dark, with a peculiar smell. Pen set the clothes on the counter, and the shop woman told over them with quick fingers, and named a price.

"Pen," muttered Desdemona, "let me do this."

"If you don't embarrass me," Pen muttered back. The shop woman gave him a strange look, but then his mouth began a sharp, though polite enough, negotiation that resulted in due course in a sum double what he had first been offered.

"Good," said Desdemona. "Let us look around a little."

Abandoning the counter, they went to the shelves and piles. Obligingly, Pen sorted and dealt. "Can you even see what you're doing?" he murmured.

"Oh, yes. You could, too. Wait . . . now try."

Pen squinted, and the shadows seemed to retreat. The view wasn't really an improvement. But somehow, from these unpromising heaps, he pulled some quite fine discards, if torn or discolored in spots. Granted the elegant blue brocade doublet with the three-inch gash in the front, set around with brown stains, was a bit disturbing.

"We can set these to rights," Desdemona promised.

"Isn't that what you call uphill magic?"

"Only a very little. Can you sew?"

"Not especially well, no."

A brief silence. "We believe you will find that you now can."

Pen set back several items that seemed too gaudy, to Desdemona's disappointment, but at last they agreed on a small pile of what she assured him were men's garments, the likes of which Pen had never seen at Jurald Court, nor Greenwell either. The silk-weavers here seemed to set a high standard for local castoffs, certainly. Back to the counter for another negotiation, and in a few more minutes, Pen left the shop not only with the additions to his wardrobe, but with a goodly supply of coins. Even when he turned over Tigney's half, there would be some money left over.

Someday, he promised himself, *I shall have new clothes, from a real tailor*. Though how he was to get to that someday, he had no notion.

Heading back downhill, they passed a bathhouse. Pen stopped and eyed it. "Pleasures of the body, eh?" *Clean and warm* surely qualified. Not to mention *shaved and trimmed*.

"Superb idea!" said Desdemona. "But not that one. There's a better one farther up near the palace."

"It looks tidy enough . . . "

"Trust me."

The voice he'd come to recognize as Mira of Adria said something, which he tried but failed to not-understand. *If you would but put him under my direction, I could show him how to make a fortune in a place like this* seemed to be the gist of it.

Pen chose not to pursue the remark.

The bathhouse near the palace-and-temple precincts was intimidatingly large, compared to the one in Greenwell run out the back of a woman's home, but not too crowded at this time of day. Pen visited its barber for a serious shave and a trim of the ragged ends of his hair, then the men's side for a thorough lathering with scented soap of head and body, a sluicing rinse with a bucket of warm water, and a soak in the huge wooden tub with the copper bottom, big enough for half-a-dozen men, kept heated with a small fire underneath. He oozed down in the water and lingered with his eyes half closed until the skin of his fingers began to grow wrinkly, he began to worry that Tigney might be ready to send out a search party, and he became aware that Desdemona, who seemed to be purring as much as himself, was eyeing a couple of the better-looking of his fellow bathers in a way that Pen found unsettling. Time to decamp.

Dressed, hair combed out and drying, and back on the street, he glanced at the looming bulk of the temple at the top of the hill. It was the most imposing structure in town, and the chronicle of Martensbridge that he'd read yesterday had made much of it. A temple had always crowned this high site, but the prior one, being built of wood in the style of the Weald, had burned down in one of the periodic fires. In a joint building effort of Temple and town that had taken several decades, it had been replaced by this one of stone, after the Darthacan manner. This represented not a change in lordship or worship, but a change in wealth, Pen gathered. Curious, he turned his steps not downhill, but up.

He walked all the way around it, marveling at its size and stately proportions, then peeked through the tall pillared portico. No ceremonies seemed to be in progress, and other lone worshipers were trickling in and out, so Pen ventured within. As the space opened up before him, he realized that the old wooden Greenwell temple was a mere hall by comparison, despite its abundant woodcarvings. Or maybe a barn.

The holy fire on the central granite plinth had a round copper hood and chimney, made rich with delicate hammered designs, to carry the smoke out of the worshipers' eyes, with the result that the domed roof was not smoke-blackened. A ring of arched windows below the dome let in light. The space was six-sided, one for the broad entryway and one for each of the five gods, opening to domed apses that must, could one see the temple from the top, make it look like a grand stone flower.

The niche for the Lady of Spring, whose season this now was, was redolent with offerings of fresh blooms. A few serious-looking townsmen were praying in the niche of the Father of Winter, god of, among other things, justice. Judges, lawyers? More likely litigants, Pen decided. An impressively pregnant woman knelt on a cushion before the altar of the Mother of Summer, praying perhaps for a safe delivery, or possibly just for the strength to stand up again. The Bastard's niche, between the Daughter's and the Mother's, was presently empty.

Pen went by habit to the altar of the Son of Autumn. Only two fellows were there before him. The younger man, looking like a military recruit, knelt on one of the provided cushions, his hands up, palms out and fingers spread. Praying for luck? An older man lay prone on one of the large prayer rugs, arms out, hands clenching, in the attitude of deepest supplication. It was mere fancy that Pen imagined him a veteran, praying for forgiveness, but he couldn't shake off the impression.

He picked out a cushion behind them and got down onto his knees without quite knowing what he was praying for. Or should be praying for. Or even Who he should be praying to. So he prayed for the safety and well-being of his family, and of all on the Jurald lands, and poor half-cheated Preita as, he was reminded, he had promised to do. Ruchia? Hardly the right god. He signed the tally, rose, and carried his knee cushion over to the Bastard's niche.

Kneeling again, he realized he'd forgotten to pray for himself. How temporary was the transfer of his affairs to this new god? The Bastard was the master of disasters; supplicants more often prayed to *avert* His attentions, like paying a mercenary company to route around one's town.

Would praying for knowledge be safe? Pen was certainly desperate for it. But the white god was the author of some pretty vicious ironies, as far as the prophecy-stories associated with His gifts told. Praying for the soul of Ruchia seemed late off the mark, as she was signed by her funeral miracle to be in His hands already. Pen contented himself with hoping she was happy there, whatever that meant in that profoundly altered state beyond death.

On impulse, Pen decided to pray for Desdemona. Granted, demons were already creatures of the god, though whether escaped prisoners or servants seemed unclear. Maybe they could be either, as one man might be good and another bad, or a man might go from bad to good or the reverse at different times of his life? He became aware that she had grown very quiet, like a tight, closed ball inside of him.

Demons, unkillable and, it appeared, immune to pain, did not fear much, but they feared their god, and the dissolution they would suffer if they fell back into His hands. Pen would too, he decided, if going to the gods meant his destruction and not his preservation. However it was that souls were sustained in the hands of their chosen gods. Or choosing gods.

Praying for her safety and well-being must cover it, since neither were possible without that substrate of continuing existence. A well-practiced prayer that he knew how to do. So he did, whispering the words aloud.

In all, he was relieved that no one answered.

He unfolded himself and went back to the portico, pausing a moment to take in the view up the lake. He wondered if that distant gray smudge sticking out into the water from the left shore might be Clee's castle birthplace—not on a crag, for a change, but using a small island to provide it with a free moat.

Uncertain which of the descending avenues to take back to the Order's house, Pen called softly, "Desdemona . . . ?"

No answer. She seemed still locked up inside him. Pen wondered if the gods really *were* more present in their temples, for all that the divines taught that They were always equally present everywhere. And if demons would know. Pen pursed his lips, then slipped into a silk mercer's shop at the top of one street.

Most of the goods displayed were far beyond his means, but he negotiated for a bit of ribbon about the length of his arm without doing his little stock of coins too much damage. He found the mirror provided for customers to hold the cloth up to their faces, and braided the blue silk band through his queue. He turned his head and waited.

"Pretty!" murmured Desdemona.

Aha, that's fetched her out. He must keep that trick in mind. He said only "Thank you," and went back to the street, where he was then able to ask himself for directions. *No wonder sorcerers have a reputation for being strange.* That silent speech, if he ever gained the knack of it, would be a great convenience. Swinging his bundle of new old clothes, he started off.

A couple of housemaids giggled and blushed as he strode by, which Pen ignored. A glum and elderly washerwoman, shuffling along, looked up, and her wrinkled face broke into so unexpectedly sweet a smile that Pen had to smile back, and offer her a little bow. A shave and a hair wash worked on women of all sorts, it seemed. Which, since Desdemona might well be described as women of all sorts, was . . . opportune.

Turning down the steep street fronting the Order's house, he saw Clee walking up it accompanied by a tall, black-bearded, soldierly fellow leading his horse. Pen finally saw what the term *richly caparisoned* meant, for it was a very well-dressed horse: saddle and bridle carved and stained and set with silver; its saddle blanket, admittedly atop a more practical sheepskin, of embroidered silk. He thought of Desdemona's horse lecture, and was amused.

Two mounted guardsmen and a groom followed, reins slack. The bearded fellow bore a sword, in a town where very few men carried them, and a jeweled band on his hat.

Not much apart from the near-identical color and cut of their hair marked the two men as related. Clee was lanky, his hands thin and ink-stained, his clothing a knee-length townsman's gown with trousers in a simple cut and fabric. His companion was thickset and muscular, his hands broad, suitable for maintaining a grip on a weapon in defiance of blows, his riding leathers heavy and less elaborate than what his horse was wearing. Pen suspected the straight black hair had actually borne a helmet at some point. Tough, solid, unsmiling.

Clee looked up and saw Penric, and his head went back in surprise; after a moment, he beckoned Pen nearer. The pair stopped to let him come up.

"Penric! I would like you to meet my brother, Lord Rusillin kin

Martenden. Rusi, this is our visitor, Lord Penric kin Jurald, from the valley of Greenwell."

Lord Rusillin spread his hand over his heart in the courteous gesture of a comrade of the Son, offering Pen a reserved nod. Pen smiled and nodded back, though he couldn't quite bring himself to touch his lips in the sign of the Bastard. "Five gods give you good day, my lord."

The carved mouth made an effort at a smile. "Lord Penric. One god is giving you a difficult time, by what my brother tells me."

Clee had gossiped about his condition? Pen supposed it was unusual, and therefore interesting. He couldn't think Learned Tigney would like that. But then, very few people were as determinedly uninformative as Tigney. Pen managed, "So far, I have taken no harm from my accident. And it's won me a trip to Martensbridge at the Temple's expense, which I cannot fault."

The smile grew more genuine. "You should join a mercenary company if you really want to see the world."

Was Rusillin recruiting? That was one way for a lord to maintain his estate, certainly. "My brother Drovo did that," said Pen.

"Good for him!"

Affability did not seem to come easily to the man, but Pen sensed he was trying. He therefore let this go by, struggling to remember what all he'd said to Clee about Drovo. By Clee's lack of a wince, Pen hadn't got round to mentioning his brother's final fate, ah, that was right.

"Rusi collects and leads a company of men for the Earl Palatine of Westria," said Clee, confirming Pen's guess.

"A mercenary company that could find good uses for a sorcerer," Lord Rusillin remarked, "though the Temple does not often release theirs to such services. The sorcerer might find such tasks profitable as well."

Pen cleared his throat. "I'm neither a sorcerer nor Temple-sworn, at present. Or only an infant sorcerer. I acquired my demon less than a fortnight ago, and they are much weakened for a time by such transitions, I've learned. And I've had no training at all. So I'm afraid I'm not much use to anyone, just yet."

"Hm. There's a shame." Rusillin gave him a kindly look, or perhaps it was pity.

"Well," said Pen, extricating himself before Clee's brother could start in on any more direct military propositioning, "I should report in to Learned Tigney. He'll be wondering where I went. Honored to meet you, my Lord Rusillin."

"And you, Lord Penric."

He watched Pen keenly as he went inside, bending his head to make some remark to Clee that Pen did not hear, though Clee's lips twitched. Pen was pleased that the two half-brothers seemed to have a reasonably fraternal relationship despite their differences in estate. There was certainly plenty to tempt Clee to envy, were he inclined to it.

He wondered if Desdemona had found Rusillin's powerful figure impressive.

Pen went upstairs and settled with Tigney who, remarking sternly on his lateness, received as strict an accounting of Pen's time as of his coins.

"Desdemona seemed to like the bathhouse," Pen told him. "I hadn't known creatures of spirit could partake of pleasures of the body quite so simply."

Tigney's lips thinned in his beard. "So dangerously, if the demon becomes ascendant. They devolve into fascination and excess, with no thought for preservation. As a man might ride a stolen horse to death."

Controlling a wicked impulse to whinny, Pen excused himself to put his new treasures away and return to his station in the library.

The following afternoon, Pen had grown so absorbed in a Darthacan chronicle of Great Audar that he almost missed his chance.

The librarian had gone out, but a scribe and two acolytes were still working. They left one by one as Pen was perusing an account of the massacre at Holytree that seemed vastly different than one he had read from a Wealdean writer. He only looked up when Desdemona, with some effort, made his mouth say, "Hey!"

"What?"

"Now's your moment. To the cabinet."

Pen set his volume down and hurried over to it. "Wait. It's still locked." He wasn't going to try to force it; the lock was sturdy, the woodwork was fine, and the destruction would be obvious.

"Put your hand on the lock."

Baffled, Pen did so. A surge of heat seemed to flow from his palm. Within the metal mechanism, something clicked.

"Could you always do that?" he asked.

"Not for the first few days." He had the sense of a convalescent tottering happily around a room after too long abed, delighted to be working weakened muscles again.

"But . . . Tigney must know. Hasn't he told the librarian?"

"To be sure, which is why you have never been left alone here. This oversight will not last. So hasten."

Willingly, Pen did so. The cabinet door creaked wide.

The contents were slightly disappointing; a mere two shelves of volumes, less than forty in all, the other two shelves bare. Nothing sparkled or growled or seemed to need to be chained like a vicious dog. His hands reached out eagerly. "Which one?"

"Not that, no, no . . . that one."

"It's not the thickest."

"No, but it's the best. Three-fourths of what's here is rubbish. Now close up. She's coming back."

Pen swung the door shut; the latch clicked. He set his hand to it. "And lock up again?"

"We can't do that."

"Wait, why not?"

"Locking increases order. Too advanced for you right now."

The disorder that would result if the librarian thought to check the lock was a bit frightening to contemplate, if one wasn't a durable demon. Pen scurried back to his bench, shoved the filched volume into his tunic, and opened his Darthacan chronicle once more. The words seemed to dance before his eyes, and the volume tucked under his heart to burn. Footsteps sounded from the hall.

"Don't leave right away," muttered Desdemona, "and *don't* make a show of it, or offer limping explanations. Go out exactly as you always do."

To Pen's relief, the first one back was the scribe, who gave Pen a cordial nod and took up her quill again. The librarian, returning a few minutes later, looked around as if satisfied and went to her desk, where she took up a perpetual copying task that she fitted in between other duties, much like a woman with her knitting. Pen read two more pages without taking in a word, then rose, tucked the parchment slip with his name on it into the page where he'd stopped, and set the volume on the librarian's desk with his usual "Thank you."

She nodded back, with a mildly approving look, and Pen made his escape.

Unsure where else to hide, Pen went back to Clee's room; to his relief, the dedicat was out. He closed the door, set a chair in front of it to slow anyone entering, jounced down on his bed, and opened the stolen book. *Borrowed* book. It wasn't as though he meant to take it out of the house. And he certainly meant to put it back. Undetected, by preference.

Essentials of Sorcery and the Management of Demons, the title page read. *The Work of Learned Ruchia of Martensbridge, Senior Divine and Sorceress of the Bastard's Order. With Aid from Learned Helvia of Liest and Learned Amberein of Saone. Volume One.*

"Hey," said Pen, indignant. "You wrote this!"

"Not we," sighed Desdemona. "Ruchia's doings. We would not have had the patience. And a tedious great deal of work it was, too. We threatened to throw her off a bridge, once, if she would not finish it up and be done."

Distracted by this, Pen found his next sentence jammed up in his mouth. When he had untangled his tongue, he asked instead, "Could you have?"

"No," sighed Desdemona. "Not her. Neither from a bridge nor from our being." She added after a little, "Best rider ever."

"Couldn't you just tell me all this?"

"Your voice would grow hoarse, and Tigney would wonder." Another pause. "The Temple offers many warnings about demons, and they are not all *wrong.* You may trust Ruchia. Also, you will not be able to waste precious time *arguing* with her."

Taking the hint, Pen turned to the first page. This text was handwritten, not printed from woodblock, which made it easier to read, but also made him worry about how few copies might exist. He tried to settle himself and pay attention, and not read so fast in his excitement that he failed to take it all in.

After a time, he asked, "Desdemona, what does she mean by *enhanced perception?*"

"Hm. Can you juggle?"

"I can manage three balls. I have trouble with four or more." And there had been strong domestic objections to his attempt to try it with burning brands, like the acrobat he'd seen in the marketplace.

"Find three things. Or four."

The room was not well supplied with balls, apples, or other substitutes, but he finally rolled up two pairs of socks. "So, and?"

"So, juggle."

The three sock balls went as usual; the four, after a brief encouraging run, ended with Pen fishing dust-smeared sock balls out from under the beds.

"Now, again," said Desdemona.

The sock balls rose—and slowed. They curved in the same trajectories, but Pen felt he might almost take a sip of ale between having to attend to each. His hands moved more languidly, though, and with more effort, as if he were stroking through water.

"That was fun," he said, collecting all four out of the air and stopping.

"We can't keep that up for very long," said Desdemona, "but it is useful in a pinch."

"Should I wish to take up the trade of a marketplace juggler, I suppose."

"It works as well for dodging blows. Whether from fists or blades."

"Oh." Pen thought this through. "Could I dodge arrows?"

"If there are not too many."

"Could I snatch arrows out of the air . . . ?"

"Only if you were wearing thick gloves."

"Could I—"

"Pen?"

"Yes?"

"Keep reading."

"Ah. Yes."

After a time he asked, "Could I shoot fireballs from my fingertips?"

Desdemona vented a long-suffering sigh. "No. You may light very, very small fires."

Pen pulled over the candle stump and held his forefinger to the black wick. "Show me." A moment later, he snatched his hand back. "Ow!" He sucked on the scorched finger. The flame licked up, smoked, and steadied.

"I see it will take you a little practice," she said serenely. He thought she was laughing at him, but it was hard to tell. He was reminded that *she* didn't have to feel the pain.

"I confess I don't see much advantage over flint and steel or a spill. Unless you didn't have them, I suppose."

"You may also do the same from across the room. Or across the street." She added after a moment, "Fire is beloved of the god. You only need a very, very small flame, shrewdly placed, and the fire will do the rest. With equal ease, you can light a candle—or burn down a city."

Having no desire to burn down a city, Pen dismissed that last. "I wish I'd had this skill when struggling with all those rainy campfires, when we were up in the hills trying to make meat out of sheep. I would have been the most popular man on the hunt."

Desdemona was silent for a moment, then said, "It is one of many skills best kept discreetly hidden. For if it is known, any accidental fire within a mile could be blamed on you. And no way for you to prove your innocence."

"Oh."

"In fact, most of the skills are dual-edged that way."

Pen digested that. Was that one more reason that real Temple sorcerers were so quiet and elusive?

He turned the next page.

It was the succeeding afternoon before he could steal another session with the book, feigning to be going up to his room to work on repairs of his new old clothing. After the first few chapters, all seeming very practical, Ruchia's prose grew denser, and the subtleties of what she was trying to describe more slippery.

"I don't wholly understand what she's trying to say about the magical friction," he complained to Desdemona, who had been silent for so long he'd wondered if she'd fallen asleep.

"Hm. Pull that candle over, and light it and blow it out a few times, as fast as you can."

He did so, fascinated with the process. He still found it easier to point when making the little flash shoot up where he intended, though not with his hand held so close. He could dimly sense how, with practice, he might not even need that aid. After a dozen rounds of the exercise, he shook out his hand, which had grown uncomfortably hot even though he'd not touched the flame. He rubbed it with the other.

"Feel that, do you?"

"Yes?"

"If a sorcerer demands too much strong magic of his demon, too quickly, his body will go beyond mere fever to its own destruction."

Pen's brow furrowed. "Are you saying a sorcerer could *burst into flames?*"

"Mm, no, the body is too wet for that. He would more just . . . burst. Like a grilled sausage splitting its casing."

Pen stared down at his torso. "Yech. Does this happen *often?*" Surely any demise so spectacular would have been talked about more.

"No, not really. Usually the sorcerer will pass out before that. Perhaps suffer the usual aftereffects of a bad fever. But it is certainly possible in *theory*."

Pen wished she didn't sound so enthusiastic about the idea. Revolted but not deterred, he returned to the book.

A long while later, he frowned and thumbed back to the title page. "Where is volume two? *What* is volume two? Should I have it? Is there a copy in that cabinet?"

"There is, but it is beyond you for the moment. It is mostly about the application of sorcery to medicine."

He wrinkled his nose, staring at the page. "Did Learned Helvia and Learned Amberein help Ruchia with that part?"

"Oh, yes. Ruchia also consulted with another physician or two from the Mother's Order, on the more obscure points."

He considered the timing. It didn't add up. "Wait. Were Helvia and Amberein still *alive* at the writing?"

"Not exactly. Maybe in the sense that their knowledge survived the way Ruchia's voice has survived on those pages. Ruchia still credited them anyway, by way of a memorial. She spent the most time on the second volume, by way of restitution, she said, for the unplanned loss of us from the Mother's hand."

Pen wondered if there was a very disappointed young physician somewhere, missing, due to Pen's roadside accident, the Temple demon she or he had been promised. "Can I learn all of that?"

"Perhaps. In due course. You would do well to spend some time studying with the Mother's people first before trying much. But how much of your life do you really wish to devote to treating people's worms?"

"Leaving aside the views of the worms, healing seems a safer sort of magic than some of these other things."

"Oh, no. It is by far the most dangerous. And the most subtle. Most dangerous because most subtle, we suppose."

"I suppose . . . if anything went wrong . . . is it possible to kill a person by magic?"

"No," said Desdemona firmly, but then, after a long pause, "Yes. But only once."

"Why only once?"

"Death opens a door to the gods, through which they can, for a moment, reach into the world directly. The demon would be naked and helpless before our Master, and be plucked out like an eyeball before the sorcerer could take a breath. And be delivered to the Bastard's hell, and its utter destruction."

"Even if it were not murder, but, say, a medical accident while trying to treat a person? The intent not harm, but good?"

"That is part of what makes the practice so challenging. And not for the novice."

Pen curled up atop his blankets and hugged his knees. "Desdemona—what happened to Tigney's demon? Do you know?"

A sense of deep discomfort. "Yes, for Ruchia supervised it."

"What, then?"

"The theory is covered four chapters on."

The last chapter in the book, Pen realized. "Yes, but I want the story. The short tale, at least."

A long silence. Surly? Uncertain? Untrusting . . . ?

Pen drew breath and said more firmly, "Desdemona, tell me."

Compelled—so, he *could* compel—she reluctantly replied, "Even at the beginning, he was overmatched with a demon too strong for him. For a few years, all seemed well, and he reveled in his new powers. But then his demon ascended, and made off with his body. He fled to Orbas. It took the Temple a year to find him, subdue him, and bring him back."

"And?" he prodded, when she did not at once go on.

"And they brought him before the Saint of Idau."

"The town of Idau possesses a saint? I had not heard of such."

"A very specialized saint, dedicated wholly to the Bastard. Through him, the god eats demons, and so draws them back out of the world."

"What happens to the sorcerer?"

"Nothing, save whatever grief he may suffer at the loss of such powers. However balanced by relief at the return of his own control. Tigney," she said bitterly, "recovered entirely."

Pen's face scrunched. "Desdemona—did you *witness* this event? This . . . eating?"

"Oh, aye."

"What was it like?"

"Have you ever witnessed an execution?"

"Once, at Greenwell. There was a man hanged for robbing and murdering on the road. Learned Lurenz took us, he said, so that we might learn the true wages of crime. Just the boys, though."

"And did you?"

"Well . . . highwaymen did not seem so thrilling to me after that."

"Just like that, then, I expect. If you were a demon."

"Ah." It was Pen's turn to fall silent.

He was several pages farther on when Desdemona said, "But if you ever try to take us to Idau, we will try to fight you. With all our powers."

Pen swallowed. "Noted."

Pen was closing on the end of the same chapter, a little stiff from sitting, when the door rattled. Swiftly, he thrust the book under his pillow and took up the bit of half-done mending he had ready for such an occasion, but it was only Clee.

"Ah, there you are," said Clee. "I was looking for you."

"Does Learned Tigney want something of me?" *Finally?*

"Not at all. But my brother Rusi has invited the both of us to dine with him at Castle Martenden this evening."

Pen's interest was caught, despite his frustration at being interrupted in the middle of a difficult passage. Castle Martenden, it was said, had never been taken by force of arms, although that might partly be because no great wars had yet come to it, merely local squabbles. Which could be as fatal as any wider struggle to those involved, no doubt.

"I should like that. But, tonight? It's a long walk."

Clee smiled. "Rusi is a better host than that. There are horses waiting for us outside the gate."

"Are we to stay the night?"

"There'll be a good moon later, so if the weather holds fine, we need not. But Rusi will provide all that we need if we decide to delay till morning."

Gratified both with the prospect of escaping this narrow house for an evening, and an opportunity to see so fascinating a fortress, Pen hurried to don what of his new clothes were now usable. Clee gave him no opening to better hide Ruchia's book, unfortunately, as he waited politely for Pen to ready himself, and then ushered him out the door before him.

"I should ask leave of Learned Tigney," Pen remembered as they started down the stairs.

"No need," said Clee. "I already have. You aren't a prisoner here, you know."

And yet not quite free, if Clee was detailed to be his duenna. The scribe was, by way of being Tigney's private secretary, trusted with his correspondence; also with his captive, it seemed. Pen wondered if Clee also worked with the ciphers, and if it would be wrong to ask him about them. "Good." Giving Learned Cautious no chance to reverse his ruling, Pen followed Clee directly out to the street.

A brisk walk brought them to the old stone bridge; upstream and down, several millwheels turned and creaked in the steady outflow. They passed over the arch and through the lesser half of Martensbridge. This part of town was devoted to serving the caravans that came down from the north passes, and boasted warehouses, tanners, saddlers, smiths, and lodgings for travelers who wished to stay close to their goods. Beyond the gate that served the road flanking the lake, they found a small livery. Two horses waited, bespoke and already tacked up. They seemed better mannered than the usual rental remounts.

Watching Clee swing readily into his saddle, Pen asked, "Are these your brother's beasts?"

Clee nodded, and reined around confidently to lead Pen onto the road north. They walked their mounts along side by side for a while, threading local traffic; farm carts going, at this hour, mostly home from the markets, animals being walked to their fates at city butchers.

"Were you taught horsemanship as a child?" Pen asked.

"Yes, we had all the usual castle sports. Castle Martenden was a good place to grow up. I wasn't apprenticed to the Order till I turned fourteen, as directed in our father's will."

The usual age for such placements. "Had the old lord a large family?"

"Not very, to my benefit. Rusi and I were the only boys. Rusi's elder sister is long married, and mine chose the Daughter's Order, and now teaches at a Lady-school down the valley of the Linnet."

"It sounds a reasonably happy family life, then." Pen hoped Clee would hear the delicate inquiry in that; or, if he didn't, so much the better.

Evidently he did, for his lips turned up, wryly. "Rusi's lady mother always treated us children fairly. And Rusi is my elder by a decade. So even if his parents had died in the opposite order, and our father had married my mother, very unlikely considering her station and lack of dower, I still would not be the heir. Nor greatly suited to the task."

"You aren't jealous of Rusillin's rank?"

Clee eyed him sidelong. "I'd have been a fool not to have thought of it, and a greater fool not to have thought better of it. Are you jealous of your brother Rolsch?"

"No," Pen realized, never having considered it quite like that before. "Rolsch plagued me in many ways, when I was growing up, if not how Drovo did—he was enough older to be above such humor, I think, as well as not being naturally inclined to it. But I never wanted his place. Still don't."

"That's fortunate, then."

As the road grew less crowded farther from town, Clee led them first to a trot and then to an easy canter, and Pen followed, heartened to have found another commonality with the prickly dedicat. After about an hour's ride in the late spring afternoon, the waters sparkling to their right and the hills rising to their left, they rounded a curve of the lake, and the gray bulk of Castle Martenden loomed up before them.

It perched on an islet only a dozen paces out from shore, its walls seeming to grow out of the rock that was its foundation. High and solid and forbidding, they followed the contours of the islet's bounds. This had resulted in something other than foursquare, though four round towers with conical slate caps jutted up at its corners, with a fifth for luck over the drawbridge.

The village of Martenden straggled along the road, a mere farm hamlet, though the fields and vines climbing the slopes beyond looked fair enough. It offered a smithy, an alehouse, a leather-worker's, a carpenter's shop, and a small inn for travelers too soon benighted to push on to the city at the lake's end. Clee followed his glance.

"Its earlier lords had more hopes of this place," he observed, "but they were all siphoned away by the Temple and the city merchants."

"Mm," said Pen. "I expect the city exploits the river for its mills, as well. And it is the logical end-point of lake traffic."

"There is that."

Clee led them right up to the small arched bridge and drawbridge, clopping across and returning the salute of a soldier standing guard with easy familiarity. Door and portcullis were all blocked open on this peaceful day. Inside the court, paved with fitted flagstones, the place was not so bleak. Arched porticos with stone columns ran along two sides of the irregular space. Atop them two stories of wooden galleries overlooked this light well, suggesting that those living within did not actually have to grope about in darkness at all hours. As they dismounted and a groom hurried up to take charge of their horses, Lord Rusillin himself came out on a balcony, saw them, and waved. He made his way down an end staircase, boots scuffing in an alert man's rhythm, to the courtyard.

"Ah, you have secured our guest," said Rusillin amiably to his brother. "Any difficulties along the way?"

"None whatsoever," Clee assured him.

Making the hand-over-heart salute, he went on to Pen, "Lord Penric. Welcome to Castle Martenden."

"Thank you for your invitation, Lord Rusillin. I was most interested to see it." Pen looked up past the galleries toward the battlements. "And from it."

Rusillin smiled. "Our supper is almost ready. But we could certainly take you up to the sentry walk."

The castle's lord led them back up the stairs he had descended, and from the third floor over to a short set of stone steps. Pen followed eagerly, Clee bringing up the rear. Then onto the walkway behind the high, crenellated outer wall. Pen leaned over to gaze up and down the lake, imagining being a sentry here, on the watch for enemies. Or, he supposed, merchants' boats laden with rich cargo from north or south, but he had not heard Castle Martenden accused of lake piracy.

Ten miles distant to the south, he could just make out the walled city. The lake curved slightly here, narrowing, then its northern arm struck out an even longer distance to the smaller town that overlooked its headwaters, lacking a princess-archdivine to raise its status and its walls, but doing well as an embarkation point for trade. Beyond the curve, a pair of small green islands decorated the blue surface, home, he understood, mainly to goats, sheep, and a few reclusive religious mystics. The westering sun breathed a golden glow over it all.

"Beautiful," Pen said, awed. "Has this place ever been besieged in your time, Lord Rusillin?"

"Not in mine," Rusillin replied easily. "My father fought off an incursion of the Earl of Westria, in his day, but at the ridges and along the roads. His troops never reached here. Or Martensbridge, little though the town remembers."

"Yet now you work for Westria?"

Rusillin's lips stretched. "The earl palatine learned his lesson. Far better to have us with him than against."

Jurald Court really was a farmhouse, compared to this, Pen conceded.

"What lies beneath?" Pen asked, turning back to look down into the paved courtyard, grown shadowed as the light angled.

"You'll see the lower levels after supper," Rusillin promised. "There is an interesting water gate off the main stores. Very useful for bringing goods in and out."

"I suppose this place would never run short of water in a siege," Pen mused. "Another advantage over a crag."

"To be sure," Rusillin agreed, and led them back to the stairs. He pointed out a few more militarily useful features along the way, sounding as house-proud as any goodwife. Were the goodwife enamored of serious mayhem.

They walked, boots sounding on the boards, along the third-floor gallery to what proved not a lordly dining hall but a small chamber. Two slit windows on the lake side, framing an unlit fireplace built into the stone wall, provided a faint illumination, and Pen blinked, tempted for a moment to call on Desdemona's seeing-in-the-dark skill, but his eyes adjusted soon enough. Good wax candles, only one frugally lit, graced an age-darkened sideboard crowded with covered dishes. Clee went to share the flames around among the holders there and upon the round table set only for three. The lord meant to have the luxury of privacy tonight with his interesting guest, apparently. At his brother's polite request, Clee took the role of server, cheerfully and without resentment. Smiling, he offered Pen the pewter basin to wash his hands first.

The repast was rich in meats and thankfully sparing of cheese: venison, slices of beef, racks of lamb, and a whole chicken were presented, which Rusillin carved with the speed and dexterity of a surgeon accomplishing an amputation. A stew of spiced root vegetables, any winter-stored tiredness masked by their buttery sauce, and a salad of fresh spring greens improved the variety still more. The wine was pale yellow, sweet, and from kin Martenden's own land, Pen learned. The two brothers, Pen noticed, drank sparingly, so he tried to do the same, for all that each took turns topping up his glass.

Plainly primed by Clee, his host exerted himself to draw Pen out about his youth at Jurald Court. Pen chose not to spoil the mood by mentioning Drovo's death, but he did ask questions in turn about the mercenary life, wondering if his brother had found it satisfying before its truncation. Talking about his command, Rusillin sounded more like Rolsch than like Drovo, more calculations and logistics and complaints of dubious suppliers than thrilling tales of heroism. Garrison life ran mostly dull, but Rusillin's company had seen bloodshed in two clashes over a disputed valley on the earl palatine's far borders, and in one peasant revolt over, of all things, an attempt by the earl to eradicate packs of feral dogs plaguing the region.

Rusillin topped up Pen's glass again, with an encouragement to drink pointed with assorted toasts. Pen remembered that Drovo had been at a drunken party with his friends when they'd been recruited in Greenwell, though he had defended his choice with vigor even after he'd sobered up. Could a man be made dead drunk and drafted into mercenary service the way the king of Darthaca had once been rumored to press sailors during one of his wars? Surely it would be easier to run away from a mercenary company than from a ship at sea. He wet his lips and smiled cautiously through the toasts.

Rusillin then inquired genially about Pen's accidental acquisition of Desdemona. Pen told the tale, again; the repetition was beginning to seem more like the memory of a memory than the thing itself. Clee was very interested in the details of his swoon, which Pen on the whole was unable to supply. Growing a touch morose, perhaps with the wine, Pen dwelt on his broken betrothal.

"Does the pretty Preita await you?" asked Rusillin.

"I doubt it," sighed Pen. "Her parents were no doubt entertaining better offers for her hand by the time I rode out of town."

"Mm, sad."

Clee made to refill his glass in consolation, frowning to find no room. "And has the demon awoken within you?"

"A little," Pen confessed, reluctant to recount such lunatic experiences before this company. And he could hardly describe Ruchia's book to Clee, deep in Tigney's confidences.

"So it survived the abrupt transfer all intact?" said Rusillin.

"Oh, yes. Seems to have."

Clee pressed more meat upon him which Pen, stuffed, was compelled to refuse. "I can hardly hold any more of your abundant hospitality, my lord," he apologized.

"It was the least I could do. I have one more indulgence to offer."

Rusillin went to the sideboard and came back with three goblets fashioned of the pale green glass of the district, passing them around with his own hands like a very superior butler. They proved filled with a golden liqueur scented of flowers. Pen had thought such things were served in smaller vessels, but the lord of Martenden seemed not a man to stint his table.

"Try this cordial. It is distilled by a woman in our own village." Rusillin saluted Pen with his glass, and sipped, as did Clee.

Pen lifted his own goblet in grateful return toast. As he set it to his lips, a voice inside his head began, *Penric, Penric, Pen, pen, penpenpen Pen! Pen!* It sounded as panting and effortful as someone breaking through a brick wall with a sledgehammer. His eyes widened, and he smiled in concealment of his confusion.

Desdemona . . . ? What? he tried back.

Take only a small sip, and hold it in your mouth. Don't swallow. Be ready to spit it into your napkin.

Not knowing what else to do, or why, he did as instructed. The cordial was on the whole pleasant, very sweet and complex, but with a bitter undertaste.

Aha. Syrup of poppies only. We can handle that. Drink, then, but very slowly. Do not betray your knowledge.

Why not?

Because we want to see what transpires.

Ruchia, Pen recalled, had been a spy. Trusted agent. Who sailed troubled waters, whatever *they* were, aside from a prime example of Tigney's maddening vagueness. Pen felt he had embarked all unknowing into a very strange storm.

The liquid in his mouth acquired an even nastier taste, and Desdemona whispered, against the evidence of Pen's senses, *Good. It is made safe. Now swallow.*

Pen gulped, and managed, without choking much, to say "Most interesting. It smells of chamomile blossoms."

"Yes, I believe that is one of the ingredients, though the goodwife guards her recipe even from me. Chamomile is said to be very soothing." Rusillin sipped from his own goblet with evident pleasure, and regarded Pen benignly. When not laced with syrup of poppies, the stuff was evidently a deal more palatable.

The conversation grew more desultory as Pen slowly drank. The two brothers were now watching him with all the attention of a cat or a dog, spoiled by tidbits at the table, tracking every morsel their master ate, waiting to pounce on a prize. When Pen yawned, not really feigned after the meal and all that untainted wine, they swayed with it. Pen's body grew warm, though the room was cool as the lake-light from the slit windows faded to gray and shadows of evening encroached, and he undid the collar of his tunic.

Finishing his glass, Pen remarked, "Very soothing indeed, my lord."

"I shall tell the goodwife how much you enjoyed it," Rusillin promised, and took the glass away again to the sideboard where, his back to the room, he refilled it.

Clumsy, opined Desdemona. *I suspect poisoning guests is not in his usual line. Though I suppose greater subtlety would be wasted on you.*

And why was she an expert? Pen had no trouble producing a frog-eyed goggle as Rusillin handed him a second glass. Its undertaste was even more bitter than the first.

They're not taking any chances, are they? mused Desdemona, as the stuff turned vile in his mouth.

Now what should I do? asked Pen, starting to panic. *I'm going to throw up soon.*

Keep playing along. You may now start to feign a drunken stupor. I'm sure you've witnessed such things.

Not only witnessed, but experienced, if only the once. Wine-sickness, like a hanging, had been a salutary lesson he'd taken to heart at a young age.

"You could use this cordial as a bedtime composer," Pen remarked, letting his speech slur.

"Truly," said Clee, sipping along with him from a glass in which the level had barely dropped.

Pen yawned again, more widely. "Sorry, m'lor'," he muttered, and let his head fall, pillowed on his arms. Silence fell around the table.

Bastard's tears, he demanded of Desdemona, *now what?*

Stay limp. If they think their ploy effective, they will not bother to bind you. A considering pause. *Not that bindings are any great impediment, but why make extra work for us?*

Rusillin's voice finally came, "Is he out? Check his eyes."

Clee lifted Pen's head painfully by the hair, and pulled back an eyelid. Pen suppressed a yelp and tried to make his eyes roll up.

"Not wholly," Clee judged, accurately, "but I expect this will do." He took a fraught breath. "Are you ready?"

"Yes. Let's get the business over with."

Between them, they lifted Pen from his chair and supported him, an arm dragged over each brotherly shoulder.

"Ha," huffed Clee. "Lord Cowherd is not as light as he looks."

"These wiry types can fool you, sometimes," Rusillin observed. "I was beginning to think he was never going to fall over."

For conspirators, they didn't sound very passionate, Pen thought. Or even very excited. He felt a bit indignant about that. The fright was all on his part. He let his eyes slit open.

Together, they manhandled him out onto the gallery, now deeply shadowed with the evening though the sky was still pale, only the first stars showing. Down a back stair. Past the level of the courtyard, and down a darker, narrower stair, the walls partly dressed stone, partly seeming carved out of the living rock. While Clee supported Pen's half-limp form, Rusillin lifted a ring of keys from his belt and unlocked a stout wooden door. They dragged Pen through, and Rusillin turned and locked it again.

Shouldn't we be trying to escape? Pen asked urgently.

Soon. There are two of them. The chance must be good, or it is likely to be wasted.

There were two of him, too, Pen thought, or perhaps thirteen depending on if you counted the lioness and the mare, but he still felt outnumbered. He felt outnumbered just by *Rusillin.*

Pen wasn't sure if they'd brought him to a cellar, a storeroom, an armory, or a dungeon. The long chamber seemed to partake of all those descriptions. The roof was supported with pillared arches of stone, graceful enough for a minor Darthacan temple. High on the lakeside wall, a line of thin, iron-barred windows like half-moons let in the last of the silvery twilight. A bundle of pikes rested off the floor in a pair of wooden cradles. Barrels and crates were stacked all around, but along one wall lay a pile of old straw, with several sets of ugly manacles hanging down. That the irons were unpeopled and rusty was not all that reassuring.

The brothers dragged Pen to the far end of the chamber and let him down, rather gently, to the cold rock floor. He twitched and half rolled, and caught a glimpse of the nearby water gate. From this side, it was a stone ramp down to a broad, low arch above the lake, which lapped gently at its base. A barred portcullis, raised at present, protected the opening in the thick walls, and a further set of heavy doors were pulled back. On the ramp, a skiff was drawn up half out of the water, its oars shipped. Faint reflections rippled on the curving roof of the chamber.

"Let's have a better light for this," said Rusillin, and Clee pulled a tinderbox from his belt pouch and went to kneel by a row of part-used tallow candles set up along the edge of the ramp and shielded from drafts by coarse glass vases. Half-a-dozen smoky yellow lights soon sprang up, which, Pen realized, made hardly a difference to him. Another advantage lost to delay?

When Rusillin turned his back for a moment, going to rummage among his stores, Pen seized the chance to turn his head, but the only other item of interest in view was an old wool-stuffed mattress flopped on the floor nearby, a blanket and pillow piled at its foot. *So why aren't I laid on that?* If it was where kindly kidnappers kept their victims while waiting to sell them on to some evil merchant rowing in from the lake, shouldn't it be over by the manacles?

He forced himself to stay limp, if still slit-eyed, as the brothers came back to gaze down at him in a moment of contemplation.

"That was easy," said Clee. "As you said, let him walk to us. Like a calf to the market."

"Bit of an innocent, I'd say," said Rusillin.

"Bit of a fool. Well, Lord Cowherd." Clee prodded Pen with his toe. "Sorry about this, but needs must drive."

"He'll feel no pain. You, or I?" Rusillin held up a long, wicked war-knife, obtained from somewhere among the stored armaments. Its edge gleamed new-honed.

"It's your trade. Probably your reward, if the demon jumps to you."

"Those are the odds, correct? The demon always jumps to the strongest man in reach, you said."

"So Tigney claims."

"In that case, why did it not jump to one of those temple guards the sorceress trailed?"

"Can't guess." Clee shrugged. "He did say it was the most powerful demon he'd ever overseen in all his stable. You have to wonder why it jumped to the divine, back in her day."

"It shall like its new home, I daresay," said Rusillin tranquilly.

They're not trying to kidnap me. They're trying to kidnap Desdemona!

So Pen wasn't the merchandise, from the robber lord's point of view; he was just the wagon. *I thought a demon could not kill and hope to survive?*

Other way around, said Desdemona. *A sorcerer cannot kill with magic and keep his demon. But he can certainly be killed, and lose it. If it jumps in time.*

So was he to be summarily unbetrothed a second time, before he lost his life? He felt madly bereft in prospect. Surely a demon must prefer a powerful captain, who would lead it to the feast of all chaos on a battlefield, over, over clumsy *Lord Cowherd*. The epithet stung.

Not, said Desdemona tensely, *if we scramble. Now, Pen.*

As Rusillin's thick fingers made to close on his throat, and the blade descended, candlelight flickering along its quite excessive length, Pen jerked and rolled away.

"Bastard's teeth!" Rusillin swore. "I thought he was out. Clee, grab him!"

Pen pushed to his knees, then to his feet, as Clee made an oddly slow swing at him. He evaded the dedicat and looked for the door, but

Rusillin was already in the way. He slashed at Pen's belly, which barely twisted out of reach in time. Pen dodged around a pillar. Rusillin dodged the other way. Clee cut him off, seizing him around the shoulders. "Gah, he moves like a snake!"

Rusillin lunged.

As the blade approached Pen's belly, a spiral of rust ran up its length; by the time the hilt rammed home, as slowly to Pen's eye as a bead falling through honey, it had shattered into a thousand bright orange flecks that burst into the air like dandelion fluff, and about as lethal.

"What!" Pen and Rusillin both grunted, practically in unison.

Fire, said Desdemona cheerfully, *takes many forms*.

Clee still clutched him from behind. Pen wrenched away. Rusillin tossed away his hilt, grabbed up a pike, and swung it between Pen and his goal.

"Demon, capitulate!" cried Clee. "We offer you a better master! Tigney means to betray you to the Saint of Idau! I copied out the letter! Aid that fool you ride at your own peril!"

Desdemona, as excited as a hunting dog let loose upon its prey, seemed to hesitate, freezing within Pen.

Pen, backing away from both men, tried frantically to counter. "But which master? Have you thought it through? Whichever one of you she takes will fall helpless in a swoon, and the other can cut his throat again." Could he divide his enemies?

Rusillin grinned horribly, swinging his pike around. "I think not. If it jumps to me, Clee still cannot take my lands nor my command, so his risks are doubled. If it jumps to him, well, I am just as pleased to skip the risks, and have a loyal sorcerer secretly in my service, whose rewards will be rich."

"You *can't* imagine we were so stupid as not to work that out in advance," chided Clee, also grabbing a pike and getting between Pen and the door. Together, both men strove to back him up, jabbing and feinting and allowing him no escape. They seemed ruffled, but not enraged. It felt very strange to be murdered so indifferently. Rusillin, Pen thought, would be just this cold and level-headed in battle, perhaps *had* been.

Surely any Bastard's demon must prefer so potent a soldier.

"What," jeered Desdemona aloud, "and have to look at *your* ugly face in every mirror till we found a way to throw you off? The Bastard my Master spare us that!"

"Des, don't *bait* them!" yelped Pen, horrified.

Clee blinked in confusion, but held his block. Rusillin's brawny arms drew back his heavy pike, preparing for a lethal lunge.

Pen set their hair on fire.

Clee dropped his pike and yelled. Rusillin, made of sterner stuff, tried to complete his lunge first, his pike's hooked blade banging and scraping into the stone wall where Pen had been an instant before.

Every trouser tie, buckle, and toggle on both men's clothing worked loose at once. Rusillin's next lunge was much impeded by his trousers falling down around his thighs, catching him up; Pen swore Desdemona *giggled*. As both men staggered around beating out the flames on their heads and tripping over their clothing, she cried, *Make for the water gate!*

Pen ran down the ramp, tried to push off the skiff, which didn't budge, saw Rusillin out of the corner of his eye hopping furiously toward him, and shot through the low archway. The water splashed cold around his ankles, calves, thighs, *crotch, aaah*! He wailed, "But Des, *I can't swim!*" as his next step landed on nothing, and he plunged over into a drop-off as steep and sudden as the castle wall's rise above him.

That's all right, said Desdemona smugly. *Umelan can. Let her guide you.*

Umelan made it known in a violent surge of revulsion that she was not used to waters this cold, nor a body so lean and unbuoyant, but somehow Pen floundered to the surface and began a dog's paddle out into the growing darkness. He blinked water out of his eyes and swiveled his head, looking for the direction to shore.

Make for the opposite bank, Desdemona advised. *Rusillin will be sure to have men out searching the nearer one for you before long.*

"I can't swim that far!" Pen gasped.

If you relax and slow down, you will find that you can.

Pen kept paddling. Gradually, his strokes lengthened, and his trailing legs found a rhythm like a frog's which, if they did not propel him much, at least did not impede him. His frantic gasping steadied.

Until he heard Clee's voice, too close behind him: "There he is! I can see his hair in the water."

Pen turned to find the shadowy silhouette of the skiff putting out from the water gate. Two men, it seemed, could shift its weight where one man could not. The oars creaked and screeched in their locks as Rusillin pulled mightily. Could Rusillin beat Pen down with an oar and drown him? Hook him with a pike and drag him back to the castle like some long, unwieldy fish?

Now, that wasn't bright, murmured Desdemona happily. Pen's body warmed in pulsing waves, in the cold water.

Clee, standing to peer toward Pen, a pike gripped in his hands like a harpoon, swore in surprise as his foot went through the bottom of the boat. He lost his hold on the weapon, which sank, weighted by its big steel blade. The oarlocks worked loose, and the oars skittered along the thwarts; Rusillin cursed. The skiff settled sluggishly.

Over the high castle walls, a voice floated up in a frightened bellow: "Fire! FIRE!" Other voices took up the chorus.

Rusillin looked out into the darkness after his retreating prize, back over his shoulder at his other threatened treasure, and, using one oar as a paddle, began to turn his water-weighted craft around.

"Rusi," said Clee in an alarmed voice, "I can't swim either!"

"Then you'd better grab that oar and get to work," Rusillin snarled. "The other fool will drown in this cold soon enough."

At that point, it was really *redundant* for Rusillin's oar blade to snap off as he dug it into the water.

Very quietly, Pen turned on his back and began paddling in the opposite direction.

The moon was rising over the eastern hills by the time Pen pulled himself up over the rocks, crawled a few paces, and flopped down in some lovely soft mud. He was chilled through and wheezing. He never wanted to move again.

At length, curiosity overcame his torpor, and he made the effort to roll onto his side and peer back across the lake. The sparks and orange glow that had been soaring from the castle like a chimney fire had finally stopped, ah. *That was a nice castle,* he thought sadly. *Too bad.*

Rough justice, murmured Desdemona, sounding nearly as exhausted as Pen. *If you want the other kind, you shouldn't draw the attention of the white god.*

"Did Ruchia do things like this?"

Not often. She was too astute to let herself be cornered. Desdemona seemed to consider. *After the first few lessons.*

She added after a little, *If you lie here longer, you will perish of the cold, and all my night's work will be wasted. Also, I do not wish to be stuck in a cow.*

Pen pulled himself to a sitting position. "You could have had Clee."

I'd rather the cow.

"Or Lord Rusillin." Why had she not chosen Rusillin?

Get up, Pen. Walking us out of here is your work.

Pen climbed to his knees, then to his feet. Then, skirting around a few incurious cattle, to what passed for a road on this steeper eastern shore, more of a rutted farm track. He stared north up the length of the lake, south down it. He bore no risk of getting lost, exactly.

We could go north, Desdemona observed. *We could go anywhere.* A pause. *Except Idau.*

"I can't say that I've ever longed to see Idau." Or even thought about its name on the map, where it appeared as a dot no bigger than Greenwell, some fifty miles west of Martensbridge and just over the border to the lands of the earl palatine. "But all my things are back in Martensbridge. And I never finished the book. And Tigney must be wondering where I am by now. Do you think he really gave Clee leave to take me to the castle?" Could Tigney even have been a conspirator? Uncomfortable thought.

Hah. Tigney might have given you leave to go beyond the town walls—never us.

"You suspected something? Even then?"

Mm. A very noncommittal . . . non-noise. *We were sure something interesting must be afoot. We didn't know what. We could not speak aloud in front of Clee, nor yet silently to you.*

"Are all demons this curious? Or did you get that from Ruchia?"

Ruchia and we . . . were a very good match. Unsurprising, since we chose her. Desdemona feigned a yawn. *You walk. We'll nap. Wake us when we arrive.*

Pen sighed and started south, boots squelching as he stumbled over the ruts. This night was going to be interminable.

The sky had turned steely, though the sun had not yet chased the moon over the eastern hills, when Pen came again to the Martensbridge town gates. Early market traffic already made them lively. The gate guard scowled at Pen, and began to recite the restrictive town rules about vagabonds.

"I bear a message for Learned Tigney at the Bastard's Order," Pen said, picking the not-quite-lie most likely to explain both his appearance and his urgency. "The boat had a mishap. I have traveled all through the night."

The name of Tigney and the Order seemed to be the master key. Pen found himself trudging again up the steep street as the sky melted to bronze, then muted gold.

The surprisingly awake-looking porter answered his pounding at the door and gaped at him in amazement. "Lord Penric!"

"Good morning, Cosso. I need to see Learned Tigney. At once." He'd had plenty of time to think, while he'd stumbled through the dark, of how to explain the night's doings, and why a powerful local lord had tried to murder him. Indignation had given way a while back to unease. Now that he was here, all his fine furious speeches seemed to run through his numb fingers like water.

"I believe," said the porter, "that he wishes to see you. Though I can't say you are expected. Come up."

Cosso ushered him straight to Tigney's work chamber, where candles burned low and guttering in their sockets.

"Learned, Lord Penric is here." Cosso gave way, pushing Pen before him, then took up a guardsman's stance by the door, his face quite wooden.

Tigney sat at his desk, his quill molting in his fingers as he fiddled with it. Pen was alarmed to see Ruchia's book laid out on the writing table, but much more alarmed to find Clee there before him. Both Temple men looked up at him in shock.

Tigney was dressed for the day—no, for yesterday. Clee wore a close cap over his remaining hair; howsoever he had put himself to rights after a night of attempted murder and, presumably, firefighting, he was rumpled up again by a ten-mile ride in the dawn. Still, he had to look better than Pen. *At least I've stopped dripping.* Pen would be enraged at the sight of him, but he was just too tired to muster the emotion.

"Well, well," said Tigney, putting down the quill and steepling his fingers. "Has the committee for the defense arrived?"

Verbal sparring was beyond Pen by this point. He said simply,

"Good morning, Learned. Yesterday afternoon, Clee told me you had approved an invitation by his brother for me to dine at Castle Martenden. They gave me a drugged cordial, and took me down to the storeroom and tried to murder me. They wanted to steal Desdemona. I broke away, and swam the lake, and now I'm back." He squinted. That seemed to cover most of it. "Oh, and I'm afraid we may have set the castle on fire, but they shouldn't have tried to spit me on those pikes." He squeezed his eyes shut, and open. "And I'm sorry about the boat. But not very."

Tigney, canny and cautious, raised his chin and regarded Pen. "Whereas the tale Clee has just told me was that your demon ascended and beguiled him to take you to the castle, where you went on an arsonous rampage, stole a boat, and either escaped or drowned. You are supposed to be halfway to the border of Adria by now."

Pen considered this. "Much too far to walk."

"It is two men's word again one's," said Clee, who had overcome his first horrified paralysis. "And him a stranger in this place."

Stranger than you can imagine. Pen raised a finger. "Two against two. Me and Desdemona. Unless you count her as twelve, in which case I can make up a jury right here."

Tigney rubbed his forehead, doubtless aching, and glowered at them both. "That one of you is lying is self-evident. Fortunately, I have another witness. In a sense." He motioned to the porter. "Cosso, please fetch our other guest. Apologize, but make him understand it is urgent. Ah—tell him Lord Penric has come back."

The porter nodded and went out.

Clee, heated, said, "Learned, you cannot be thinking of taking testimony from the demon! It is utterly unreliable!"

Tigney stared dryly at him. "I do know demons, Clee."

Clee either had the sense to shut up, or was temporarily out of arguments. Pen was pretty sure this was not the scene Clee had been picturing when he'd hurried to lay his tale before Tigney. If he had really thought Pen drowned, a not-unlikely outcome, why had he come to make these accusations, rather than holing up with his brother? Maybe Rusillin had thrown him out? Clee certainly had been the one to pass along the gossip about Pen's arrival in town. Which of the brothers *had* been the first to broach the demon-stealing scheme?

Minutes passed. Pen sat down on the floor. Tigney started to say something, then made a never-mind gesture and left him there.

Finally, a bustle sounded from the hall; the porter's voice soothing, a new one querulous. A short, stout old man wearing a stained white dressing gown and stumping along with a stick entered the room. Tigney, who had left Clee and Pen standing, hurried to set him out a cushioned chair. His hair was white and receding and combed back to a thin queue; his face was as round and wrinkled as a winter-stored apple, but not nearly as sweet. He might have been a retired baker with bad digestion. He thumped down in the proffered seat with a grunt, and stacked his hands on his cane.

Inside Pen, Desdemona *screamed*. And wailed a heartbroken, *Ah! Ah! We are undone! It is the Saint of Idau!* Pen felt a desperate flush of heat through his body, and then she curled into so tight and despairing a ball within him as to nearly implode.

"Blessed Broylin." Tigney bowed before him. Then, after a moment, he thumped Clee on the back of the head and shoved it down as well. Coming up wincing, Clee crouched and backed away, signing himself and mumbling, "Blessed One . . . " Clee seemed nearly as surprised as Desdemona, if more frozen. No one could be as frantic.

Tigney glowered down at the boggled, bedraggled Pen, but then just shook his head.

So was this to be the second lethal ambush Penric and Desdemona had faced in the space of less than a day? Ambush it clearly was meant to be, crafted by the cunning Tigney no doubt. No wonder he hadn't troubled to tutor Pen. He must have been planning it for a week, to get this creaky old man transported here from Idau in secret. How else could he corner and arrest such a powerful demon, except by surprise? And Pen had walked her right into it. Should he get up and try to run? *Could* he get up, let alone run? *We should have gone north after all. Oh, Desdemona, I am so sorry . . .*

"So, Blessed." Tigney gestured to Pen. "*Is* his demon ascended?"

The old man frowned unfavorably at Pen, who looked up at him in dismay, but said, "No. Not a bit. All your panic seems unfounded, Tig. Entirely not worth what that vile cart did to my back, rushing me here."

As the gray eyes squinted down, Pen was abruptly caught in that gaze, as if he were looking through two pinholes at a blinding sun, as if something huge and ancient and *present* lay just around some corner of perception. He couldn't look away. He couldn't run away. He thought he might even want to crawl *toward*. That elderly and unprepossessing body seemed worn like a stage costume, insubstantial and deceptive as gauze, over, yes, only a man, but also a channel to something that was . . . not a man. Not anything Pen had ever expected to meet face-to-face alive, even through such a screen.

It came to him that every prayer he'd ever said or mumbled or yawned around before had been by rote. And that he'd never be able to pray like that again.

"Can you compel his demon to speech?" Tigney asked the saint.

"If I can persuade it to stop howling in fear, perhaps."

Clee, unwisely, tried, "But can you compel it to speak the *truth*?"

The old man eyed him. "Don't know. D'you think I could compel you?"

Clee wilted. But, driven by whatever desperation, he essayed: "If the demon is not ascended, then Lord Penric's behavior is his own, mad or criminal to repay begged hospitality with arson and destruction. And he should be brought before the judges for it."

The old man snorted. "And how do you imagine the magistrates of Martensbridge could arraign a sorcerer against his will?"

Tigney cleared his throat. "Even if it is not yet ascended, I fear that it's only a matter of time. Learned Ruchia's was the most formidable demon in the whole of my experience. Much too powerful for this raw young man, however well-intentioned he may be. Blessed, I take full responsibility for my Temple-sworn duties, and I must ask you, as a matter of prudence, to take this danger out of this boy and the world."

Pen, listening intently, his stomach curling, tried pointing out, "But I'm not Temple-sworn. I'm really only a guest here."

Clee said poisonously, "In your case, that's hardly a recommendation."

Tigney just shook his head.

It came to Pen that for all the talk of accusations and magistrates, arguing like a lawyer was not what was called for now. If there was truly a god immanent in this chamber, it wanted another mode of speech altogether.

Pen climbed up on his knees and shuffled over to face the saint. Inside him, he thought Desdemona wept, despairing as a woman mounting a scaffold. Tigney made an abortive motion as if to restrain Pen, but the old man merely regarded him curiously, without fear.

Pen opened both hands and raised them, as he might have done before a temple altar, with less cause. It occurred to him that the attitude of supplication was identical to that of surrender on a battlefield.

"Blessed, if I speak, will the god hear?"

The sheep's-wool eyebrows twitched. "The gods hear you at all times, speaking or silent. You hearing the god . . . that is more rare."

Pen decided to take that for a typical obscure Bastard's *Yes*. He swallowed, thought of bowing his head, but then decided to look up. At, or through, those terrifying gray eyes.

"Lord God Bastard, Mother's Son, Fifth and White. Please spare Desdemona. She's a *good* demon." Pen considered that descriptor, in all its ambiguity—good for *what*?—and decided to let it stand. "She has no life save through me, and, by your leave, please . . . please let me serve her in her need." And, in what was surely the most foolhardy impulse of his life, even beating out Drovo's drunken oath to the military recruiter, added, "And Yours."

Tigney shook his head, back and forth, once, slowly.

The Saint of Idau raised his hand and laid it on Pen's forehead, in some beginning malediction. His lips parted. Stopped. His look grew inward for an instant more deep than long. Fathoms deep. The eyebrows climbed in surprise. "Huh! There's a first." His hand dropped back.

"What?" said Tigney, nearly squirming with anxiety. "The white god takes the demon, yes?"

"No. Spits her back. Says He doesn't want her. At least not yet."

Tigney blinked, stunned. Pen's breath caught. *What, what, what . . . ?*

Clee protested, "But you must!"

The saint eyed him sourly. "If you want to argue with the god, go to the temple. Not that you'll get much save sore knees, but it'll spare my ears." He made to lever himself up with his cane.

Pen cried aloud, "*Wait*, wait, what . . . Blessed, what does that *mean*?"

The old man eyed *him* glumly. "It means congratulations. You're a sorcerer." He pursed his lips, and added more judiciously, "The gods do not act for our ends, but for Theirs. Presumably, the god has some interesting future in mind for you—for you two. This is not a blessing. Good luck. You'll need it."

Tigney, aghast, said, "But what should we *do* with him?"

"No idea," said the saint. He paused. "Though it would likely be prudent not to let him get killed on your doorstep."

His eyes still wide, Tigney said, "He'll have to be sworn into the Order."

The saint's lips quirked up. "Weren't you listening? He just was." He wrinkled his nose. "Though not, I suppose, to the *Order* as such . . ." He shuffled toward the hall, grumpily mumbling, "Ah, Lord Bastard, my *back* . . ."

At the doorway, he turned around. "Oh." He pointed to Penric. "That one tells the truth"—his finger swung to Clee—"that one lies. Have fun sorting out this tangle, Tig." His cantankerous voice floated over his shoulder: "*I'm* going back to Idau."

Clee was taken away by a couple of husky dedicats, Pen was not sure to where. With more painfully sincere politeness than heretofore, Tigney suggested Pen might like to rest in his room a while. Pen, swaying on his feet, did not demur, and neither did Desdemona, who had gone very silent indeed.

All Pen's meager possessions had been turned out and strewn across his bed, though nothing save Ruchia's book appeared to be taken. Clee's things were in no better form, and for the first time, realizing Tigney had known nothing, Pen wondered what the divine had first made of it all when both men had gone missing last night. He wasn't quite able to muster sympathy.

He cleared his bed without ceremony, stripped out of his clammy clothes, stole Clee's blankets to throw atop his own, and climbed in, more exhausted than he'd ever been even after the most futile, sleet-soaked hunt. When he slept, he dreamed uneasily of fathomless eyes.

He woke in the early afternoon, ravenous, and went to beg food in the kitchen, where dedicats or acolytes who had missed meals were, depending on the mood of the servants, sometimes allowed charity. His extended to dry bread, some pretty good beer, and a random but generous assortment of leftovers from lunch. *Hunger makes the best sauce*, he remembered his mother intoning to him, vexingly, but there was nothing left on his plate but a smear by the time he'd done.

A dedicat found him there, drooping over his place. "Lord Penric," she said. "Learned Tigney begs you will attend upon him upstairs."

She led him not to Tigney's workroom, but to a larger chamber at the back of the house. Pen hesitated in the doorway, taking in the intimidating committee assembled around a long table. Tigney was present, and two older divines in the robes of the Bastard's Order, but also one in the neat black gown of the Father's, black-and-gray braid on the shoulder, with a notebook and quill before him. A bulky man whom Pen guessed by the chain of office around his neck was a city magistrate sat next to him. A middle-aged woman in a fine silk gown, protected by an over-robe of scarcely less elegant linen, tidied a stack of papers, and rearranged her own quills and ink. All stared back at Pen.

The saint had apparently gone back not to Idau, but to bed, for he sat fully dressed in plain townsman's garb on a cushioned chair in the corner, eyes half closed as if dozing. Pen did not feel the god within him now, to his relief. The immense absence did not seem to leave an empty space, precisely, so much as one reserved, freed of all life's clutter and waiting for its Guest again.

Tigney rose and ushered Pen to a chair at the foot of the table, facing the room's window. He could see all the interested faces around the board, and they could see his even better.

"Learneds, Your Honor, milady." That last, by Tigney's respectful nod, was directed to the woman in silk. "I present to you Lord Penric kin Jurald of the valley of Greenwell, as discussed." Tigney did not present Desdemona. Pen thought she was awake, within him, but still very silent; exhausted, cautious—a mode, he was beginning to realize, not characteristic of demons—still afraid of the saint?

Tigney sat to Pen's left; the magistrate straightened up and frowned down the table. "This committee is here assembled to inquire into the unfortunate events of last night," he said, formally. If he'd been trained as a lawyer, Pen suspected he could parse more implications out of that. Not a trial, yet—inquest, was that the term? The magistrate went on, "We have thus far taken the testimony of Learned Tigney and Blessed Broylin of Idau, and the testimony and confession of Dedicat Clee."

"Did Clee finally stop lying?" Pen asked Tigney.

"Mostly," Tigney grunted. "We think."

In his corner, the saint snorted softly, but did not look up.

"There remain some points of confusion and uncertainty," the magistrate went on. Pen did not doubt it. "In aid of their resolution, we request that you take oath before the gods of the truth of your tongue, and recount what you experienced for our records."

Pen gulped, but, coached through the wording by the Father's divine, readily did so. He couldn't think of anything he wanted to lie about anyway. Maybe he was still too tired.

Under the prodding of the magistrate, Pen repeated his account of the events of the past day, in a deal more detail than his first bald report to Tigney. Quills scratched furiously. Every once in a while, another member of the committee would ask some shrewd or uncomfortable question, by which Pen began to grasp what a gullible idiot he had been. Remembered terror and outrage yielded to some embarrassment.

At least he was not alone in that last. The magistrate asked Tigney, "Why did you choose to lodge Lord Penric in Dedicat Clee's room? Was there no other choice?"

Tigney cleared his throat. "No, but Clee was, I thought, my trusted assistant. The two were of a like age. I thought Clee might keep an eye on his doings, maybe draw him out and find any falsehoods in his tale. And report to me."

Pen's eyebrows scrunched. "You set him to spy on me?"

"It seemed prudent. Your story was . . . unusual. And as you yourself have found, some men will do questionable things in hopes of gaining a sorcerer's powers."

Pen thought throat-cutting went a bit beyond *questionable*, but the Father's divine looked up from his note-taking and asked, "If Dedicat Clee had not been placed so close to temptation, do you think he might not have generated his scheme in the first place?"

Tigney shrank in his seat. After a long pause, he muttered, "I do not know. Maybe not."

The woman in silk and linen pursed her lips, her own busy quill pausing. "In all your observations last night, Lord Penric, was there anything to tell you which of the brothers first originated the plan?"

"I'm . . . not sure," said Pen. "Up till the castle caught fire, they seemed very united and, um, loyal to each other. Lord Rusillin seemed more willing to abandon the hunt at that point, but then, he thought I was about to drown in the lake. In his, er,"—not *defense*—"so did I." Pen blinked. "Is there any word from Castle Martenden today? I mean, apart from Clee. I couldn't tell if he'd come back because his brother had thrown him out, or to prepare some ground on Rusillin's behalf." If the latter, he had certainly failed. Mucked it up beyond all repair, possibly. Pen could hope.

"That will be another point to clarify," the woman murmured, her quill scratching again. "Or maybe not." A slight, strange smile turned her lips. "Dedicat Clee claims the notion was his brother's, over a dinner with too much wine."

"But then, he would," observed one of the other senior divines. By her slight frown, the woman did not seem to find this helpful.

"Will Lord Rusillin be arrested, too, like his brother?"

"We are looking into the practicalities of that," said the woman.

Unlike Clee, Lord Rusillin, ensconced in . . . whatever was left of his stronghold, had his own armed men, which must certainly make the task more challenging to a town constable. Pen didn't get the idea this disturbed her as much as it did him.

The committee ran out of questions as Pen ran out of answers, and, sucked dry, he was released.

Tigney escorted him out. "I have many urgent things to attend to as a result of all this," he said, waving a hand about a bit randomly, if appropriately. "I should be grateful if you would keep to your room a while longer, Lord Penric. Or at least to this house."

"What's going to happen to me?"

"That's one of the things I must attend to." Tigney sighed, and Pen wondered if he'd had the benefit of a nap this morning. Probably not. "Apparently, you are meant to keep your demon. You might even have been intended to *get* your demon." He looked troubled by this thought, not without cause. "Blessed Broylin either would not or could not say."

Emboldened, Pen said, "If I am to stay in, can I have Ruchia's book back? And the run of the library?"

Tigney began to make his usual negative noises. Pen added, "Because if I don't have anything to read, and can't leave the house, I will have no way to pass the time except to experiment with my new powers."

Tigney grimaced like a man chewing on an unripe quince, but shortly thereafter Pen, grinning, climbed back to his room with the book clutched firmly in his hand.

He was back reading in the library the next morning when Tigney himself came to find him.

"Lord Penric. Please dress yourself"—Tigney looked him over—"as best you can, and make ready to accompany me up the hill. Our presence is requested."

"Up the hill?" said Penric, confused. Some local argot?

"At the palace," Tigney clarified, confirming Pen's guess and alarming him no little bit.

He hurried through a better wash from his basin, combed and retied his hair with the blue ribbon, and skinned into the least dire selection of clothing left in his pile. Shortly after, he found himself climbing up the steep street in Tigney's wake. The divine, typically, did not say much. Pen supposed he would learn all for himself, firsthand, and gritted his teeth in patience.

The palace, with all its offices, was a rambling structure of rose-colored stone extending over three buildings behind the temple. It was no fortress like grim Castle Martenden; if the city walls did not hold, its own would not slow a determined attack for long. Its upper facades were rich with windows. They were admitted to a side entrance, where a servant in the livery of the princess-and-archdivine escorted them up two flights not to a throne room, but to a workroom reminiscent of Tigney's, though several times larger. On the lake side, four tall doors set with glass admitted good light, and allowed the exit of occupants onto a narrow balcony. Writing tables and chairs were positioned to catch the best illumination. Several scribes were at work, who looked up curiously as they arrived, then bent their heads again to their quills.

Pen was not too surprised when the silk-and-linen-clad woman from yesterday's inquest rose to receive them from the servant at the door. "Five gods give you good day, Lord Penric, Learned. This way, if you please."

First, Penric was made to sit down and read through a long copy of his deposition from yesterday, sign it, and have his signature countersigned by Tigney and the woman, whom he finally learned thereby was the princess-archdivine's own secretary. This was repeated for two more clear copies—some palace scribe had been busy last night. It all seemed tolerably accurate and complete, from a certain point of view.

Then he was taken to the end of the room, where another aging woman sat at a desk apart, reading through a stack of papers. Her gray hair was more finely dressed, her silks more elaborate than the secretary's—though Pen was beginning to get the idea that silks were to this palace as cheeses were to Greenwell, locally abundant to the point of surfeit. Time-softened skin, slight body, yet somehow secure within herself—he didn't need Tigney to knock him on the back of the head in order to bow low when he was presented.

"Your Grace," he followed Tigney's lead in addressing her. She extended her hand in brief formal courtesy, and they each bent to kiss her archdivine's ring. She was not wearing the Temple robes of that office today; Pen wondered how she kept track of which personage she spoke for at any given moment. Rather like possessing a demon, that.

The princess-archdivines of Martensbridge were by three centuries of tradition daughters of the Hallow King of the Weald, called or perhaps assigned to this pocket palatine duty on behalf of their royal parent, though this one was, by the grind of time, now aunt to the present king. Lacking a spare or willing daughter, the office was sometimes filled by a cousin or niece; sometimes elected from the Daughter's Order. Like all things human, the princesses had varied over time in their abilities, but everything about the orderliness of this place spoke well of its current ruler.

There was a sad shortage of crowns and robes about the princess-and-archdivine today, to Pen's disappointment, though she did wear some handsome jewelry. Power without panoply, but he was grateful for the informality when she gestured and her secretary brought two chairs for her guests.

As they settled themselves, Pen a bit gingerly, she said, "So, this is your problem child, Tigney." He nodded ruefully. Her shrewd gray-eyed gaze went to Pen. "Learned Ruchia's demon is now within you?"

"Yes, Your Grace?" Had she known Ruchia?

Evidently so, for she sighed and said, "I had once hoped that she would become my court sorceress, but there were other calls upon her skills. And I'm afraid she found my modest court too dull." Pen wondered if she saw him as a poor exchange, though as her gaze dwelt on him her expression softened.

Deciding he was addressing the princess, just at the moment, he essayed cautiously, "I am sorry about burning down your castle, Your Grace."

Her lips curved up, slyly. "Ah, but Martenden is not my castle. Kin Martenden formerly owed fealty to kin Shrike, who died out heirless a generation ago, leaving Martenden orphaned, or perhaps rogue. A freedom of which the current lord's father, and Rusillin himself, have taken undue advantage. Four times has that castle blocked or seized traffic on the road and the lake during disputes with the city. The city council has been trying to buy out the lordship for fifteen years, but every time they thought him cornered, he's turned about, most lately with his mercenary schemes. Stealing young men away from this country, more cruel than any tax he has paid, or more often not paid, to us. Castle Martenden has been a bloody thorn in the side of the royal free city for *years*."

"Oh," said Pen, beginning to be enlightened.

"Lord Rusillin is weakened and off balance as never before, and best of all, he did it to himself. This is not an opportunity I or the town mean to let slip away. Nonetheless, the campaign, being tricky, will take a little time and much cooperation." She grimaced at that last word. "That being so, we think it well for you to be put out of his reach. Rusillin is not a *forgiving* sort of fellow."

"Er?" said Pen. Tigney sighed.

The princess nodded to Pen. "I understand you took an irregular holy oath yesterday. If you will make it a regular one today, the Temple of Martensbridge will undertake to send you to the white god's seminary at Rosehall. There you will receive the divine's training that most Temple sorcerers complete *before* they are offered the responsibility of a demon. Better late than never, I suppose."

Pen gasped. "Rosehall? The Weald city with the university? That's three hundred years old? The *famous* one?"

Tigney cleared his throat. "The seminary, while associated with the university corporation, has its own specialized faculty, one of the very few authorized to oversee the training of Temple sorcerers. Nonetheless, you would be expected to take some lectures from the other body. Since you are starting all askew. I cannot imagine it will be easy. For anyone involved."

The princess—or perhaps it was the archdivine—smiled. "If the Bastard's Order at Rosehall can't handle a little disorder, they have taken oath to the wrong god. But it will give time for this young man's superiors to take thought, and judge him fairly." She considered. "Some prayers for guidance might not be a bad idea, either."

Pen wasn't sure if the tightness in his chest was his own excitement, or Desdemona. He gulped. "Your Grace. Learned. May I—I need to talk with—there are two affected here. May I have leave to go apart, and speak with Desdemona?" He wasn't sure they could manage silent speech just now, and he had no wish to sound demented in front of this high lady.

The princess raised her well-groomed eyebrows. "Desdemona?"

"It's what he's named his demon," Tigney muttered to her.

"He's named it?" The eyebrows stayed up. "Unusual. But yes, Lord Penric, if you feel you need to." She gestured toward the balcony. "Take your time."

As Pen slipped through the glassed door and closed it behind him, she and Tigney leaned their heads closer together.

Pen gripped the carved wooden balustrade and stared out over the town, the river, the bridges and mills, the long lake. The pale line of the peaks on the farthest horizon.

"Desdemona!" he nearly squeaked. "Rosehall! The university! Me, to be a learned divine! Can you even imagine it?"

She said dryly, "All too well. Four of my riders before you have been down that road, although three of them before my time. Thankfully."

"Even better! It would be as if I had my own tutor living inside my head! How easy could it be?"

"Mm, I'm not sure how similar the study in Brajar or Saone is, or was, to Rosehall."

"I hear the students at Rosehall have great freedom in the city."

"If you like drunken, rowdy parties, I suppose."

"And don't you?"

He thought she smiled, or might have, had she possessed lips. "Perhaps," she admitted.

"I could be the first *Learned* in my whole family, as far back as I know. D'you think my mother will be pleased?" All right, his imagination was getting a little ahead of events, here. But he would send a letter home with Gans, telling her, since it appeared the Temple was going to send him off posthaste.

"Mm," said Desdemona. "While in general mothers are quite happy to brag about their children rising in the Temple, there is a *slight* problem with those who take oath to the white god. Women fear it might reflect on their own marital fidelity, in the minds of some of their gossips."

"Oh," said Pen, taken aback. "That seems very unfair, given it was my *father* who—never mind."

"Your mother will be pleased for you in her heart," Desdemona promised him. Somewhat airily, he felt, given that the demon had still been insensate when he'd last seen Lady Jurald. But with good will.

"Will you—" He stopped. *May I go* was an absurd question to ask, *Will you go with me* even more so. He wasn't back arguing his case with Rolsch or his mother, after all. *Habits.* "Will you be pleased?"

"Pen," she said, in a quiet tone he'd never heard from her before. He stilled, listening.

"You looked a god in the eyes and bore witness for me, by which alone I am preserved." She took a deep breath, through his mouth. "You looked a *god* in the eyes. And spoke for *me*. There is nothing in my power that I will ever refuse you, after that."

He took that in, to his ears and to his heart. Swallowed. Nodded shortly, staring unseeing at the far-distant peaks.

In a few minutes, when he was composed again, he went back inside to kneel before a princess and pledge his future.

PENRIC AND THE SHAMAN

PENRIC AND THE SHAMAN

I

FIVE GODS, but vultures were huge when seen at this distance.

The bird cocked its pale head on its sinuous neck, peering at Inglis like a nearsighted old man, as if uncertain whether he was its enemy or its . . . breakfast, judging by the graying of the scudding damp sky overhead. It shuffled back and forth, its pantaloon-feathers stirring on its legs as it raised one talon-tipped foot and contemplated its dilemma. The hooked yellow beak seemed to take aim. Inglis opened his parched mouth and gusted a harsh hiss, like the fire in a blacksmith's forge when the bellows blew. The bird skipped back a pace, raising vast brown wings, as if it were a villain in a play swirling his cloak just before declaiming his defiance to fate.

Fate, it seemed, had Inglis at bay now. Run to ground. He scratched at that hard ground with a gloved hand, leather cold and stiff, but grubbed up only snow. Not enough light yet to see if there was much blood on it. The steep vale he had climbed out of last night was a shadowed gulf, the ice and the rocks a mosaic of white and black streaks, the scrubby trees vague claws. His head ached abominably. He had thought that a freezing man was supposed to go numb, but his trapped leg continued to throb. One last heave failed to shift anything. Angled downward on the slope, he had no strength left to pull himself upright and try to get some better leverage.

The vulture hopped again. He wasn't sure what it was waiting for. Reinforcements? They contemplated each other for an unmeasured time.

A dog barked, getting closer. Not mere yaps, but deep woofs, as if sounding from a chest the size of a barrel. A sharper bark joined the first, and another. The vulture flapped and heaved itself into the air, retreating, but only as far as a nearby bare-branched tree, as the dogs rushed up. Surely he was hallucinating—there could be no Great Beast *here*, but the deep-voiced dog was the size and shape of a wolf, and the wolf in Inglis's blood seemed to sing out to it. It shuddered in canine ecstasy, licking his face, rolling in the snow and waving its paws in the air only to jump up and lick again, as the other two swirled around him, whining and yipping. *Do you imagine I am your god? No gods here . . .*

Voices.

"What is it?"

"Something dead, looks like. Arrow, you idiot beast! Don't *roll* in it, you'll stink up the hut fair fierce—again . . . "

"Oh. It's a man."

"Anyone we know?"

Shadowy shapes moved around him. Someone dragged off the dog, but with a menacing growl it wriggled free, then began nosing him again.

". . . No. Traveler."

"What's he doing this far off the pass road?"

"Getting his fool self killed, looks like."

"He took this track, alone in the dark, in this weather? Practically qualifies him for a suicide, I'd say. The Bastard's bait for sure."

"Should we haul his carcass down to Whippoorwill? Might be a reward or something."

A thoughtful pause.

"Eh, nor there might not be, and where's the point to that? Collect the reward now, save steps. Strip him and let the carrion birds give him a sky burial. It can make no difference to *him*."

"Well, it's about time somebody gave us a god's-day gift."

Ah. The vulture's reinforcements have arrived.

Hands, plucking at his clothes. "Good cloth. Good boots—help me shift these rocks, and I bet we can get both of them."

"Might have to cut off the smashed one."

The leg, or the boot? No, they'd want the boot. Maybe the leg . . .

"Riding boots. So where's his horse? Think he was thrown?"

"Figure we could find it? It might have a pack, with more goods."

"He'd have to have been leading it, on this slope. Might have slipped . . . stupid to try to climb in those boots." A pause. "I don't see it down below."

"It'd be dead meat if it were . . . get *off* him, Arrow, you fool dog!"

Hands at his belt. "There's a purse! . . . Ah, piss. Not much in it."

"Fancy knife hilt. Hey, think those're real jewels?"

A snort. "Martensbridge glass, maybe."

They pulled at the sheath, trying to tug it free. Inglis's eyes unglued; he reached deep and found his last reserves, flinging his voice like a javelin: **"Don't touch my knife."**

A mad scramble back. "Bastard's teeth, he's still alive!" The lesser dogs went into paroxysms, barking wildly, and had to be beaten off him. The great dog went flat, ears and tail down, whimpering, licking his face and neck with abject servility. But the hands that had been tugging at his knife did not resume their attempted scavenge. *Sacrilege.* His powers, it seemed, had not wholly deserted him in craven company with his hope, faith, and courage.

"Father and Mother. *Now* what do we do?"

The very question that had been plaguing him for five hundred miles. Scraping for the last residue of truth left in him, he got out, **"Take me home."**

He wept, he thought, but he no longer cared who saw it. Perhaps the gray dawn was false, because the world around him darkened once more.

II

"I'M *BORED*," whined Desdemona. "Bored, bored, bored."

Penric, as soon as he regained control of his lips from her, smiled down at the page across which his quill was carefully making its way. "Destroy a flea."

"We slew every flea in the palace precincts *weeks* ago. And all the lice as well."

"And I'm sure everyone here would be grateful to you," murmured Pen, "if they knew." He had learned early on in his association with his demon, which had gifted him with the powers, though not yet the learning, of a Temple sorcerer, to be discreet about the deployment of their magics. He deployed his quill in the setting down of the next three words in Darthacan, glanced up at the volume in the Wealdean tongue he was copying, and translated the next line in his head, cross-checking to be sure it *was* the next line, and not one up or down from it. He'd ruined not a few pages by that inattention.

He pressed his lips closed to prevent interruptions while he unloaded the complex medical phrase, then rolled his shoulders and stretched. "Your part will come soon," he said tranquilly. "Just three more lines and this page is done. You shall like that."

"It was only diverting the first hundred times. After that, it was as bad as worms."

Desdemona, formerly, had been the possession of a Temple physician-sorceress of the Mother's Order, devoted to medicine and the healing arts. Two such women, actually, in her long succession of riders. Which was where she had picked up her mastery of the Darthacan tongue, passing it in turn to him, and of medicine as it related to sorcery, in which Penric was . . . making slower progress.

"I shall not make you treat people's worms."

"You made us treat *bookworms*."

Penric arranged another sentence in his head, and studiously ignored her till it was transferred. She did not try to interrupt, having learned by experience that however droll fouling his lines might seem to a demon of disorder, it just sent him around to start over at the beginning, and then she had to endure her tedium twice as long.

At her next chance, she said, "At least ask the princess-archdivine if we can ride courier for her again this week."

"Des, it's *snowing*." He glanced up at the fine glass window of his tiny, but private, work chamber on the palace's fourth floor, which let the light in and kept the vile weather out. In his not-that-long-ago youth at Jurald Court, his family's home at the feet of the great mountains that bounded the Cantons on the north, he'd been sent out in the snow to hunt or check the trap lines. Sitting indoors with a blanket over his lap, lifting nothing heavier than a feather, was *much* nicer, even as he'd discovered that the small muscles of the eyes and hands could get just as fatigued as big ones.

Last line. He sat up, read the page down once and up from the bottom once, matching it almost line-by-line to the original— Darthacan was a *fluffier*, if more structurally logical, tongue than Wealdean—and rose to collect the next wooden printing plate from the stack.

He had devised this process while studying at the Bastard's Seminary at Rosehall, adjunct to the great university in that Wealdean town. Poor scholars had to rent, and share, their frightfully expensive books, which had led to much brangling over turns, a couple of memorable fistfights, and one stabbing. Which Pen could never mix into because it would have been *unfair*, not to mention that few fellow students, once they learned of his sorcerous-if-untrained status, challenged him . . .

". . . more than once," Des murmured smugly.

Des was getting disturbingly good at reading his thoughts, these days. *Practice, I suppose.* He was a bit peeved that the process did not seem to be reciprocal, though he had certainly grown able to sense her moods—*so many, many moods*—and had become almost unthinkingly fluent in their silent speech. When they were alone, he tried to let her chatter on aloud with his mouth as much as she pleased, which seemed to help keep her in a good humor. Bad idea when *not* alone, since their conversations all took place in his voice. To the confusion, and a few times violent offense, of their auditors.

He pulled the next prepared wooden plate off the stack at the end of his worktable, and carefully arranged his new page face-down across it. As habitually as when sitting down to dinner, he blessed the work with the tally of the gods: touching his forehead for the Daughter of Spring, his lips for the Bastard, his navel for the Mother of Summer, his groin for the Father of Winter, and spreading his hand over his heart for the Son of Autumn. And then tapped his thumb twice more against his lips, for luck. Sitting up straight, he said, "Ready, Des?"

"You hardly *need* me for this, anymore," she griped, but flowed into alignment with him nonetheless.

He passed his hand above the plate. A stink of wood rot and burning arose from it, along with a puff of steam mixed with smoke.

His hand heated, pleasantly taming its cramping. His carefully calligraphed page grayed into ash.

He took up his brush and whisked away the ash and crumbs. Raised upon the surface was left a perfect mirror replica of his page, ready to turn over to the palace printer for making anything from a few dozen to hundreds of copies. The work would have taken an ordinary woodcarver the better part of a week, and wouldn't be nearly so fine. He could produce ten plates a day, and it was only that slow because he'd not yet figured out how to perform it with anyone's writing but his own.

The trick of it was in the destruction of the handwritten page, so that there was no net gain in order. Uphill, creative magic was costly; downhill, destructive magic was cheap. What happened to the plate afterward in the hands of ordinary men did not seem to impinge on this demonic summation. He could do this all day long.

The princess-archdivine had been delighted with his new skill, when he'd first shown it to her, and now used him regularly for her official pamphlets. In between those interrupting assignments, he was permitted to get on with the task of his heart, reproducing Learned Ruchia's two-volume work on sorcery and medicine to be distributed to the Bastard's Order throughout the Cantons and the Weald—and, soon, Darthaca and Ibra. (And after that, perhaps Adria and far Cedonia? Des moaned in prospect.) And to which he had added a short epilogue detailing his new technique—*A Codicil by Learned Penric of Martensbridge, Sorcerer*, he had proudly headed it—which should multiply its effect yet further. He owed Ruchia that living memorial, he thought, for death-gifting him with her demon, however inadvertently.

Well, inadvertent from his point of view, hers, and her demon's. He was uneasily unsure about the intentions of the white god that she, and now he, served. Though so far, Penric seemed to have been let get on with his life free of holy molestation.

At a cautious knock at his workroom door, Pen called, "Enter."

A palace page in the blue tabard of a dedicat of the Daughter's Order poked her head in, though only a few wary inches. She jerked back and waved a hand before her nose, grimacing, as the smoky fug of Pen's labors wafted out into the corridor. "Learned Penric, sir. The princess-archdivine bids you attend upon her in her private cabinet."

"Now?"

"Yes, Learned."

Penric waved amiable acknowledgment. "Very good. I'll follow presently."

The girl whisked away, and Pen rose and set his tools in order.

Hurrah! said Des. *Something new? An outing? An airing . . . ?*

"More chores, more likely." Pen closed his door and made his way down the corridor.

The princess-archdivines of the royal free town and hinterland of Martensbridge were, by law and long custom, appointees in the gift of the distant Hallow King of the Weald. The town's charter from him, and fealty to him, were what made it royal; the distance was what made it free, Penric suspected. Save for one or two lapses that they had managed to repair by strategic marriages, bribes, and a few armed clashes, the high house of kin Stagthorne had held onto the throne through the past several generations of elections. The current holder of the Martensbridge benefice had thus been, by the turning furrows of time, first daughter, then sister, then aunt to the succeeding kings.

Princess-Archdivine Llewen kin Stagthorne was now a slight, shrewd woman of sixty, who had carried out her duties to the Temple in this pocket palatine realm with the firm hand of a frugal housewife for some thirty years. As Penric knocked at the door to her private cabinet, one floor down from his own and adjacent to her chancellery, and was bade to enter, he found her dressed in the five-colored holy robes of her Temple office. Presumably she'd been caught either on the way to or from some ceremonial task. She was flanked as usual by her secretary, a woman of like age—and shrewdness—in the silks and linen and fine woolens appropriate to the palace precincts.

A strange man was also present, not nearly so finely clad. Above middle height, broad-shouldered, fit; perhaps thirty years of age? Brown hair, gray eyes. Face and hands red and chapped with cold; recently shaved but not, given his road-reek, recently bathed; riding boots cursorily cleaned of mud. Pen might have taken him for some urgent courier, but for the distinctive gray doublet with the brass buttons peeking out from beneath his thrown-back black cloak.

What's a Wealdean Grayjay doing here?

The man eyed him in turn, then palpably dismissed him. Penric advanced to kiss the archdivine's ring, held out perfunctorily to his inky fingers, and murmured, "How may I serve you, Your Grace?"

"Well, let us find out. Pull up a chair, Penric." She nodded to the wall, where a few stools for favored visitors or supplicants were lined up. Unfavored ones were kept standing. The Grayjay had already been granted one, and the secretary another; the princess-archdivine occupied her carved seat, perhaps not accidentally reminiscent of a throne, and the only one supplied with a cushion. Supplicants were not encouraged to linger, not out of any high-nosed pride on the princess's part, but because there were always other supplicants waiting.

Llewen went on mildly, "How goes your latest translation?"

"Well, Your Grace. Another two weeks of *uninterrupted*"—Penric made sure to emphasize that last word; Desdemona snickered silently—"work should see it ready to send out into the world after its sister volumes. I'm starting to think about its Ibran-language edition. Some recent medical texts in that tongue would be useful for reference, if they might be obtained for me. Helvia and Amberein gave me the Wealdean and Darthacan terminology, but Aulia of Brajar was no physician. And also, she may be out of date."

The strange man's hand clenched in impatience upon his knee. "*Your Grace . . .*" squeezed out between his lips, protest constricted by politeness, or perhaps the prudence of a man who hadn't yet had his wish granted.

"Ah," said the princess. "Permit me to introduce Senior Locator Oswyl, agent of the Father's Order in Easthome. He is here, he tells me, on a mission of close pursuit, complicated by some very peculiar aspects, for which he earnestly begs the support of a sorcerer."

Senior Locator was a title of a Temple Inquirer of middle rank; not the lowly man-at-arms of a mere Locator, nor the heights of an Inquirer or, more dizzyingly, Senior Inquirer, who were normally learned divines, but something betwixt and between. Although the name of his Order's home chapter, from the royal capital itself, added some tacit clout. Penric sat up, interested, and offered the man a friendly smile and a little wave of his fingers. He did not smile back.

"And this is Penric, my sorcerer," Princess Llewen went on, with a nod Pen's way.

Oswyl's eyes widened. In a voice of unflattering surprise, he said, "*That's* your court sorcerer? I was expecting someone . . . older."

And better dressed, perhaps? Penric was very fond of his hard-earned white robes of the Bastard's Order, and wildly proud of his shoulder braids marking him as a divine and a sorcerer, but he had quickly learned not to wear them while at work. At least not when yoked with a demon of disorder with a questionable sense of humor. As a result, most days he went about the palace precincts looking the tattered clerk Oswyl had evidently taken him for. Since the palace denizens knew who he was by now, this was not usually a problem. He could turn himself out as a showy, and laundered, ornament to the court well enough when someone gave him warning . . .

Thinking of his incomplete translation, Pen stifled his leaping curiosity and offered, "You could try Learned Tigney of the Bastard's Order on Stane Street. He is the master and bailiff of all Temple sorcerers in this archdivineship." Not that this secretive company numbered many. Nor did that number include Penric, who owed fealty directly to the princess-archdivine in return for his late schooling.

"I *started* with Tigney. He sent me *here*," growled the Grayjay, sounding frustrated. "I told him I needed someone *powerful*."

"I trust," murmured the princess, "you do not judge so quickly by appearances in your inquiries, Locator."

Oswyl went a little rigid, but swallowed any attempt at answering this observation, *yes* or *no* being equally hapless choices.

Feeling faintly sorry for the man—he'd run into the sharp side of the princess's tongue himself a time or two, though never without having earned it—Penric offered peaceably, "So what do you need this powerful sorcerer for, sir?"

The princess waved her beringed hand. "Tell the tale again, Locator. With a bit more detail this time, if you please. If something so dangerous has entered my lands, I need to understand it."

Oswyl took a long breath, of a man about to recount the same story for, by Pen's guess, the third time in a day. At least it ought to be well-practiced. He at last addressed Penric directly: "What do you know of the Wealdean royal shamans?"

Penric sat back, or aback. "Not a great deal. I've never met one in person. Their society is engaged in an attempt to recover something of the Old Weald forest magics, thought to be stamped out in the conquests of Great Audar. Except brought under the disciplines of the Temple, this time."

The Darthacan conquest of the Weald had taken three hard-fought generations, five hundred years ago; three generations later, Audar's empire had all fallen apart again in internal discord. But when the Darthacan tide receded, the Temple remained, and the old forest tribes, shattered and scattered as much by the passage of time and the progress of the world as by Darthacan arms, never reestablished themselves. Why the restored, if much changed, Wealdean hallow kings had sponsored this antiquarian revival when they had perfectly good Temple sorcerers at their disposal, Penric did not know, although the interested scholar in him felt a sneaking approval.

"The shamans' magic is a human creation, or at least, rising from the world instead of descending, or escaping, from a god as demons do," Penric went on. "In the old forests, tribal shamans were said to invest their warriors with the spirits of fierce animals, to endow them with that strength and ferocity in battle. The making of a shaman partook of this, only more so. The spirits of animals were sacrificed into others of the same kind, generation after generation, piled up until they became something more, Great Beasts. Invested at last into a person, the spirit of such a creature brought its powers to him not"—he cleared his throat—"not unlike the way a demon of the white god does for a sorcerer. Despite the very different origins of the gifts."

Humph, said Desdemona, but did not contradict this.

As Penric drew breath, the princess held up a stemming hand. "Penric is quite fond of reading, and will happily share all he learns. But perhaps not all at once? Go on, please, Locator."

The Grayjay pressed his forehead, as though it ached, and grimaced. "Right. The first the Father's Order at Easthome was told of this case was after that mess at the funeral, which was late off the mark. We should have been called out when they first found the body. Howsoever. I was dispatched to investigate and report on a suspicious death at the estate of one of the minor branches of the kin Boarford family, about ten miles outside of the capital. Not the home of the earl-ordainer, thankfully, although for that I suppose they would have sent a more senior man.

"As I—eventually—worked out the chain of events, one of the scions of the family, a young man with military ambitions named Tollin kin Boarford, had purchased a wild boar captured alive from some hunters. He'd kept it for some weeks in a sty on the estate. His older brother thought that he had plans for some boar-baiting show, because instead of making any attempt to tame it, he teased it to make it wilder. Although I suppose either plan would have been equally stupid. But when Tollin was found one morning in the sty, shirtless and with his belly ripped open, and the boar bled dry with a knife in its throat, it seemed to the servants and family death by plain misadventure. The boar was butchered and fed to the dogs. Tollin's body was washed and wrapped and made ready for his funeral rites at the old family temple on the estate, conducted by the local divine.

"Which was where everything went wrong, because none of the funeral animals signed that any god had taken up his soul, not the Son of Autumn, which would have been expected, not the Bastard, nor any other. As far as his family could tell, he had become a sundered ghost, and no one knew why. The divine, *finally*, sent for help."

But instead, they got this Grayjay, Desdemona quipped. Penric pressed his lips closed.

"There was not much to see in the sty, and the boar was eaten by then, but I did, with some argument, get the family to allow me to unwrap and examine the body. Where I was apparently the first to notice that, in addition to the ghastly goring of his abdomen, there was a slit of a knife wound just under his left breast. Shifting the event from misadventure to murder."

"Huh," said Pen, impressed.

"At that point, I reexamined the knife, and determined that it was not only too wide to have made the wound, it was too wide to fit in Tollin's belt sheath. Not his blade at all. And after a search of the sty, its environs, and pretty much the whole estate, no other knife of the right dimensions was found. Carried off, it seemed, by whoever had stabbed him to the heart."

Huh, said Des, less unimpressed. She seized Pen's mouth to inquire, very much in Learned Ruchia's cadences, "Could you tell which injury came first, the knife wound or the goring?"

Oh, now that's an interesting question, Pen commented, deciding to forgive her for the unauthorized interruption, not least because Oswyl glanced across at him with a shade more respect.

"I could not. I'm not sure it would have been apparent even if I had been able to see the body when it was first found. But I took the knife and my inquiry to Tollin's friends. None of them recognized the blade, but at last I learned that Tollin had also been comrades with a royal shaman, one newly invested with his powers. A younger son of the northern kin Wolfcliffs."

The princess nodded. "That branch of their kin has been noted for supplying royal shamans since Good King Biast revived the practices, a century before my birth. Or so it was when I last lived at the king's hall in Easthome."

The Grayjay nodded back. "It's still so. This shaman, Inglis kin Wolfcliff, was said by his friends to have been trying to court Tollin's sister, without much success. When I went looking for him, I discovered that he had vanished out of Easthome, without leave from his superiors, the day after Tollin's death. No one knew where or why. They did identify the knife found in the boar as a ritual sort, but with no signs of the uncanny on it.

"Which is when I persuaded *my* superiors to issue an order for Inglis's arrest. And the wherewithal to carry it out, which was harder to extract. Inglis seems to be an ordinary-looking fellow—middling stature, dark hair and eyes, early twenties—of which I found there is a vast brotherhood on the roads this season, none of them well remembered by anyone. Fortunately, he rode a fine flaxen mare, a gift from his family upon the occasion of his investiture I was told, which was noted by every ferryman and inn stable boy from the lower Stork to the Upper Lure all the way to the Crow. Which was where we found the mare, lamed, sold to an inn hoping to resell her to a breeder. And our quarry vanished into air."

Penric cleared his throat. "Knowing what you pursued, shouldn't your superiors at Easthome have requisitioned you a sorcerer before you started out?"

Oswyl's jaw tightened. "They did. A sorcerer, six royal guardsmen, and three grooms. Upon the Crow River Road, we had a . . . strong difference of opinion as to which way Inglis might have fled. Learned Listere held out for his having made for Darthaca or Saone, to the east, to cross the border out of any jurisdiction of the Weald. I thought north, if for the same reason, making for the mountain passes out of these hinterlands into Adria or Carpagamo."

The princess raised her chin. "If so, the shaman is out of his reckoning. The passes were blocked by snow a week ago. They don't normally open again until spring. Unless you think he outraced our late-autumn blizzards?"

Oswyl's lips unpressed unhappily. "From the Crow? If so, he would have had to be flying, not walking. My hope is to find him bottled up above your lake somewhere, stranded like a laggard merchant."

"So where is your Easthome sorcerer now?" Penric prodded.

"Halfway to Darthaca, I suppose," growled Oswyl. "And all the troop with him, as they refused to be divided."

That is a very determined Grayjay, Penric observed to Desdemona, *to follow his own line though his whole pack hares off without him.*

Or a typical devotee of the Father's Order, she returned, *with a rod up his fundament and an obsession with his own rightness.*

Who is judging by appearances now? Really, the man had just covered, what, four hundred miles between Easthome and Martensbridge, along muddy roads as winter whistled in, pushing ten men to ride as fast as a man alone. And losing his race and chase by very little margin. No wonder he seemed vexed.

Penric asked cautiously, "What *exactly* are the powers of this shaman, Locator? As you and your Order in Easthome understand them to be? If I am to be assisting you in this arrest?" *Or making it for you, sounds like.*

Oswyl turned out his chapped hands. "Shamans are said to have great powers of persuasion or compulsion—in the strongest form, to be able to lay a geas upon a person that can last for weeks. The weirding voice, they call it."

Penric's lips twitched. "Sounds as if the hallow king should be making them royal lawyers, not royal warriors."

This got him a grim glare from the Grayjay. *No jokes, right. Oh, well.*

"I am also told that this voice does not work on sorcerers. Or rather, does not work on their demons."

That is actually correct, murmured Desdemona. *Remind me to tell you of the one Ruchia met on one of her missions to Easthome, who tried to seduce her.*

Did he succeed?

Yes, but not for that reason . . .

With some difficulty, Penric wrenched his attention back to the Grayjay. *Later.* And very much not only for the salacious tale.

"It's unclear to me," continued Oswyl, frowning in untrusting speculation at Penric, "what happens should the weirding voice fail with the demon but work on the sorcerer."

I will save you, Penric! Desdemona promised, in a dramatic tone. . . . *Unless, like Ruchia, you should not care to be saved.*

That one, Pen ignored. "What else?" asked Pen.

"Like their ancestors, they are supposed to be savage and merciless in close combat."

Hence the six royal guardsmen, Pen supposed. Now on their way to Darthaca. How could he face down a desperate murderer possessing, presumably, trained martial skills, in a maniacal battle-frenzy? Not that Pen didn't possess certain powers of speed and evasion, not to mention distraction, in his own right, but . . . he thought perhaps he might take his hunting bow along. The one with the heavy draw and the really long range.

Sound thinking, said Des. *I should not in the least care to replace you with whatever stray passerby happened to be around if you became careless.*

When their person died, a demon, unbound by this dissolution, perforce jumped to another nearby. Temple rites for a dying sorcerer assured that the approved recipient would be prepared and standing ready. Alas that not every sorcerer died to schedule . . . *Could you jump to this shaman?*

No. He'd be full-up.

Huh. I suppose that would leave the Grayjay . . .

Desdemona shuddered, delicately.

Confident that his demon would do everything in her very considerable powers to keep him alive—and, Pen confessed to himself (*and us,* put in Des), stirred to keen curiosity by all this lurid tale—he straightened on his stool, preparing to volunteer the services that everyone here so clearly was about to ask of him. But the Grayjay was going on.

"There was one other task for the forest mages. That was to bring back the souls of their slain spirit-warrior comrades from the battlefield, to undergo certain cleansing rites necessary for them to go to the gods. To prevent them from being sundered and lost."

"I've read a little of that," said Penric. "Those were the banner-carriers, right? As ghosts are sometimes bound to a place, they would bind them to their banners, to carry away to safety. That was *real*?"

"I . . . maybe. The thing is . . . " Oswyl hesitated. "As signed or, more correctly, not signed by his funeral miracle, Tollin was taken up by no god. He might have refused the gods out of despair, or been refused by them, and been sundered. Doomed to dissolution as a fading ghost. Or worse, involuntarily polluted by some incomplete rite, prevented from reaching his god reaching for him." Oswyl grimaced at this sacrilege.

Pen had to agree with that sentiment. To murder a man was a crime. To deliberately sunder his soul from the gods, stealing not a life but that mysterious, eternal afterlife, was sin of the darkest, cruelest sort, a theft of unfathomable enormity.

"I requested a Temple sensitive to search the estate for any evidence of his lingering ghost. She found nothing. Well, not *nothing*, there were a few sad revenants faded beyond recognition, dozens or hundreds of years old. But the distraught sundered ghost of a freshly murdered man should have been livid in her Sight, she said. Tollin's soul simply was not there."

Oswyl drew a long breath. "As Inglis took nothing on his flight that he did not own, he is not accused of theft. I think that belief may be . . . mistaken."

Penric's jaw unhinged. "You think the man stole a *ghost*?"

Or should that be *abducted*? *Ravished away*? *Taken hostage*? This crime was going to need a whole new law devised to cover it. Just the sort of hair-splitting argument the Father's Order reveled in, Pen supposed.

Hang the Father's Order, murmured Des in new alarm. *There will be more fearsome Powers than the gray company with an interest in* this *pilferage . . .*

The princess-archdivine, too, was staring in amazement at the tight-lipped locator. Had he not ventured quite so far in his prior testimony to her? He stirred uncomfortably, making a truncated wave as if to distance himself from his own deduction, but then that hand clenched closed. "None of my superiors think so. But *I* do."

III

TO OSWYL'S RELIEF, the princess-archdivine took his tale seriously enough to gift him with both the loan of her court sorcerer, and of a small troop of her palace guards, local men of the Daughter's Order whose calling was to protect Temple property and pilgrims. To his frustration, the expanded party was not readied until the morning.

He'd used the time as well as he could, canvassing the lower town across the Linnet River where merchants and caravans stopped, and where the inns, taverns, smithies, saddlers, liveries, and other businesses catering to the trade of travelers were congregated. The docks and quays servicing the lake traffic were growing quieter with the advancing season, although the lake had not yet frozen over. But in neither venue was he able to unearth any sure report of a lone traveler matching his quarry's description.

The laggard winter sun was rising gray and gold as they cleared the town gates and at last took to the main road north, skirting the lake's western margin. It had stopped snowing, leaving no more than a finger's width of dirty white trampled on the half-frozen ruts. As the town fell behind and the long valley lake widened, Oswyl stared across doubtfully at the farther shore, dark against the dawn. All farm tracks and rugged scrubland climbing the heights on that side, he'd been told, a route unlikely to be chosen by a fugitive in a hurry. But what about a fugitive wishing to hide? For all that this realm had looked small on a map, it seemed much more spacious on the ground.

No, take it logically; search the most likely possibilities first, then the lesser. He stared between his horse's bobbing ears and tried not to feel so tired.

Turning in his saddle, he checked their outriders, a sergeant-at-arms and four men, all looking sturdy enough bundled against the cold, then glanced aside at his new sorcerer. At least this one rode better than the last one, who had been a town-bred man of considerable seniority but also age and girth. This Penric looked a lean youth, with fine blond hair now tied back in a braid at his nape, and deep blue eyes whose cheer, at this hour, Oswyl found far more irksome than charming. It was hard to believe that he held the rank of a learned divine. Or the powers of a Temple sorcerer, either.

To top it off, the princess-archdivine had divided the purse for this venture, for which he was grateful, between the sergeant and the sorcerer, for which he was not. They were her own trusted men, to be sure, but just such a split in authority had been a chief source of infuriating delays in his ride from Easthome. The Temple remounts were a plain blessing, though, and he composed a prayer of thanksgiving in his mind to the Daughter of Spring for Her mercies, howsoever conveyed through Her prickly handmaiden the princess. Archdivines had seldom come Oswyl's way, princesses never; both combined in one person, who reminded Oswyl unnervingly of his most forcible aunt, had been daunting. Though her sorcerer had seemed entirely at his ease in her company, as if she were his aunt indeed.

Some ten miles down the road the cavalcade approached a handsome castle, built on an islet a little out from the lakeshore, that had been growing in Oswyl's eye and interest. As they drew even with it, Learned Penric twitched his horse aside and rode out on the causeway. The drawbridge was fallen in, its timbers blackened. The interior was shadowed, deserted and dismal.

Penric stared meditatively, then muttered, "Huh," and turned his horse back.

"What was this place? What happened to it?" Oswyl asked, looking over his shoulder as he followed.

"Castle Martenden. The clan of kin Martenden used to be something of a force in this region, for good or ill, but four years ago last spring the fortress was gutted with fire. Its lord had been charged with an, er, attempted murder, but fought his way free of the town guard and fled north over the mountains with a remnant of his men. He was reported to have raised a mercenary company in Carpagamo, but, happily, instead of returning to make trouble here, he took them on to the wars on the Ibran peninsula, where he may well have better hopes of restoring his fortunes."

The endemic wars against the Roknari Quadrene heretics in those far realms were a noted sink of landless men, both honorable ones and rogues. Oswyl nodded understanding. "But why hasn't it been repaired and put back into use by the town, to guard the road?"

"Tied up in litigation. Lord kin Martenden managed to be both attainted by the town council for his crime, and interdicted by the Temple for, er, certain impieties, so both claimed the spoils. The law courts of Martensbridge have been as good as a cockpit ever since. Townsmen take bets on the outcomes of the latest appeals."

Oswyl considered this tale, lips pursing. "Was he actually guilty of the crime charged, do you have any idea? Because . . . *interests* can have strange effects on such disputes." He frowned in speculation.

"Oh," said Penric airily, "I'm sure he was. There were warranted witnesses. And confessions."

The sorcerer then directed his attention to the hamlet on the opposite side of the road, and its shabby inn and alehouse, as a source of hot cider and information. While the troop took advantage of the former, Oswyl pursued the latter. Yes, the tapster opined, there might have been such a young man pass through a week ago, but many travelers refreshed themselves here, though few lingered, pushing on instead to the larger towns at the lake's head or foot. Not for the first time, Oswyl wished Inglis kin Wolfcliff had possessed the courtesy and foresight to be born with a large portwine birthmark on his face, or six fingers on his left hand, or grown to a giant of a man, or a dwarf, or had a limp or a stammer, or *anything* memorable at all.

"Do you think *you* will be able to identify the accursed man, should we ever come up to him?" Oswyl, exasperated, asked Penric as they mounted and headed north once more.

The youth looked introspective for a moment. "Oh, yes. If he's an invested shaman, Desdemona can't mistake him."

"And who," Oswyl went on, not less exasperated, "is this bloody Desdemona woman you keep going on about?" Wife? Sister? Leman? Not a member of this party, in any case.

Penric—*Learned* Penric, the gods help them all—blinked. "Oh! I'm sorry. I did not realize you had not been introduced. Desdemona is my demon." He smiled cheerily across at Oswyl.

"You *named* your *demon?*"

"Really, it was necessary. To keep all of her straight. She's quite a complicated person."

In Oswyl's theology, demons were not persons at all, but elemental forces of . . . un-nature. From the gods, or at least, from one god, but not by that reason holy. "I thought demons were fundamental chaos. Not capable of *being* anything."

"They all start out that way, it's true. Not anything at first. Rather like a newborn infant. But like an infant, they *learn*. Or perhaps copy. They learn from the people and the world around them, and they carry much of that learning along with them as they cascade down through time from master to master. Everything about them that might be called either good or evil comes ultimately from their human riders."

Oswyl frowned at this novel view. "I thought they were inherently destructive, and dangerous withal."

"Well, so they are, but destruction need not be inherently evil. It depends upon how cleverly it is deployed. When Desdemona was the possession of Learned Helvia, who was a physician, she destroyed stones of the bladder, a very painful condition I am told, and warts, and sometimes even tumors." He added after a distracted moment, "And worms, that were debilitating their victims. Though an apothecary's vermifuge could do that task as well."

If sorcerers were rare, physician-sorcerers were rarer still. "I have never met such a practitioner."

"I gather they are kept rather apart by the Mother's Order, to spare them for special tasks." After a thoughtful moment, he added, "Their sex, too, is something demons learn. Desdemona has been possessed by some ten women over time—plus the mare and the lioness—so she's grown quite feminine by now. She's an exceptionally old demon. It's rude to tell a woman's age, Penric!" His hand flew to his lips. "Uh, sorry. That was Des."

"It . . . talks? With your mouth? And yet it is not ascendant?"

"She. Yes, she does, and no, she's not. They can get quite chatty, among the ten of them. So if I say something strange, ah . . . it might not always be me. I should warn you of that, I suppose."

A sudden change in demeanor and speech was supposed to be one way an observer who was not a Temple sensitive could tell if a demon had ascended, seizing control of its rider's body for itself. But if the demon was leaking out *all the time*, how could it be discerned if such an emergency had occurred? Oswyl edged his horse slightly farther from the sorcerer's.

Penric piffled on, "Back at seminary I once sat down with a quill and paper and tried to work out her exact age, going back through all her riders one by one. Connecting them to some dated king's reign or public event whenever we could."

Reluctantly fascinated, Oswyl asked, "How do you keep them all straight? Or do you?"

Penric let his reins fall to his plodding horse's neck, held up both hands, and wriggled the digits, as if pleased to find them in place there. "Ten ladies, ten fingers. Very convenient."

"Ah," Oswyl managed.

"The Temple had planned to gift their star demon to another physician when Helvia died, but instead it jumped to a senior acolyte named Ruchia, who was of Martensbridge here. Oh, I see"—Penric blinked absently—"Helvia was *visiting* Martensbridge at the time. I'd wondered about that. Anyway, the Bastard's Order at Martensbridge not being slow off the mark, they promptly claimed Ruchia for themselves, and hurried her through the tutorials of a divine. In return, Learned Ruchia gave, er, extremely *varied* service to the Order and the Temple for the next forty years. She certainly seems to have traveled, in her duties. Which was how, when she had her fatal seizure of the heart some four years back, I came upon her on the roadside near Greenwell Town, and . . . here we all are."

"How old were you?"

"Nineteen."

Making him all of twenty-three, now. He still looked nineteen. Or, Oswyl might allow, twenty. At a stretch. "Were you some sort of precocious scholar, as a youth?"

"Not at all. I liked to read, but there weren't many books to be had in Greenwell."

"Yet you dashed through the learning for a divine in just four years?" It normally took six.

"Three. I came back here to the Princess-Archdivine's service last spring. You have to realize, I—we—had already been through the training for a divine four times already. In a sense. And twice for a physician. So it was more of a refreshing. I tried to talk the seminary's masters into granting me my rank fivefold on that basis, but they resisted my blandishments, more's the pity."

"I suppose . . . it was as if you already carried a tutor inside of you?" Which seemed like cheating, somehow.

Penric grimaced. "Mostly. Although Desdemona thought it was

just *hilarious* never to help me out during my oral examinations. It would have been bad for you, Penric." His brows twitched up, and his mouth, down. "Ha-ha."

Was that last an interjection from the demon? The voice sounded faintly altered in cadence and accent from the strangely sunny young man's usual tones.

"That was Ruchia," Penric put in, confirming Oswyl's guess. "Desdemona speaks with her voice a lot. I don't know if it's because she is the latest and freshest, er, imprint, or held the demon longest, or simply had the strongest temperament. Time may have something to do with it. The first three women are almost impossible to tell apart, and I don't think it's just because they shared the Cedonian language. They may be melting together with age." He stared out over the lake, pewter gray and rippling bleakly in the chill wind blowing down from the distant mountain peaks shrouded with clouds. "Altogether, I calculated my demon is just over two hundred years old. I have noted," he added, "that the demon-generations are getting longer, as this tale goes on. I find that heartening, myself. I sometimes wonder what my . . . imprint will seem like, to the next person to inherit Desdemona."

"Your head seems very, uh, crowded," Oswyl offered at last, into the rather blighted silence that followed this.

"Very," said Penric. He brightened. "But at least I never lack for tales."

"I . . . wait. Now which was Desdemona, again?" The question he'd started this interrogation with, Oswyl dimly recalled. He kept his fingers curled firmly on his reins.

"That's my name for all of her together. Like a town council of ten older sisters who issue one edict. It also saves my running down several names every time I wish to address her, like my father shouting at his children."

"I . . . see." Oswyl's brows drew down. "The sorcerer I rode with from Easthome never told me anything like this." The dour fellow had not talked much at all, in fact.

"Perhaps his demon was younger and less developed. Perhaps he does not have a very cordial relation with it, if its prior riders were not happy men." Penric's lips twitched up, and his voice shifted a betraying hair. "Perhaps you never asked—Inquirer."

Oswyl hunched his shoulders and pressed his horse into a trot.

They could not reach the next town soon enough. *And I am betting not only my mission, but maybe my life, upon this mad-brained sorcerer? Father of Winter, in this Your season, help me!*

IV

INGLIS WOKE IN DIMNESS, but not darkness. A bright square proved to be a small window on the wall of a hut, covered with parchment. On the opposite side, a rough stone fireplace gave off a red gleam and a few yellow flickers, like animal eyes peering out of a little cave. The walls were a mix of stone and logs, chinked with moss and mud. He lay tucked up in a nest of faintly reeky furs, on a floor of dirt scattered with crushed bracken. The big dog lay curled at his feet, sleeping, its paws loose and relaxed.

His boots and outer garments were gone, his chest bare. Convulsively, he felt at his waist, then sagged back down as his hand found his knife hilt. He still wore his belt and trousers. He had no memory of having arrived here, but he did have a dim recollection of someone feeding him warmed water, and of floating awake in darkness only to drown again. How much time had passed . . . ?

And do you still have all your fingers and toes, fool? That was a question he might answer. He struggled up out of the furs—bear, sheepskin, others less identifiable. His hands were stiff and swollen, but not tipped white or scabbed black. His right leg was bruised dark purple from knee to bulging ankle; he couldn't tell if anything was broken, but it did not move well. Sprained, certainly. Three of his right toes oozed, as if burned. The left foot was no worse than his hands.

How much time lost? Had he missed all of yesterday? Anxiously, he sat up straight, squinted, and began the familiar count down the red scabs crisscrossing his arms. Twenty-five, the tally of his nightmare flight. Had it been twenty-five at last reckoning? *Yes.* Had he lost a day, failed to blood his knife, like a lazy farmer neglecting to feed his pig trapped starving in its pen? Had he lost . . . everything? He pulled the blade from its sheath, cradled it in his hands like a child, crooned anxiously. Extended his senses as painfully as he shifted his body. Oh bless, the faint warmth still hummed . . . he wasn't sure if he should thank any god for it. Or if any god would ever thank him. No telling. For twenty-five days, he had not dared to pray.

Except for this. He counted down the scabs, trying to recall which arm he had used last. He'd alternated strictly, to give time to heal between assaults. Infection was a constant risk. He should whet the knife again soon, to keep it sharp and make this easier. His right hand was steadier just now; so, left arm. He composed himself as well as he could, closed his eyes, and sliced: angled, shallow. He panted, waited for his head to stop swimming, the twist of nausea to settle. Opened his eyes again. Blood flow sluggish, but maybe if he squeezed there'd be enough that he wouldn't have to take a second—

The hut's door banged open, and he flinched worse than at the cutting. Blurry silhouettes swirled against the bright mountain air beyond. He blinked through tears more from the sharp pain of the light than the gash on his arm, and the figures resolved into a woman, sheepskin cloak bundled about her, carrying a small cloth sack and a copper pitcher, and a man in leathers wearing a sheepskin vest, fleece turned inward. The dog jerked alert and growled, but the growl trailed off in a few tail-thumps of recognition.

Seeing him sitting up, the woman said, "Oh, you're awake," but then, as she came closer, cried sharply, "What are you *doing*?"

He wanted to hide knife and arms beneath the furs, but he dared not stop this once started. "Stand back!" he commanded, and, as she made to swoop on him, **"Stand back."** The dog scrambled up, fur rising along its spine. The woman stopped abruptly, staring in dismay. The man's hand froze on the work-knife at his belt.

Whispering words under his breath that were supposed to help his focus, but really didn't just now, he stropped the knife blade up and down along his arm, coating it thoroughly in sticky red. Would it be enough to buy one more day? The faint hum seemed to strengthen. *Yes. Perhaps.* He wasn't sure but what a single drop would do the job as well, but he couldn't take chances. He held the knife in his lap, trying to protect it from his intruders' shocked gazes. When the blood smears turned brown and crumbling, all life sucked from them, he could clean the blade and hide it away once more.

The woman said tremulously, "I brought you food. And drink." She held up her burdens as if in evidence.

The man, scowling at Inglis, stepped in front of her. "Suppose you just put that knife away, fellow."

Did they think he threatened them? Inglis wasn't sure he could even stand up just now, let alone attack a person. His eye drawn by the pitcher, he raised the fur across his lap and slid the knife out of sight down next to his right thigh. He licked dry lips and set both hands out atop the cover, spread and still. He most certainly didn't want to frighten off that charitable young woman. Was the man's voice one of those he had heard in his daze upon the rockslide? Vulture, or rescuer? The dog sat back down.

"What were you doing with it?" asked the woman in suspicion, coming no nearer.

"I . . . it . . . it drinks blood." He wondered if that sounded as deranged to them as it did to him.

"All knives do," observed the man, his hand not leaving his own hilt.

Not like this one. "I drink drink," Inglis essayed hopefully.

"Travelers get dry in the mountains," said the woman, in a tone of careful placation. "They think because they are not hot, they are not thirsty."

"I . . . yes."

She circled wide around him to the hearth, collected a clay cup faintly familiar from last night, and filled it from the pitcher. She extended it to him with a long reach. He took it with a hand that shook, then both hands, and gulped down its contents, an unstrained barley water flavored with mint. Invalid stuff, far from a noble beverage, but it was warm, seeming both food and drink. He extended the cup back. "Please . . . ?" He drained it three times before he stopped *guzzling.* He caught his breath and nodded thanks.

"Who are you—traveler?" asked the man.

"I, uh . . . Inglis k—" He cut off his too-famous kin name. "Inglis." *Oh. Should I have offered an alias?*

"Where were you bound?" asked the young woman. "Towards Martensbridge, or Carpagamo? Either way, you took a wrong turn."

"Pass from Carpagamo's closed," said the fellow, "Unless he was the last man to come in over it."

Inglis shook his head. He followed the dog's interested gaze to the cloth sack. Gingerly, the woman held it out to him. His clumsy fingers found it contained generous lumps of some soft white cheese, sheep or goat, captured between parsimonious slices of heavy barley-and-oat bread, and strips of dried smoked meat of uncertain origin. Venison, perhaps. Inglis, after a moment's hesitation, tore into it as if he were a wolf indeed.

After allowing the first couple of frantic swallows, the man asked, "Where's your horse?"

Around his mouthful Inglis answered, "Left her lame on the Crow Road. Then I walked."

"Oh." The man's mouth pursed in disappointment.

It came to Inglis that the young woman must have prepared this repast for him, with her own hands. He eyed her more closely over his chewing. Her face was mountain-broad, lips and cheeks rouged only by cold, her body work-lean; her youth lent her a passing prettiness. The fellow was not much older. Hunter, shepherd? Both? Up here, all men put their hands to all tasks, as the turning seasons ordered them. The two shared the light hair and blue eyes of this mountain stock, close kin surely.

"Who are you?" Inglis asked in turn after his next swallow. "Where is this place?"

The woman smiled hesitantly at him. "I'm Beris. That's my brother Bern."

Bern offered more reluctantly, "This is the summer grazing camp for Linkbeck, the village in the valley. Our hunting camp in winter."

So, he'd not traveled quite so far back in time as the place's crude look suggested. Not to the world of Great Audar's era, when these mountain tribes had held their high fastnesses against the invaders as the Wealdean forest tribes had not. Or maybe the Darthacans had taken one look at the damp precipitous country and decided they didn't want it that much. The Temple's invasion in these lands, replacing the old ways with the new, had been a slower process, more a gradual weeding out than a violent burning over. With a chance, a hope, if not a prayer, that they'd not uprooted *everything* . . .

No. He eyed the great dog, its furry triangular ears pricked as it tracked the progress of the meat strips to his mouth. *A certainty.* "That dog. Who owns it?"

"Arrow is Savo's beast," said Beris. "Had him from his uncle Scuolla this past autumn."

The dog lay down on its belly, wriggled up to Inglis, and shoved its head under his left hand. No pup, but a full-grown animal, mature—middle-aged and dignified, after a fashion. Absently, Inglis scratched it behind the ears. Tail thumping, it whined and licked at his bloodied arm.

"He seems to think he's your dog, now," said Bern, watching this play through narrowed eyes. "Hasn't left your side since we brought you in. Why is that—traveler?"

"Was Savo with you when you found me?"

"Aye, we'd gone out hoping for red deer. I'm not sure you were a fair trade, since we can't skin or eat you."

They'd seemed willing enough to skin him; Inglis trusted they would have stopped short of the eating, yes. But there had been no shaman among the hunters, or they would surely have recognized each other, and this conversation would be very different. So, not Savo.

"That knife," said the brother, Bern, looking at him sideways. "Are those *real jewels*? I bet Churr not."

Inglis had never imagined they might not be real. He drew out the knife and stared at it. The slim eight-inch blade was hafted in walrus ivory; he could feel the echo of old life in it when he held it in his hand. The beautifully curving hilt widened to an oval at the end, capped with gold, flat face holding small garnets, one gone missing in some past time and not replaced. They encircled a cabochon-cut red stone he guessed might be a ruby. *Tooth and blood, how fitting.* His blood on the steel had darkened and dried already, its life sucked in as ravenously as he'd just wolfed down hard bread and cheese. He set about rubbing off the residue on his trouser leg. "I suppose so. It was an heirloom."

The silence in the room grew a shade tighter. He glanced up to find a disquieting stew of curiosity, avarice, and fear simmering in his watchers' faces. But . . . they had brought him in off the mountain, and given him food and drink. He owed them warning.

"Why do you, uh, give it your blood?" asked Beris warily. "Is it, that is, do you think it's a magic knife?"

Inglis considered the impossibly complicated truth, and the need to quash that avarice before it created trouble—*more* trouble—and finally settled on, "It is accursed."

Bern drew breath through his teeth, half daunted, half dubious.

Beris's gaze tracked up and down the scabs on his arms. "Couldn't you feed it, I don't know, animal blood?"

"No. It has to be mine."

"Why?"

His lips drew back in something not much like a smile. "I'm accursed, too."

The pair excused themselves rather swiftly, after that. But they left the food and barley water. Arrow declined to follow, though invited with an open door, soft calls, chirps, a whistle, and firm commands. Bern circled back as if to grab the dog by its ruff and drag him, but, at Arrow's lowered head and glower, thought better of the plan. The door closed behind them.

Like most people, they underestimated the keenness of Inglis's hearing.

"What do you make of him now?" asked Beris, pausing a few paces beyond the hut.

"I don't know. He talks like a Wealdman. I think he must be out of his head."

"He wasn't very feverish. Do you think he might be uncanny? Dangerous?"

"Mm, maybe not to us, the shape he's in right now. Perhaps to himself. Churr could inherit that knife he coveted so much after all, if he goes from chopping up his arms to cutting his own throat."

"Why would a fellow *do* such a thing?"

"Well, mad." (Inglis could *hear* the shrug.)

"His voice was very *compelling*, did you feel it? It gave me the shivers."

"Mother and Daughter, Beris, don't be such a girl." But the mockery was tinged with unease.

"I *am* a girl." A considering pause. "He might be handsome, if he smiled."

"Don't let Savo hear you say that. He's already annoyed enough about his dog."

"I am not Savo's *dog*."

Siblings indeed, for then he barked at her, and she hit him, and their squabbling voices faded out of even Inglis's earshot.

He coaxed the dog up under his arm with a bribe of smoked meat. Hugged him in, stared into the clear brown eyes, then closed his own and tried to *sense*. The animal's spirit-density was almost palpable, hovering just beyond his present crippled reach. How many generations of dogs were poured into this Dog? Five? Ten? More than ten? How many generations of men had cultivated it? This could be a dog to make a shaman, immensely valuable.

And who was Scuolla, to give such a treasure away? Was the man an illicit hedge shaman, had he *made* Arrow? Intended this nephew Savo for his secret apprentice? Or was he unknowing of what he'd possessed? Horrifying, that he might be unknowing.

Appalling hope, that he might be wise.

"As soon as I'm on my feet," he told the dog with a little shake, "let's go find this ungrateful old master of yours, eh?"

Arrow yawned hugely, treating Inglis to a waft of warm dog-breath entirely lacking in enchantment, and rolled over like a bolster against Inglis's side.

V

PENRIC'S PARTY came to the town of Whippoorwill, at the head of the lake, in the early winter dusk. It was half the size of the more successful Martensbridge, and a bit resentful of the fact, but still fivefold larger than Greenwell Town of Penric's youth. Even the anxious Grayjay made no suggestion that they press on any farther this night. At the local chapter of the Daughter's Order, which lay under the princess-archdivine's direct rule, they found crowded, but free, lodgings.

Then Oswyl made the first practical use of the troop that had trailed them by sending them all out, severally, to ask after their quarry in the inns and taverns of the town. He didn't mention brothels aloud; Penric was unsure if they were tacitly implied, if he thought the fleeing murderer would make no use of them, or if he was simply respectful of the guardsmen's oaths to the Daughter's Order. All business in Whippoorwill was settling down to merely local traffic as the high roads to the northern coast countries closed off for the season.

Penric and Oswyl had just finished eating at the tavern of their choice where, alas, no one remembered a dark-haired and dark-eyed Wealdean heading north alone in the past week, though any sensible fellow attempting the passes this late might have joined one of several parties and who would have noticed him then? Oswyl was rubbing his eyes in pain at this prospect when one of the guardsmen, Baar, came back. "I think I may have found something, sirs . . . "

With open relief but guarded hope, Oswyl followed at his heels down the streets, Penric trailing, to a lesser inn just off the main north road. Its air was homey and shabby, and it mainly served frugal local countrymen.

"Oh, aye," said the tapster, when Oswyl had lubricated the man's tongue with a pint of his own ale, and his purse with three more all around for their company. "Don't know if he's the man you seek, but certainly a well-set-up young fellow with dark hair and eyes. That describes half the Darthacans on the roads—"

Oswyl nodded rueful agreement.

"—but this one spoke with a Wealdean accent, and not lowborn. I thought he must be a scholar, because he said he wanted tales, as he was writing a book. Collecting them, see."

Oswyl's eyebrows went up. "What sort of book?"

"Old tales of the mountains, uncanny ones. Campfire tales, children's stories, ghost stories. Not saints' legends, much. He was especially interested in tales of magical beasts."

"Did he get any from you?" asked Penric.

"Oh, aye! It was a busy night." The tapster looked around mournfully at his current near-empty premises. "After he bought a round or two, I think he might have got enough for half his book right here."

"Did he seem especially intent about any particular tales? Ask more questions?"

"He seemed quite pleased to get the fellows going on about rumors of uncanny animals being bred up in the high valleys."

Penric came more alert. "Do you mean, um, current rumors, not just old stories? What are they?"

"Well, there's supposed to be a man up the Chillbeck who raises specially smart dogs, very prized by the local shepherds and hunters. I've met some right smart mountain dogs, though, so's I don't know as there's anything more to it than tales and bragging."

"Did he say anything about following those rumors to their source?" asked Pen.

"No, can't say as he did. He didn't say much about himself, come to think. Contented just to listen, y'know."

Oswyl put in, "Did he ask much about Carpagamo, Adria, the passes? Anything about how to get to the north coast?"

"A man hardly needs to ask about the passes this time of year—folks scarce talk about anything else, always hoping for a late thaw and one last chance to get through. But no, I don't recollect as he did. He seemed tired. Went up to bed soon after."

"Did you see which way he went in the morning?" asked Oswyl.

"No, sir, sorry. Mornings are a busy time, getting everyone out. He went off afoot, though. No horse for him. That's why I thought, poor scholar, despite the kin-rich mouth."

Penric blinked. "You have a good ear for accents."

"Well, sir, we get a lot of travelers through, at least come summer, and they do tell their tales. Gives a man practice."

Oswyl sat back, frowning, although not at anyone here. "How many nights ago was this, again? Try to be sure."

The tapster, brows crooked with concentration, counted up on his thick fingers. "Six nights, sir. I remember because it was the evening of the horse-market day, and we had a lot of folks in from the country round for that."

Oswyl gave a grunt of satisfaction, drained his tankard, and rose. "Thank you. The Father of Winter's blessing upon this house, in His season impending."

"Go with the gods, sirs."

Learned divine though he now was, Penric did not add the Bastard's blessing, first because most people didn't appreciate the ambiguity, and second because he was incognito for the evening's scouting. And, third, ever since he had once met the god immanent—as close as his arm's reach but not, surely, anything to dare touch—he wasn't exactly *comfortable* pledging His word. It might not prove to be a safely hollow courtesy.

The Daughter's guard paced before them with a lantern as they made their way back along the dark streets to the Order's house. Penric ventured, "It sounds as if a foray up the valley of the Chillbeck might be worth the time."

Oswyl snorted. "Have you looked at a map? That valley has no good pass out of it to the north. And there are a dozen more just like it. It would be like plunging into a gigantic stone maze."

"It's not so different from my home country, just a hundred miles east of here."

Oswyl eyed him dubiously. "There will be more people on the main road."

"Strangers stand out more in the vales. People notice them. And besides, if that tapster spoke true, you've made up a few days on Inglis's lead since the Crow."

"Time I do not care to waste by haring off up blind alleys."

"Unless the blind alley turns out to be a hunter's bag."

"Hm." Oswyl paused and stared to the north where the high peaks glimmered in the night, a pale wall across the world. "I believe I was right to hold to my reasoning back on the Crow Road. I'd wager that stout Easthome sorcerer is saddle-sore and empty-handed now, somewhere in Saone." The vision seemed to give him a certain understandable satisfaction. "Why should I think your advice better?"

Oddly, Penric didn't sense that the question was rhetorical. "Because this is my home country, not his? Because why would Inglis, if the man was Inglis, ask all those questions and not pursue the pointers they gained him? Because Inglis, being a stranger here, will try the most easily reached routes first?"

"*Time*," said Oswyl, though his teeth.

"Is it so desperate? He is no less or more trapped by the snow on the passes than he would be by Chillbeck Vale. It's not as though he's been leaving a trail of bodies."

Oswyl was surprised into a noise that came as close to a laugh, if a black one, as Penric had yet heard from him. "I suppose I should not wish it."

An oil lantern hung over the Order's gates, its yellow light glittering from the snow sifted in between the street's cobbles. Oswyl motioned Baar ahead of them into the warm, with a clap to his shoulder and a low-voiced, "Well done, man." But he did not at once follow, and Penric paused with him.

"As a Temple sensitive, have you ever gone out, or been taken out, to check accusations of hedge sorcery?" Oswyl asked abruptly.

Penric, curious at this sudden turn in the talk, folded his arms against the night chill and replied, "Three times, when I was at seminary at Rosehall, I was taken along for training. Not for the working of the thing, since any sorcerer recognizes another as readily as I can tell you are a tall man, but to get a grasp on the legalities, which can become complex. For one thing, just because the accused is not a sorcerer, and they almost never are, it doesn't necessarily mean no crime has been committed, by other means or persons. I did think the false accusations, if the accuser knew them false, to be especially heinous."

Oswyl nodded grimly.

"I've not been sent out since I was made court sorcerer, as Tigney has others to call on for such routine duties. But Desdemona, after she became a Temple demon, went with her riders on hundreds of such inquiries, and found a real sorcerer involved, what—"

Twice.

"Only twice."

"As a locator, I've seen the same from the other side," said Oswyl. "In ten years, only a single case sustained, and the poor man, who'd thought he was going mad, flung himself upon the Temple's mercy and found it. But one time . . . "

He hesitated so long, Penric nearly prodded him with a, *But one time . . . ?* except that Desdemona quietly advised, *Wait.*

Oswyl glowered down the street at nothing, and finally said, "One time, we were laggard on the road. The reasons seemed sufficient—bad weather, a bridge washed out. Howsoever. We arrived at this dismal village out in the country to discover the accused woman had been burned to death by her frenzied neighbors the night before. No sign found that any demon had jumped from her pyre. She was almost certainly innocent, and if we had arrived timely, we could have disposed of the false charges forthwith, and given stern warnings to the slanderers. As it was, we faced the dilemma of trying to charge an entire village with murder. It all broke down in a sickening morass, and in the end . . . well, no justice was done there, in the Father's sight or any other."

While Penric, taken wholly aback, was still trying to come up with something to acknowledge this that didn't sound fatuous, Oswyl yanked open the door and made to step within. But as he did he growled over his shoulder, "So I *do not like* being late."

The door thudded shut like the end of an argument.

After a moment, Penric sighed and reached for the handle. *This isn't going to be so easy, is it?*

The Father's cases seldom are, noted Desdemona. *Else they wouldn't need* Him.

They rode out of Whippoorwill very early the next morning.

VI

TWENTY-SEVEN.

Inglis controlled his pained panting, and stropped the knife blade carefully over the shallow cut across his right thigh. When it was well-coated, he set it aside and scrambled around in his fur nest to pull up and tie his trouser strings. He'd found the rest of his clothes in a pile near the hearth; his purse had been unsurprisingly missing. Left boot also there, right boot ruined, cut down the shaft. If it had come off, presumably it could come back on . . . no. He sighed and abandoned them both.

It took three tries to wallow upright. Arrow sat up and watched with interest. As Inglis hobbled barefoot the short distance across the hut, the dog rose and paced along. Inglis's hand found its ruff, sturdy but not quite high enough for good support. The wooden door, secured only by a rope latch, creaked wide. He leaned on the jamb and looked around.

The morning sun was blindingly bright on the snow, which was turning slushy in some late teasing thaw, and Inglis's eyes watered. Blinking, he found that the hut was nearly at the tree line. Dark firs and pines fell away below; he could see over their tops down into the vale. The flat valley floor narrowed here, the last farms straggling up its crooked, attenuating length. A small village clustered around a timber bridge over the barely-a-river.

A few more crude huts clung to the slope near Inglis's refuge. One was plainly a smokehouse, from the aromatic haze rising through its thatch. A nanny goat with a bell hung from a leather strap around its neck wandered past, ignoring him. From somewhere nearby, he heard women's voices.

He stared down at Arrow, who gazed back, soulfully attentive. It was worth a try . . . He caressed the dog's head, and said, **"Fetch me a stick."**

The dog made a cheerful noise in its chest, too deep to be a yip, and bounded away. By the time Inglis had retrieved, cleaned, and sheathed his knife, and determined that no more belongings of his were in the hut, Arrow returned to the doorway, dragging a log as long and thick as a fencepost. He dropped it with a thunk at Inglis's feet and looked up proudly, toothy grin gaping, tail swishing back and forth like a cudgel.

Inglis was surprised into a rusty laugh. It felt strange in his throat. "I said a stick, not building timber!" Though it would make fine firewood. He ruffled the dog's head anyway. "Fetch me a **thinner** stick."

Eagerness unimpaired, Arrow bounded away again. He returned in a few minutes towing something more sapling-like. Inglis broke off the side branches and tested it. It would do for now. The snow was almost not unpleasant on his swollen, throbbing right foot. The left was out of luck. He wondered if he could beg some coverings for them. Limping slowly, he followed the sound of the voices.

In a three-sided shelter, its open face turned to the sun, he discovered a team of women at work scraping a stretched hide. One of them was the girl Beris. The other two were older. All stopped scraping to look up and stare at Inglis, although, as the dog momentarily abandoned him to snatch a pale scrap and retreat to chew on it, the one with the gray braid spared a dispassionate, "Arrow, you fool dog. You'll make yourself sick." Arrow's tail thumped unrepentantly.

"You got up," said Beris, bright and a bit wary. "Are you feeling better now?"

Better than what? "A little," Inglis managed, and, belatedly, "Thank you for your aid."

The middle woman said, "You were lucky to be found. Another few days, and we'd all have gone down to the valley, even the boys." She eyed him in curiosity. "Where were you bound?"

He wasn't sure he could explain his confusion of mind to himself, let alone her, nor how many times he'd switched his goal from Carpagamo to Linkbeck and back. He finally settled on, vaguely, "Up the vale, but I took a wrong turn in the dark." He extended his empurpled foot. "I was wondering if I might beg some rags to wrap my feet. My boots are impossible."

She made a grunt and a motion, which her companions seemed to interpret without difficulty, and levered herself up to trudge off. Gingerly, hoping he would be able to stand again without aid, Inglis lowered himself to another sawed-off chunk of tree trunk that they seemed to be using for camp chairs.

Should he try the 'poor scholar collecting stories' ploy again? It had brought him this far. Arrow relieved him of his dilemma by making another raid on the skin scraps; the woman with the gray braid made a desultory *begone, pest* gesture at him, which he eluded.

"That is an extraordinary dog," Inglis began. Did either of them realize how extraordinary? Two different flavors of blank faces regarded him in return. Beris's seemed innocent. The elder woman's might conceal more. Try manners? He attempted a smile at her, and said, "My name is Inglis, by the way."

"So Beris said."

"And you are, Mother . . . ?"

"Laaxa."

Inglis nodded, as though he cared. Her lips quirked, as though she did. "I was told one of the men who helped bring me off the trail had the dog from his uncle, Scuolla. Can you tell me where to find him to speak to?"

Laaxa snorted. "Where to find him, yes. Though I doubt he'll be speaking to you." She pointed up the valley. "He was killed in a landslide not two months back, poor old man."

The blighting of Inglis's last forlorn hope was as crushingly cold as an avalanche. "Oh." He sat in silence for a minute, too taken aback to think. He finally tried, "Was he the man who raised dogs? I was told there was such a fellow in this vale. Or did he have Arrow from someone else?" Yes, there might be one more possibility . . .

"Oh, aye, it was something of his trade. His partner was supposed to have inherited them, but they were together out hunting for meat to feed the beasts. *His* body they managed to dig out, at least. The dogs were scattered about to whoever would have them, after. So if you've come seeking to buy one, you might still have a chance."

"Did, uh, you know Scuolla well?"

"Only to nod to. He was no kinsman of mine. He kept to himself up the east branch."

He tried Beris: "Was Savo close to his uncle, do you know?"

She shook her head. "Savo's mother's a lot younger than Scuolla. I don't think they had much to do with each other even before she married and moved to her husband's farm."

He wasn't sure how to ask, *Was your neighbor an illicit hedge shaman?* without frightening them into silence. "Was Scuolla gossips with *anybody*?"

Laaxa shrugged. "He drank with Acolyte Gallin, time to time, I think."

Inglis prodded, "Acolyte Gallin?"

"He's our Temple-man, down Linkbeck." Laaxa waved in the general direction of the valley. Indeed, such a small village was unlikely to rate a full-braid learned divine. An acolyte would typically be made to do. "He serves the whole of the Chillbeck upper vale."

"So he would have conducted Scuolla's funeral rites?"

"Gallin buries pretty much everyone, in these parts."

Inglis worded his next question cautiously. "Did you hear any strange rumors about Scuolla's funeral?"

He'd hit something, because both women gave him sharp, closed looks.

"Wasn't there," said Laaxa. "Couldn't say. You'd have to ask Gallin."

Shamans came as linked chains—half shackles, half lifelines. A shaman was needed not only to culture a Great Beast, but to conduct its sacrifice into each new candidate at the commencement of his or her service. At the end of that life of service, a shaman was again needed to cleanse the comrade soul, free it of that earthly link—some said, contamination—to go on to the gods. Among the reasons for the revival of the royal shamans of the Weald, it was said, was to sustain such chains, that no soul might go sundered. Among the reasons for keeping the practices discreet and contained was to limit such risks. At his own investiture, Inglis had accepted the hazards blithely. He was anything but blithe now.

If Scuolla had indeed been a hedge shaman, as Inglis now strongly suspected, whoever had conducted his investiture was probably long dead; with luck, readied for his last journey by Scuolla himself. So who had cleansed Scuolla in turn? And might that unknown person help Inglis in his woe? *Follow the chain.*

In this high country, it was rumored, the old ways were quietly tolerated by the rural Temple hierarchies, so long as their practitioners conceded precedence and authority to the Temple, and quarter-day dues. And if the local Temple folk were not too rigidly virtuous. So was this Acolyte Gallin an enemy of the old ways, or one of the quietly tolerant? And if the latter, had he quietly helped his drinking friend's soul along by securing the services of another hedge shaman to perform those last rites? Or at the very least known where and how, and by whom, they were brought off?

In which case, the next link in Inglis's chain must be to find Acolyte Gallin. Unless this new hope should prove yet another illusion, melting away like the others as his hand grasped for it . . . the despairing thought made him want, not for the first time, to plunge the accursed knife into his own breast, and be done with this struggle. *One more try.*

Although *One foot in front of the other* was perhaps no longer a very useful self-exhortation. Inglis twisted around. The toy-like houses were only a couple of miles away, as a rock might plummet. Getting himself down the mountain in his current battered condition would be a much trickier problem.

The middle-aged woman returned, her arms full of what looked to be sheepskin scraps and sticks. One of the scraps turned out to be a simple sheepskin cap, folded over fleece-inward and sewn up one side in a sort of triangle, which she plunked unceremoniously over Inglis's head. He jerked but did not rise. "Don't let your ears freeze, lad." The absurd-looking object made a startlingly swift difference in his comfort.

Two sheepskin booties, equally simple, for his other extremities followed; she knelt to fit them over his feet as though he had been a toddler. Outer boots of woven withy and rawhide looked crude but proved clever. He suspected they would grip the snow, though he doubted they'd stand up to a long march. Neither would he, just now. He swallowed a yelp as she tied the rawhide strips on the right foot. "Aye, you've done yourself good, there."

The scraping finished, the three women undid the hide from its clamps and folded it over. Beris rose to stow it away—in a wooden sledge, tucked up in the corner of the shelter. That was how they transported their high-country produce down to the valley, Inglis supposed. Curing a sledge-load of such hides would keep a village worker busy all winter. Could it also transport a half-crippled man?

They couldn't want him to linger here, eating their reserves. It was late for losing him in a crevice. Foisting him on the charity of the village temple must surely seem a better plan.

Inglis wriggled his feet in his sheepskin slippers. "I would pay you, ladies, but I'm afraid someone took my purse."

Beris looked surprised; the middle-aged woman disappointed; Laaxa Graybraid, displeased, but "Hm," was all she said.

"I suspect he still has it, tucked away somewhere." Inglis's memories were too muddled to be sure of identifying the cutpurse by his voice alone, and anyway, whichever of his three rescuers had pocketed it, they had all watched him do so. But there was no way for the thief to spend coins up here, apart from losing them to his friends at dice. "There wasn't much left in it, but enough, I think, to pay for a ride down to Linkbeck." He lifted his hand to indicate the sledge. "With no questions asked." *And none answered.*

A little silence, while they all took this in.

Laaxa vented a pained sigh. "Those boys. I'll see what I can do."

"Thank you, Mother Laaxa."

Arrow, who had stealthily acquired a belly full of hide scrapings, now proceeded to divert his watchers by vomiting them back up again, in a loud and rhythmic paroxysm.

"Eew," said Beris.

"Dogs," sighed the middle-aged woman.

"You going to take that dog?" Laaxa asked Inglis, with a twitch of her gray eyebrows.

"I expect . . . that will be up to the dog," Inglis replied carefully.

They stared at Arrow, now sniffing his production with evident fascination. Beris hurried to shoo him off, and toss dirt and snow over the slimy pile before he could eat it again.

"Aye," said Laaxa, biting her lip. "I expect so."

VII

THE DAY'S RIDE was slowed by several stops at likely places to inquire after their quarry, all frustratingly fruitless. But it brought Oswyl's troop at length to the village where the local road split off to the valley of the Chillbeck. At the inn there, at last, Oswyl found report of a silent, dark-haired stranger who had spent the night and headed off into the hills, not four days ago. But also of a couple of parties making one final try for the main road north, and one whose destination was the last town within the hinterland's borders.

After a brief debate with the sergeant and the sorcerer, Oswyl made the decision to send two men up the main road tomorrow with strict instructions, if they found the fugitive, not to approach the dangerous man, but to set one guard to follow him and the other to double back and collect their forces. It wasn't a compromise that delighted him in any way, but no one could sensibly go farther this afternoon, with darkness impending and the horses due a rest. Oswyl gritted his teeth in endurance, and made plans to use the evening inquiring of everyone there on the nature of the country roundabout.

A little later, he tracked his sorcerer out to the field behind the inn, where the man had taken it into his strange head to seize the last light and indulge in a stint of archery. It was not a skill in which town-bred Oswyl had much experience, and he watched with reluctant respect as Penric put a dozen arrows into a distant straw bundle, then sent the inn's potboy off to collect them.

"Out of practice." Penric frowned at the straw man, at this range now resembling a pincushion, and shook out his bare hands in turn.

"They all hit," observed Oswyl.

Penric rolled his eyes. "Of course they did. The target is *standing still*. If this is to turn into a hunting party in the hills, I need to do better."

"Have you hunted much?"

"In my youth." He delivered this as if his youth had been a half-century ago.

The potboy returned with the arrows, and Penric inquired of Oswyl, lifting his weapon in tentative invitation, "How are you with a bow?"

Not good enough to make a fool of himself in front of this fellow. "I've not had much chance to handle one."

"What, did your father never take you out hunting?"

"My father is an Easthome lawyer. He never passes the city gates if he can help it." Oswyl offered instead, in pointless defense, "I have some training with the short sword."

"Huh." Penric looked nonplussed, as if the very concept of a father who did not dash around in the woods slaughtering animals personally was a novelty. "We didn't hunt for sport, mind you. We needed the game for our table."

Oswyl allowed himself a trace of amusement. "Poaching?"

"Er, no, they were all our lands. My father was Baron kin Jurald. My eldest brother is, now."

"Oh." That was a surprise. It was wrong, of course, to assume that every person of the Bastard's Order was a bastard or an orphan, or some other odd thing. But it was true often enough. Though this Penric might be one of those acknowledged by-blows with which lords littered the world. Hesitant to pursue that rude curiosity, Oswyl substituted, "How came a kin honorific to be attached to a Darthacan name?" The sorcerer's light coloration made him look entirely a creature of this craggy country.

Penric shrugged. "Some last kin land-heiress met a younger son with few prospects back home in Saone, some generations ago. His dowry didn't last, but the name and the land did." He broke off to send the dozen retrieved arrows flying back into the distant target.

Oswyl wondered if this connection with the minor nobility would give the sorcerer added insight into their outlaw. As the countryside deepened, the palace clerk seemed to be dropping away, to be replaced by . . . what? Did Penric consider himself a kin warrior, or at least half a one?

Penric might have been entertaining some similar speculation, for as the potboy trotted off again, he asked, "How much of a countryman is our murderer, do you know? Or was he also one of those men who doesn't pass the city gates?" He narrowed his gaze at the peaks that were catching and reflecting the last high light, looming much larger and closer now than back at Martensbridge.

A reasonable question. The great kin lords had town mansions, as well as distant lands like little realms. Increasingly, they also kept more convenient country estates around the capital, such as the kin Boarford manor where all this disaster had started. "I believe he grew up somewhere on the south slopes of the Raven Range, though he's been living with kinsmen in Easthome in late years."

"Hm. I was rather hoping for a city mouse, out of his reckoning in the hills. No such luck for us. A city wolf? Seems a bit contradictory." He glanced at Oswyl. "Or maybe not."

Oswyl had no idea how to respond to that. "Have you ever hunted wolves?"

"A few times, when they came down out of the hills in a starving season."

"Winters like this?"

"Oddly, not so much. Winter is a bad time for the grazers and browsers, weakening them, but for that very reason an easier one for the fanglings that hunt them."

"Did you get them? Your wolves?"

"Oh, yes. We made rugs of the skins."

Penric changed his stance, kneeling, moving, turning, as he sent the next flight of arrows on its way. One missed, and he muttered an oath. "I'd have won a cuff on my ear for that one."

"Your father's love?" Oswyl asked dryly.

"Eh, or Old Fehn, his huntsman. Who'd trained Father. They were pleased to take turns on my ears. Both very keen on taking down the quarry with a first killing shot, if possible. I thought at first it was pious mercy to the Son of Autumn's beasts, but eventually figured out no one wanted to chase all over after a wounded one. Not even me, after I'd tried it a few times."

The foot-weary potboy trudged back, handing over the arrows with a poorly concealed sigh. Penric took his stance and raised his bow once more.

The straw target burst into flames.

The potboy gave a startled yelp. Oswyl jerked back.

Penric merely looked miffed. "Oh, for—! Des, we don't set game *on fire!*" He lowered his bow and glowered at the licking orange flicker, merrily glowing in the gloaming.

"What was that?" Oswyl kept his voice level and didn't let it come out a squeal, barely.

"Desdemona thinks my hunting skills are inefficient. Also, she is bored and wants to go in." He sighed and returned his unloosed arrow to its quiver. His mouth opened and vented a voiceless laugh. He added, peevishly, "I don't know how Ruchia put up with you, really, I don't."

Penric pulled his purse off his belt, dug into it, and handed over a coin to the potboy, now quivering like a restless pony. "Practice over. Off you go." The boy absconded the instant his fingers closed over his payment, looking worriedly back over his shoulder a couple of times in his hasty retreat to the inn yard.

Oswyl wondered to what god he should be praying for luck in *his* chase. Not that any god had ever answered his pleas, whether on his knees by his bed as a boy, or prone in the Temple as a man. He stared glumly at the sorcerer's braided blond queue, pale in the growing shadows, as the man unstrung his bow and reordered his gear, then followed him back inside.

The village of Linkbeck lay high up its vale, past what seemed to Oswyl's Wealdean eye impoverished farms, tending to rocky, tilted pastures rather than grain fields. The cows were fat enough, though, the barns big and solid in fieldstone and dark-stained timber, the houses in a like style, with pale stones scattered over their wood-shingled roofs. The excessively tall mountains loured over all, winter white at their tops, while the valley road was still sodden with autumn mud beneath a crunching, frozen crust. The aspiring river ran green and foaming beneath the wooden span that gave the settlement its name.

The sorcerer pushed his horse up beside Oswyl's as they approached the outskirts, if the half-dozen houses on this side of the river could be so grandly dubbed. "So what is your plan?" Penric inquired—diplomatically, since coming this way at all had been *his* plan.

Oswyl shrugged. "Start with the local Temple divine. Such shepherds tend to be most knowing of the folk about, and will have what news there is." In this backwater, not much, Oswyl suspected, but Penric was right that strangers would stand out; a few villagers working around their places turned to stare as the party rode past. The guard sergeant cast polite, reassuring salutes at them.

Penric cleared his throat. "It might be best not to mention my calling, at first. Or my rank. The former tends to make me a distracting novelty in places like this, rather like a performing bear, and the latter would get either daunted deference from rural Temple folk, or elicit every complaint they have of their superiors who neglect them. As if they could draft me as their messenger."

And neither would speed Oswyl's inquiries. "What should I name you, then?"

Penric tilted his head. "Your assistant, I suppose. Your local guide. Not untrue."

It seemed a curious reticence from a young man who had seemed proud enough of his rank back in the princess-archdivine's palace. Better, Oswyl supposed, than the off-balance swagger one sometimes observed in those newly promoted to tasks above their weight. They clopped over the bridge and turned onto the main street, where they soon found the local temple. It was built in a style not unlike the barns and houses, fieldstone and dark timber, if taller and six-sided. A little crowd was gathered under a broad portico running the full length of the front, and Oswyl stopped his horse short, flinging up a hand to halt his party. After another moment, Oswyl dismounted to wait more respectfully. Penric followed his lead, coming to stand beside him and watch.

A funeral was in progress, and had reached its most delicate stage, the signing of the gods, or god. Upon a bier decorated with evergreen boughs, a shrouded figure lay. At the head stood a middle-aged man in the five-colored robes of a divine—no, an acolyte, by the single braid looping at his left shoulder. At his sign, what was plainly the family of the deceased shuffled back out of the way to stand attentively along the wall, and the holy animals and their grooms waiting at the side came alert.

A young man had a pet raven perched upon his shoulder, clearly intended as the representative of the Father. A youth, surely a close relative, held a copper-red dog on a leash, its long fur brushed to a silky shimmer, as plainly the emblem of the Son. A leggy girl gripped the lead of a fat white pony, its shaggy hide curried as well as it could be at this season, looking quite appropriate as a beast of the Bastard. An older woman cradled a placid mama cat, marked only by the green ribbon signifying the Mother around its neck, and a younger girl clutched a squirming kitten, objecting to a like ribbon in blue for the Daughter.

One by one, the acolyte motioned the handlers to the bier. The raven, held out hopefully on the young man's arm, evinced no interest in the proceedings, and hopped back to its shoulder perch. The kitten continued its war with its ribbon. The pony sniffed briefly, causing the people lined up against the wall to stiffen in dismay, but then pulled away, tugging to get its head down and crop some weeds growing up at the corner of the portico. The red dog also sniffed, waving its tail genially but without any obvious excitement. The mama cat jumped down from the woman's arms and curled up neatly upon the chest of the deceased—an elderly grandmother, apparently—and blinked placid gold eyes. A general ripple of relief ran through the mourners, briefly stayed when the dog pulled back, but it was evidently attracted by the cat, not the dead woman, and was swiftly discouraged by a possessive hiss and a swipe of claws.

In great city temples like the ones at Easthome, the signing of which god had taken up the soul of the dead had economic as well as theological significance, as Orders devoted to individual gods took possession of the family's monetary offerings for prayers for the dead. Here, there was likely only one altar table, the colors of its coverings changed out seasonally. It was perhaps shrewd showmanship that had inspired the acolyte to offer the Mother's beast last, rather than cutting things short by beginning with the obvious. Poor these people might be, but not, therefore, paltry.

"That red dog . . . " muttered Penric out of the corner of his mouth to Oswyl.

"What about it?"

"I think we've come to the right place."

"How so?"

But the sorcerer only made a *wait* wave of his hand, vexingly, although he continued to look around with keen interest.

The acolyte intoned a short prayer and signed the tally of the gods. The half-dozen burliest men of the family took up the bier and bore it off up the street, and the grooms collected their animals and headed in the opposite direction, quickly losing their formal demeanor. The acolyte, making to follow the bier, glanced uncertainly at Oswyl's party and paused. The woman who had repossessed the mama cat came to his side.

"May I help you, sirs?" he said.

"My name is Locator Oswyl, and I am on a mission of inquiry from Easthome," Oswyl began. As the man jerked his head back in alarm, Oswyl quickly added, "I want to ask after any strangers you may have lately heard about in your district, but we can wait till your duties are done, Acolyte, ah . . . ?"

"Gallin," said the acolyte, looking less alarmed but more curious.

"Uh, perhaps my wife, Gossa, can take you in and make you comfortable till I return?"

It wasn't clear which of them he was asking, but the woman, looking equally curious, relieved the cat of its ribbon and set it down, shooing it away with her foot. She bobbed a curtsey at the unexpected visitors. "Indeed, sirs. Follow me."

The children with the animals also paused to stare. Penric cast a special smile at the girl with the white pony, touching his thumb to his lips in a blessing of the white god; the girl looked surprised at this courtesy. Gossa directed what were ever-more-obviously her offspring in assorted directions, the girl with the kitten to stop playing and run ahead to put the kettle on.

The guardsmen with all their horses were sent in the wake of the girl with the pony. Oswyl stepped aside to instruct them, once they had settled the beasts in the temple's stable around back, to spread out through the village and make inquiries as they had done at every stop so far, then hurried to catch up with his reticent sorcerer and the acolyte's wife. Such Temple spouses were often as much the servants of the gods as their mates, if through their mates. She must be a source of local news as good as Gallin.

The acolyte's house was next to the temple, and had little to distinguish it from others along the village street, although the front windows were set with glass, not parchment. It held a cramped but cheerful air suggesting more children than money. The kitchen was set to the back with a sort of parlor-study in front, doubtless where the acolyte performed his spiritual counseling, and to which the visitors were conducted. Oswyl had thus to wait till his hoped-for informant returned from her domestic domain to begin his inquiries. The young girl approached the smiling Penric to show off her kitten, which the sorcerer duly held in his lap and admired. Stroked by his long fingers, it purred like a cogwheel. Oswyl trusted no one else noticed the faint patter of dead fleas drifting off the beast when it was handed back. Oswyl attempted a smile as well, but it apparently lacked the blond man's magic; he was offered no kitten.

Goodwife Gossa, assisted by her dekittened daughter, bustled back in to offer ale, tea, and bread and butter. Penric politely made the sign of the tally before they partook, by way of blessing, which won a smile from Gossa this time. Oswyl's hopes that she might also offer information were quickly dashed, however. At his now-well-practiced queries, she shook her head in regret. No strangers that she'd heard of had arrived in the vale in the past week, or month for that matter. Oswyl cast Penric a reproaching glance.

Penric, undaunted, said to Gossa, "That red dog of your son's. Where did he come by it?"

"Ah, he's a pretty beast, isn't he? But it's a sad tale. The old fellow who raised him was killed in a rockfall not two months back. Some of his dogs had to be dragged away from the place—after days—they mourned him so hard. It was impossible to dig him up to bury him again, so my husband held his rites on the spot. But . . . " She hesitated, then was interrupted when Gallin came in.

He shrugged off his five-colored robe, which at this range Oswyl could see was a bit threadbare, hung it on a wall peg, and sat to take hot tea with weary gratitude.

"These gentlemen are looking for strangers come to the vale," she informed him, "but I've not heard of any. Have you?"

The familiar, frustrating headshake. "Not too many ever come up this far. We mostly take our own goods to the market at Whippoorwill. A few men from there come up in the summer to trade in animals or hides or cheese, but they aren't strangers."

"I was just starting to tell them about old Scuolla," his wife put in.

Gallin straightened, setting down his mug. He asked more eagerly, "Did someone finally get my letters? Or read my letters? I'd sent to my superiors in Whippoorwill twice, but have got no reply yet. And written to the divines in neighbor vales. One said he could not help, and the other . . . was less helpful." Gallin grimaced. "My prayers have fared no better."

"Help with what?" asked Oswyl.

"My ghost problem," said Gallin simply.

Oswyl sat back; Penric sat up. "Ghost problem?" he encouraged their host.

Oswyl was not without curiosity, but this side-issue seemed nothing to do with his ever-more-delayed pursuit. His new hope was to extract his party from this local hospitality and get back to the main road by nightfall. Yet Acolyte Gallin seized the opening like a swimmer grasping a rope.

"That luckless old man. I wasn't sure at first, mind you, even with the behavior of his dogs. Not all of them, just his two favorites—Arrow, a fine big fellow, and Blood, that you saw. After the rockslide it seems Arrow had run to the nearest farmyard and barked his head off, till they drove him away by pelting him with stones. Blood stood guard, I suppose you could say, back at the slide, barking and howling. Then that big dog ran all the way into town and found *me*, and whined and carried on and wouldn't be hushed. As the beast seldom left Scuolla's side, it didn't take a Cedonian sage to figure out something was badly amiss. I saddled my horse and followed him up the road, and then the hunting trail, and then, well. Big slide. Took down a lot of trees. I'd heard the crash echoing down the vale earlier that morning, but when no alarm had come, I'd dismissed it. It didn't take me long to find the remains of Scuolla's apprentice, and one of the other dogs, its back broken, sadly, but it had been too late for either of them from the first. A gang of men from the village, later that afternoon, had no better luck at finding Scuolla, though we did uncover one more dog, and buried both beasts properly, no skinning. I did insist on that, for respect." He nodded to himself. Neglected by his Temple supervisors in this remote vale, Gallin had perhaps taken to self-supplying their absent discipline or praise. Oswyl tried not to sympathize.

After a long, thoughtful, silent inhalation through his nose, Penric came out with, "And how long had you known that old Scuolla was a hedge shaman?"

Intent on recapturing the conversation by offering suitable condolences and then hurrying their leave, Oswyl swallowed his words so fast he coughed. *What?*

Gallin cast the young man a closer look than heretofore. "I've served in this vale for over twenty years. I found out what he was early on, but not so early that I hadn't had time to learn his kin and his ties, and that there was no harm in him. I take my first duty to be to souls, not laws. And to learn as well as teach, or what else do the gods put us in this world for?"

"Indeed." Penric made the tally sign; coming from a full-braid Temple divine (even one who'd left his braids in his saddlebags), it seemed to Oswyl strangely more than a mere assenting shrug.

Reassured by this reaction, Gallin went on: "My trust was repaid five-fold, through those years. Scuolla was as pious a man as any and more than many, and he and his dogs were an aid to all in need, lost or hurt, in flood or fire or famine and a hundred smaller tasks. In time, I came to think of him as my good left hand here in the vale, without which the right could not grip half so well."

Gossa, nodding in confirmation to all this, put in, "That's why we don't understand about his funeral." She made a *go on* gesture at her husband.

Penric's eyes narrowed. "It took place at the rockslide, your goodwife said?"

"Aye. There was no getting down to his body. For a time we thought the dogs might find him, or later, our noses, but he was too deep for the last and the dogs, well, the dogs never settled on a consensus. Or settled at all—very disturbed they were, right to the last. In the event, no god signed to taking up his soul, or at least none we could discern, though we made the trial five times, till the holy animals began to bite and scratch and kick and it grew dark."

"Could he have escaped the fall somehow?" asked Oswyl, ensnared by this tale despite himself. "Run off for some reason?" The dead companion was suggestive, to a suspicious mind.

Gallin huffed out a breath. "I wondered about that, too, as things went on. But it doesn't stand up to the witness of the dogs."

In his past investigations, Oswyl had found many mute things to give testimony that shouted; he supposed he must now add dogs to that list. At least his superiors could not chide him for not swearing them in. "Sundered, then."

Gossa made a fending gesture in front of her bodice, and scowled at him as fiercely as one of his aunts about to correct his legal rhetoric.

Gallin shook his head and went on, "By every sign, Scuolla was sundered, and I don't think he should have been. I know he would not refuse the gods. And if the Son of Autumn, to Whom he'd made devotions all his life, didn't think him good enough somehow, well, there's still the Bastard. So where was He? Where were any of Them?"

An unanswerable question that Oswyl had confronted many times in his career. He bit his lip.

"The thing is," put in Gossa, "everyone round about now takes that rockslide for haunted, and avoids it."

Penric laced and unlaced his fingers a few times, then seemed to come to some decision. "So this hedge shaman, working with dogs as the medium of his art, died uncleansed of the Great Beast that must have given him his powers. And now his soul is lost between the worlds, a sundering unwilled by either the gods or the man."

"You know so much of such things, young fellow?" said Gallin, startled.

"I'm, ah, something of a Temple sensitive myself, as it happens." His smile had gone a little stiff. "I knew the moment I saw the red dog that there had to be a shaman in this tale somewhere. It is partway to being made a Great Beast, did you know?"

Gallin cleared his throat. "Blood's a very intelligent dog. Well-mannered. Good with all the village children. Took to being a holy animal with no trouble at all."

"I daresay."

"So . . . you didn't come here in answer to my letters . . . ?" The acolyte seemed reluctant to give up this hope.

"Not to your letters, no." Penric bared his teeth in a brief, ironic grimace, an edged look Oswyl had not seen in his face before.

Gallin confessed, "I'd thought to find another hedge shaman for Scuolla, somewhere up or down the mountains, to perform their last secret rites for him. Him seeming out of reach of my prayers. Scuolla had his Great Beast from the shaman here before him, long ago when he was a young man, and performed the cleansing for his mentor in turn when he died. He was bringing along his own apprentice, but he'd not invested the man with his powers yet as far as I know. Well, I do know, for Wen's soul was signed taken up by the Son at his funeral the day after the tragedy."

Gossa nodded. "Plain as plain, that one was. Greatly to his family's relief amidst their grief."

Oswyl began, "I should explain something more about the fugitive we hunt—" but Penric flung up his hand, interrupting him.

"Wait just a little on that, Locator, if you please."

It didn't please Oswyl much, but Penric was turning to Gallin. "How far is it to this maybe-haunted rockslide of yours?"

"About five miles up the East Branch road, or thereabouts. An hour's brisk ride." Gallin squinted intently at Penric. "You say you are a Temple sensitive. Can you sense ghosts?"

"Ah . . . with a bit of special help, yes."

"Can you get that help?"

"I carry it with me."

Gallin grew eager. "Could you—would you—would you be willing to ride out to the fall with me, and sense what you can? It would put my mind to rest." He reflected. "Or not, but at least I'd *know*."

Such an expedition couldn't be back till nightfall, Oswyl calculated. They would be stuck in this village till *tomorrow*. "*Time*," he gritted under his breath.

Penric's glance flicked up. He murmured back, "You could go on without me."

"No. I can't."

"Well, then." He turned to the acolyte. "I'm willing to take a look, yes. I can't make any promises."

Gallin actually clapped his hands in relief. "We can be off as soon as the horses are saddled."

"We should take the red dog," added Penric.

Gallin stilled. "Ah. Aye." He rose to lead the way, pausing only to grasp his wife's hands in a farewell. At least the goodwife eyed them all more approvingly, as they clumped out after him.

VIII

PENRIC STUDIED THE DOG, Blood, as it cantered along behind the acolyte's horse. It wasn't undog, or not-dog, or even, really, terribly uncanny. It was just . . . more-dog, a peculiar density of itself.

Can you show me more? he asked Desdemona.

You are seeing what I am seeing, more or less, she replied. *Turnabout being fair play.*

Hm.

Oswyl nudged his horse up beside Pen's on the rutted wagon trail— it was unduly flattering to dub it a road. After a moment he murmured, "You really can sense ghosts?"

"Desdemona can. I don't have her share the sight with me unless I ask. It's distracting, especially in old places where many people have died over the years." When first this skill had come to him, a few months after Des had moved in, he'd tripped himself up dodging around things no one else could see, much to her amusement, till he'd worked out how to get her to shut it off. Some people had thought he'd been taken with fits. The real explanation hadn't improved things by much.

"Can all sorcerers do so?"

"I imagine it varies. Those possessing younger or less experienced demons may be less adept."

"I wonder that my Order does not requisition them more. The ability to interrogate the dead . . . would be most helpful in the instance of a murder."

"Mm, not as much as you'd think. Most souls go at once to their gods, when severed from their bodies. It's the god who is present at the funeral, not the person. An invoked messenger." An odd thing when Pen thought about it, that so great a Presence should stoop to so small a task.

Oswyl frowned in what Pen was beginning to recognize as professional frustration. As distinguished from the dozen other ways he could frown.

"In any case," Pen consoled him, "it would be hard for the sensitives to correctly interpret and report what they see. Even a fresh ghost still holding the form of its body can't speak. The sundered soon grow muddled, like an old man who's lost his wits along with his teeth. They exhaust the ability to assent to their god by the time they exhaust their ability to refuse. Which is what makes them sundered, I suppose." Indifferent, beyond attachment or pain, attenuating into pale smudges, and then, at length, gone. Pen wasn't sure he could convey how disturbing this process was to see, midway, without being frightening, exactly. Well, not after the first brush.

You squeaked in terror, said Des.

Did not, Pen thought back. *That was just a yelp of surprise.* The ghosts, once understood, had seemed less horrifying than his first fear, that he was hallucinating or going mad. Still, not comfortable.

Gallin turned his horse aside onto a narrower trail, weaving up through the trees, and Pen and Oswyl fell into single file behind him. After a damp, scrambling time, Blood bounded ahead, whining, and the steep woods opened out abruptly onto the rockfall.

Rockfall was a serious understatement, Pen realized. The slide was perhaps a hundred paces across and three times that in height, a fan of debris including boulders the size of wagons, mud, and a tangle of uprooted and snapped trees. At its wide foot, the local stream had backed up and routed around; at its narrower head, a raw and ragged new cliff marked where it had heaved itself out of the mountain's weakened side. He imagined being caught under the roar, not knowing whether to run forward or back, so screened by the trees on the shuddering path as not to know either was equally futile till too late.

The three horsemen all pulled up at the edge, but Blood sprang onward, scrambling over the treacherous footing, sniffing and uttering small yips. Penric did not at first see what the dog sought, and then, at a shift from Desdemona, did.

Oh.

The old man sat on a boulder midway across the scree and a little down from where the path was cut off. He wore the common garb of workmen in this country, boots, trousers, rough-spun shirt, a capacious sheepskin vest fleece turned inward and hanging open around him. A short-brimmed hat was pushed back on his head, a few feathers stuck in its band. Penric could not discern their hues, for feathers, clothes, and the man who wore them were all faded to a colorless translucency.

As Pen watched, Blood made his way, not quite unerringly, to the man's side, and whimpered and yipped around him like a dog sniffing around a badger's den that was too small to enter. The man smiled faintly and lifted his hand to stroke the dog's head. The beast calmed and sat, silky tail waving like a signal flag.

Pen dismounted and handed his reins to Oswyl. "Hold my horse, please."

"Can you see anything?" asked Gallin anxiously.

"Oh, yes." Pen turned and began to clamber across the debris.

"Be careful!" called Gallin. "It could be unstable!"

Pen waved understanding.

Incurious as an old idler on a town square bench, the man watched him approach. Pen's gloves saved him from tearing his hands as he tested each hold, seeking balance rather than suspect support. He was breathing heavily by the time he arrived at the boulder and found firm-ish footing. He stared down at the revenant, who stared back up but then returned his attention to his worried dog.

"Master Scuolla," Pen tried. "Shaman, sir."

The man seemed not to hear. But he had noticed Pen, and was most certainly interacting with the dog. A sundered soul some, what, two months into its dissolution ought to be a lot more vague than this. More distanced.

He looks as if he hasn't been dead more than a few days, Des agreed. *Have you seen anything like this before?*

Des shook Penric's head. *The only shaman I ever met was very much still alive.*

Can you reach him any more directly?

No more than we have done.

Feeling rude, Pen tried passing his hand through the man's head. Any chill was indistinguishable from the mountain air. The man lifted his face as if to a passing breeze, but then returned his attention to his dog, who fawned on him.

Des had gone quiet. Pen stood back and thought. His thoughts were extremely uncomfortable. The most uncomfortable of them was that this called as much for the skills of a divine as a sorcerer. He made the five-fold tally, and tried to compose his mind in prayer. Asking his god, or indeed any of the gods, for a sign seemed a madly dangerous thing to do, but in any case no sign was forthcoming. In the silence, he stared across the scree at Acolyte Gallin, and contemplated the disquieting notion that maybe he wasn't supposed to be the supplicant, here. Maybe he was supposed to be the *answer.*

But old Scuolla needs a shaman, not a sorcerer. And while Locator Oswyl had been trying to lay hands on his fugitive shaman for weeks, so far they'd come up empty.

Well, if the dead man had lingered here for two months, he probably wasn't going anywhere else immediately. Though time was clearly not his friend. Pen called to Blood, who ignored him, and made his way, slipping and sliding, back across the rockfall to the horses.

"Could you sense anything?" asked Acolyte Gallin.

"Oh, yes. He's there, all right. Communing with his dog, although not much with me."

Oswyl blinked at him, startled, and stared across at Blood licking the air by what must appear to him a bare boulder. Licking at Scuolla's ghostly hand, his tongue sliding through it in chill confusion.

Gallin signed himself, looking distraught. "He is sundered, then."

"Ah . . . " said Pen. "Maybe not yet."

"Surely it is too late . . . ?"

"I can't claim to know what's going on, here. My first guess is that his shamanic powers allow his spirit to still draw some nourishment from the world even though separated from his body. But it's been a long time. He seemed . . . it's hard to explain . . . tired. I think he's still fading, but more slowly than other men would."

"Then there's still a chance to save him? If a shaman might be found?"

"If a shaman might be found, it would still be worth a try, at least."

Gallin's breath huffed out, as he stared across to where Blood lingered by the side of his old comrade and friend. "If there are any such powers hiding elsewhere in these mountains, my letters should have brought me some word by now."

Not your letters. Your prayers. And Penric wasn't going to say *that* out loud.

Oswyl was acquiring a whole new frown, as he perhaps made some of the connections Pen just had. Or at least noticed the excessive amount of coincidence starting to pile up. As a locator, he was surely suspicious of coincidences. As a divine, Penric was too, but in a very different way. He remembered the shrewd gray eyes of the Saint of Idau, and the white god who had once looked through them at him. *At us.* Desdemona, remembering with him, shuddered.

"In any case, we can do nothing more here right now." Pen retrieved his reins from Oswyl and swung himself back up into his saddle.

Gallin called Blood, who didn't come until Scuolla's ghost made a releasing sort of *go on* gesture. The acolyte then offered the hospitality of the Linkbeck Temple to Oswyl's party for the night—Linkbeck lacked an inn as such, although Gallin assured them he could find beds for all among his villagers, no need to camp in the stable loft. He looked back over his shoulder as they turned onto the path again, and breathed in a hesitant undertone, "Not hopeless?"

Penric wasn't sure to whom that was addressed, but answered, "I am not certain. Locator, perhaps the time has come to explain the full story of the man we seek."

Oswyl gestured assent, but did not begin till they turned back onto the wagon track and he could ride side-by-side with Gallin. Penric fell behind, listening. Gallin made exclamations at all the expected high and low points, till Oswyl, drawing toward the end of his account, let fall a *Learned Penric.*

Gallin turned in his saddle and stared in astonishment. Penric returned a wary smile and a little wave of his fingers. He was unsurprised when Oswyl finished and Gallin dropped back beside him, brows crooked in new inquiry. It was embarrassing when a man twice his age looked to *him* for answers, especially when he didn't have them.

"You are really a sorcerer, and a full-braid divine?"

Pen cleared his throat. "Long story. But all Temple sorcerers must undergo a divine's training and oaths. We seldom take up the duties of a regular divine, though."

Gallin seemed to consider this, sidelong. "Does your Order *have* regular duties?"

Pen puffed a laugh. "Good question. We go where we're needed, I think."

"And yet you were not sent?" Gallin asked as Oswyl reined back to Penric's other side, trapping him in the center of their attention. The acolyte looked across: "Either of you?"

Oswyl shook his head.

Penric said slowly, "I think we may no longer be hunting. We may be trapping. If that innkeeper told us true, Inglis kin Wolfcliff seeks another shaman. Find the nearest one, and he may come to us." Come, be brought or be driven—this game would not evade such Beaters as Penric had begun to suspect were in play.

Gallin said plaintively, "But why should a shaman *seek* a shaman? What could a royal shaman, even a disgraced one, possibly want with a mere country hedge shaman?"

Another good question. That their quarry sought such a practitioner had been enough to direct their pursuit. Maybe he should have thought a step further . . . ? Des snorted.

Oswyl's logical mind was starting to work on the question. He offered tentatively, "He seeks to take refuge with someone who will hide him?"

Penric threw in, "Or perhaps he plans a suicide, yet does not want to be sundered like poor Scuolla." Yes, suicide must pose a problem for such an invested person. Some suicides sought sundering, but many another was hurrying to the hoped-for refuge of their god. The Temple spent a good deal of effort trying to discourage that particular approach to divinity.

Oswyl chewed this over, looking as though he did not like the taste. "Beyond my mandate," he said at last.

But not beyond mine . . . in principle. Another disturbing thought. Today seemed unusually full of them.

At the sound of hoofbeats, Penric looked up to see a rider cantering toward them. After a moment, he recognized one of their guardsmen, Heive.

"Sirs!" he called, reining in before them. "Daughter be thanked, I found you. Goodwife Gossa and my sergeant beg that you return at once. A stranger has come to the village, and he could be the man we seek. Dark hair and a Wealdean accent, at least, though oddly dressed, and I couldn't swear to his age."

"You've seen him?" said Oswyl, rising in his stirrups in excitement. "You haven't tried to approach him, have you?"

"No, sir," said Heive fervently. "He came to the acolyte's house, seeking him, he said. Goodwife Gossa told him you were out on an errand and sent him to wait in the temple, and for me to ride for you. The sergeant and Baar are watching the building from a distance. He'd not come out by the time I left."

"We'd best hurry," said Gallin in a voice choked with alarm, and led the way, kicking his horse into a canter. Oswyl was right on his heels. Penric and Heive fell in behind; Blood ran after them. Pen was suddenly glad he'd brought his bow along, rather than leaving it with his saddlebags in the temple stable.

At some risk of bringing in the horses wet and winded, they made fast time back to the village street, finding it bare of villagers. They stopped a few houses away from the temple. The guard sergeant waved from where he hunkered down behind someone's garden gate, and pointed to the temple door. "Still in there," he mouthed.

Oswyl returned a silent salute. They all dismounted. Blood, panting and muddy, made a lunge for the temple doors. Gallin grabbed him by the scruff of his neck and hauled him, whining, to his house, where Gossa could be seen peeking through the front window, beckoning urgently at him. Pen unlaced his bow from his saddle, strung it, and shrugged on his quiver. The other two guardsmen joined them. The armed party made its way quietly to the temple portico.

Oswyl gestured Penric ahead. "All right, sorcerer," he muttered. "Go on."

Wait, what, all by myself? "Wouldn't it be better for us all to rush him at once?"

The expressions on four faces seemed to disagree with him. "If this is a false lead," said Oswyl, "you are the one man among us who can tell at a glance."

Gallin and Gossa came out the door of their house, to stand holding hands and watching Pen anxiously. Pen swallowed, nocked his arrow, and stepped into the dimness of the temple's interior.

Light me, he thought to Desdemona, and the shadows fled from his eyes, leaving his vision clear.

The man lay prone on the wooden temple floor, just this side of the cold fire plinth, arms out in what would be the attitude of deepest supplication, except he was not aimed toward any wall shrine in particular. Penric wasn't sure if he was seeing prayer, or exhaustion. He was unshaven and wore a grab-bag of garb, townsman's clothing but a peasant's woven-withy boots, and a mountaineer's sheepskin cap. One hand gripped a long stick. By his side lay a huge dog, black and tan, head down on crossed paws in an attitude of canine boredom. Its head came up at Pen's approach, triangular ears pricked; its tail thumped desultorily on the boards, although it also growled. Perhaps both it and Pen were equally confused?

If Blood had been more-dog, this one was even more so, dense with presence. *This is a Great Beast. Not so, Des?*

Impressive, she conceded.

"Sit up," Pen commanded, in what he hoped was a convincing arresting-officer voice; "But don't get up."

The man jerked to his knees, grabbing for his stick to support his stance. His sleeve, falling back, revealed an arm crisscrossed with long, vicious-looking scabs. The knife at his belt glowed with strange power swirling like an aurora, not in Pen's eyes but in Des's. He stared wildly at Pen, mouth falling open as he drew sudden breath. The dog stood up and growled with what seemed a lot more authority than Pen had mustered.

"Inglis kin Wolfcliff," said Pen, certain now of what he faced. And then had no idea of what to say next. This whole scene was so sideways to any of his preconceptions about the man, anything he might have rehearsed would have been worthless anyway. As neither man nor dog launched himself at Pen's throat, he eased the tension on the string and let his bow droop, but still held it ready. "We've been looking for you."

IX

INGLIS USED HIS STICK to climb to his full height, although his right leg, much abused by the trip down the mountain this morning, threatened to buckle from the pain. The man before him seemed a blond apparition, inexplicable. **"Go away,"** Inglis tried.

The intruder just tilted his head. "Good attempt, wolf-man. A bit misdirected. Although wouldn't 'Give me your horse' seem more to the point?"

How did he *know* . . . ? And then, however badly his powers were crippled, Inglis recognized the fellow for what he was. And, five gods, or should that oath be *Bastard's teeth!*, he *was*. His spirit-density was stunning. "Sorcerer." Inglis was confounded by hope and fear. And by hurt, and heartache, and exhaustion, and his long, futile flight. "Temple, or hedge?" Or, five gods help them all, rider or ridden? Surely any demon so powerful must be ascendant? Could Inglis persuade it to . . .

"Temple through and through, I'm afraid. You are not more surprised than I was." He glanced aside at Arrow, who had shifted to stand at Inglis's right hand. "How did you come by one of Scuolla's dogs?"

"It found me. Up on the mountain. When I was lost, trying to find a shortcut to the Carpagamo road. It won't stop following me." Wait, how did he know of Scuolla?

"Ah. Huh." The blond man's lips crooked up in a smile of . . . dismay? "Did it bring you here, do you think?"

"I . . . don't know." *Had* it? He glanced down at the big dog, his companion for days. Inglis had assumed the animal was attracted to him because he was a shaman invested, and it had somehow confused him with its prior master. *Maker.* "I came looking for . . . " He hardly knew what, anymore.

"You came looking for Acolyte Gallin, I understand. Why?"

"An old woman up at the summer grazing camp told me that he knew Scuolla. I thought he might know . . . something."

"Did you know Scuolla has been dead under a rockfall for the past two months?"

"I was told that, too."

"And did she tell you that he was a hedge shaman?"

"No. I . . . guessed it. From the dog."

"Hm." The sorcerer seemed to come to some decision. "I have a senior locator outside, who has ridden all the way from Easthome in pursuit of you. Do you surrender? No more shaman tricks, no running away?"

What could this man do if he refused? "I'm not running anywhere." Inglis grimaced. "I mangled my leg on the mountain."

The sorcerer looked him up and down. "Ah. I *see*. Yes, mountains will do that."

Inglis hung on his staff, feeling sick. "They in Easthome seek me as a murderer?"

"Locator Oswyl is a very precise man. I'm sure he'd say he seeks you as a *suspected* murderer. No one is going to hang you on the spot, you know, without all those judicial ceremonies his Order is so fond of. Everyone has to dress up, first. Not to mention what could be some fraught theological complications." He added, "I think you had better give me your knife, for now."

"NO."

He went on with unimpaired weird cheer, "That's Tollin kin Boarford's ghost wrapped in it, yes? So Oswyl was right. I shall like to know, later, how you managed that. Speaking from my calling. Both of them, come to think."

"I'm not going to use it to stab anyone." Inglis's voice was hoarse. "Else."

"Yes, but my colleagues won't know that. Once things are more settled, I may even be able to give it back into your care. You've been faithful so far, haven't you? You've brought it a long way." His voice had gone soft, persuasive. Sensible. "Why?"

"I sought a shaman."

"You are a shaman."

Inglis vented a bitter laugh. "Not anymore."

The blond man looked him over. Or *through* him? "Surely, you are."

"I *tried*. I *can't*. Can't enter the trance." His voice, rising, fell. "I think it is a punishment. Maybe from the gods."

The sorcerer raised his eyebrows. "So why not take your problem to your shamanic superiors at court in Easthome? They were *much* closer."

"I *killed* Tollin," Inglis said through his teeth. "I could not go back there and face . . . everyone."

The sorcerer took a quick glance over his shoulder. Yes, there were some other men hovering outside the door. No other exits. *Trapped. How?*

"Oh? I was told he'd been disemboweled by a boar. Did you stab him before, or after?"

"After. It was . . . it was a mercy cut." Inglis shuddered at the memory of the knife blade going in, the pressure and the give in his hand, all mixed up with his visions as he'd descended from the plane of symbolic action, exhilarated to have completed his first investiture, to have made a fierce spirit warrior in truth. Tollin's agonized face . . . "He was screaming." *It was unbearable. I had to shut him up.*

"He could not have survived his injuries from the boar?"

"No. Gods, no."

"Why didn't you go for help then?"

"It was very confusing in that moment. He must have planted his knife in the beast's neck even as he was being ripped open. I captured its spirit and passed it into Tollin before I came back to, back to, to the sty. To the blood." His wolf-within had been wildly excited by the blood, nearly uncontrollable. Inglis could, he supposed, have claimed that he'd lost control of his powers in that moment. He'd considered that defense, on his long ride north. *But I didn't. Not really.*

That came later.

"Came back . . . out of your shamanic trance?"

"Yes."

"Did you mean to bind his spirit to your knife?"

"No! Yes . . . I don't know. I don't know how I did that." Well, Inglis knew *what* he'd done. He'd been taught about the banner-carriers, hallowed Old Wealdean warriors who were charged with carrying away from the field of battle the souls of their fallen spirit-warrior comrades. And the souls of those dying but not yet dead. The fatally wounded must have included kinsmen, friends, mentors. Had those mercy cuts, to sever the soul from its body and bind it to the banner for that strange rescue, been as horrible for them as it had been for him? *I think it must.*

"Was this investiture Tollin's idea, or yours?"

"His. He'd badgered me for weeks. But none of this would have happened if I hadn't agreed to try the rite. I wanted to test my powers. And . . . and then there was Tolla."

"His sister, yes? Oswyl mentioned her. I gather your courtship was not prospering. So why not use your weirding voice on her directly?"

Inglis glared at him, offended. Arrow growled.

"Nah, nah." The sorcerer gave a dissimulating wave of his fingers. "You have a romantic heart, I see." As Inglis glared harder, he went on, "I'm Learned Penric of Martensbridge, by the way. Temple sorcerer of the Bastard's Order, presently serving the court of the princess-archdivine, who assigned me to this Grayjay . . . " He jerked his head toward the doorway.

That near-youth was a Temple divine? Yes, he had to be, to be entrusted with his demonic passenger. Beyond Learned Penric Inglis saw another man entering the temple hall. Three more clustered behind him, two armed with short swords and one with a cavalry crossbow, and following them, yet another fellow—middle-aged, shabbier, anxious.

"What kept you?" Penric, still not turning, asked of the lead man behind him. Keeping Inglis in his eye. But Penric's sturdy hunting bow was now dangling disregarded from his hand. He slid his arrow back into his quiver.

"I didn't want to interrupt," said the first man. "Your inquiries seemed to be faring well." His accent was pure Easthome. Beneath his cloak, Inglis made out gray fabric and the glint of brass buttons. *The locator.* The armed three were Temple guardsmen of some sort, Inglis supposed, dressed in a mishmash of local winter woolens and bits of blue uniform.

Penric at last glanced back to the doorway. "And here is Acolyte Gallin, shepherd of this valley," he continued, naming the older fellow, who was gaping at Inglis in inexplicable amazement. "The very man you sought. Now that you have found him, what?"

"I wanted to find what shaman in turn had cleansed Scuolla." Inglis swallowed. "Discover if he could also free Tollin. Cleanse him so he is not sundered. We were both fools together, but Tollin does not deserve *that.*"

Gallin stepped forward, looking pole-axed. "I prayed for a shaman. And here you are, right *here*—!"

Penric, watching Inglis stare back in bewilderment, put in with a helpful air, "Scuolla has not been cleansed, because no other shaman could be found. But he is not yet sundered. I'm not sure what sustains him. I suspect he may be drawing some spiritual nourishment from his dogs."

Inglis's black yelp was scarcely a laugh. "Then your prayers must have been heard by the Bastard, Acolyte Gallin. To bring you a shaman who *can't work his craft* . . . !"

The sorcerer-divine pursed his lips, as if seriously considering this jibe. "That just might be so. He *is* the god of murderers and outcasts, among His other gifts." He added under his breath, "And vile humor. And rude songs."

"*I can't cleanse anyone.*" Too polluted himself by his crime . . . ?

"Not in your current state of mind, clearly," said the sorcerer. His tone had grown easy, friendly. Had he understood *any* of this? "I think . . . "

Everyone in the temple hall seemed to hang on his breath.

"We should all go have dinner. And get a good night's sleep. Yes."

Oswyl and the guardsmen stared at Penric in startled disbelief, as if he'd just proposed they all grow wings and fly to Carpagamo, or something equally bizarre.

"That sounds very sensible." A slight quaver in Acolyte Gallin's voice undercut this endorsement. "The sun is already gone behind the mountains."

"Aren't you going to magic him?" the lead guardsman asked Penric, nodding warily at Inglis. Inglis couldn't tell if that was something he'd wanted to see, or to be far away from.

"I don't think I need to. Do I?" Penric, smiling, held out his hand to Inglis, palm up. Waiting for him to surrender his knife, which would be surrender indeed. "By the way, how are you keeping Tollin from fading?"

For answer, Inglis mutely held up both arms, letting his sleeves fall back.

"Oh," said Penric, quietly.

"Blood holds life even after it leaves the body," said Inglis, his voice falling unwilled into the cadences of his teachers. His own despair added, "For a little while."

"Mm, yes, one sees why your Darthacan ancestors were frightened of the forest magics," murmured Penric. "It's written that the old shamans worked some very strange effects with blood. Rather a different affair if using someone else's blood, and not one's own, I imagine. Theologically speaking." His smile was unwavering.

Inglis's weary will was not. With fumbling fingers, he picked out the rawhide ties securing his sheath to his belt, and handed the knife across. Penric touched forehead, lips, navel, groin, and spread his fingers over his heart, *Daughter-Bastard-Mother-Father-Son*, completing the blessing in full before taking it. Sorcerer he might be, possessed of fearsome powers, but in this moment the full-braid divine was clearly ascendant. He didn't hold it like a weapon. He held it like a sacrament.

He sees.

Lightheaded to the point of passing out with this release from his deathly burden, Inglis fell to his knees, burying his face in the thick fur of Arrow's neck, gasping against tears. The dog whined and tried to lick him.

From outside the temple, a woman's voice cried, "Blood, you fool beast! Come back here this instant!"

A copper-colored dog with muddy paws rushed into the temple hall. Inglis nearly fell over as Arrow jerked away from him. For a moment, he gathered himself to break up a dog fight, but the two animals exchanged greetings with happy yips and whines, circling around to sniff each other's nether parts. Old friends, it seemed.

And another survivor of the rockfall? The red dog was thick with spirit-density, although not nearly so much as Arrow. Halfway to being a Great Beast; doomed to be sacrificed at the end of its life into a new puppy, to continue layering up its powers. Inglis wondered if Scuolla would have made sure it was a long and happy life, by dog standards. The good natures of both beasts suggested so.

The two dogs then turned their attentions to Inglis, swarming around him, nosing and licking and nearly knocking him over again. He was surprised into an almost-laugh fending off Blood leaning up trying to taste his face.

A woman trotted into the hall and halted beside Gallin. Middle-aged, careworn, clearly his helpmate. "He broke out when I opened the door," she wheezed.

Learned Penric, watching the play in amusement as Blood fawned on Inglis, rubbed his lips and murmured, "Take witness of the dogs, Locator?"

Oswyl just looked exasperated. "This benighted case is the strangest I ever worked on. And I'm going to have to *report it all* when I get home, you realize?"

Learned Penric's blue eyes crinkled as he grinned. "You'd best pray for eloquence, then."

IN OSWYL'S PRIOR INVESTIGATIONS, requisitioning support from the local Temple usually meant finding his bed and board at a chapterhouse of one of the Orders, or a pilgrim hostel attached to the main center, or at least a recommended inn. Linkbeck did not boast any of these, nor a jail, nor a secure lockup in some outbuilding, nor even manacles on the cellar wall of a crumbling stronghold. His prisoner must needs remain under the direct supervision of the sorcerer at all times. This resulted in their having to impose on the domestic hospitality of Gallin and Gossa; mostly, as it turned out, Gossa.

Oswyl was deeply uncomfortable with bringing a maybe-murderer-mage into their home, but the couple seemed to take it in stride. An extra trestle table to increase the seating by six was swiftly set up by Gallin and his sons. Gossa had apparently handled sudden refugees from disasters in the vale this way many times before, driving her children and the servant girl, whom Oswyl had last seen leading the Bastard's white pony at the funeral, this way and that. It didn't take her long to draft the guardsmen as well, easing Oswyl's conscience slightly. Oddments of food appeared spontaneously, as if in a tale of an enchanted castle, dishes sent over by neighbors to supplement the family's fare.

All the chaos coalesced in a surprisingly short time in seating twelve to dinner, plus the two dogs lurking under the table, whether following Inglis or in hope of scraps. Learned Penric looked discomfited when asked by the acolyte to bless the meal, but he delivered the formula with a seminary-trained grace, which seemed to please their hosts. The soup was hardly watered at all.

Inglis was a blot of silent misery in this active company. Perhaps feeling the contrast, he did exert himself to politeness, belying his unkempt brigand's looks. Someone had taught him table manners, certainly. Oswyl grew aware that Gallin, too, was watching the shaman closely. His dark presence was daunting enough that no one tried to draw him into the table talk, more to Oswyl's relief than otherwise. Perhaps to make up for this, Penric, seated on his other side from Oswyl, contributed an unexceptional tale or three, especially after the women found out he served at the princess-archdivine's court in what they evidently thought of as exotic, distant, romantic Martensbridge. The sorcerer seemed as much an object of muted wonder as the murderer; Oswyl was not used to his inquirer's menace being so eclipsed.

After a brief post-dinner consultation with Oswyl, Gallin and Gossa sensibly sent the children off to find beds with the neighbors, and kept Oswyl's party all together in their house. Gossa faltered at a social dilemma: Learned Penric obviously had to be offered the best bedchamber, but Inglis perforce must accompany him there, Oswyl wanted to keep a close eye on both, and the dogs would not be parted from the prisoner. Gossa almost drew the line at the dogs, but Penric charmed her into a reprieve, promising her they would not leave fleas in her beds.

Oswyl pulled Penric aside on the staircase. "Do you think he could control those dogs? They could prove as much a weapon as his knife."

"I suspect the dogs may have their own design. Or someone's design," Penric returned in matching quiet tones. Earlier, he had tied the thongs of the knife sheath around his neck and tucked the knife out of sight in his shirt; he now touched his chest. "And Gossa has bigger knives in her kitchen. This is a hostage, not a weapon."

"Do you think Inglis may attempt escape? He claims to have lost his shamanic powers, but he could be lying."

"Or mistaken," murmured Penric. "Or have mislaid them. I'm

rather counting on mislaid, but we'll have to see. Anyway, with that bad leg of his we could catch him at a leisurely stroll."

"Unless he steals a horse."

A weird little smile turned Penric's lips. "I think such a ride could prove strangely unlucky for him. Don't fret yourself, Oswyl. He may be the best-guarded prisoner you've ever taken."

Penric sounded a bit full of himself on this point to Oswyl's ear, but there were also the three temple guardsmen now being variously distributed with bedrolls between their room and the doors. And the shaman was plainly exhausted. The real danger might well come later, as he regained strength and balance. Oswyl shook his head and followed Penric up the stairs.

Although the bedchamber to which Gossa conducted them was a tidy-enough refuge, no room in this house was spacious. Now containing a washstand, wardrobe, bed, pulled-out trundle bed, bedroll, three men and two large dogs, it seemed even smaller. Gossa handed Oswyl the taper, pointed out the brace of candles on the washstand, bade them goodnight, and shut the door upon them. Oswyl improved the lighting somewhat when he lit the candles, although not the smell, as they were tallow.

Penric politely yielded first turn at the washstand to Oswyl. The prisoner came a pointed third. The sorcerer, who moved like a cat in the shadows, also preempted Oswyl's intent to assign beds by plumping himself down on the trundle, and the dogs capped it by nosing Inglis to the bedroll and disposing themselves to either side of it. Inglis lowered himself awkwardly, with a pained grunt. Oswyl would have put the sorcerer on the floor in front of the door, and the prisoner between them.

"So, Inglis," Penric began. "I am something of a physician, although not presently sworn to practice. I think I might do a little for that leg of yours, if you'll let me have a look at it."

"Is that wise?" asked Oswyl, startled. To him, Inglis's injury had seemed as good as a leg-iron.

"Oh, yes," said Penric cheerily. "We've destroyed enough fleas in this household to balance a *week* of healing." He glanced at Inglis, made a brief wave of his hand, and added, "And lice."

Inglis, sounding stung, said, "I slept in some vile inns. And I haven't had a chance to bathe properly for a month."

All right, he *sleeps on the floor,* Oswyl revised his plan. And then wondered if Penric had misunderstood him deliberately.

Inglis scrubbed a hand through his ragged hair, then swallowed a startled oath. In this light Oswyl couldn't see the rain of dead bugs, but he could hear the faint patter as they hit the floorboards.

Fluidly, Penric slipped to Inglis's right side, shoved Blood out of the way, and sat cross-legged. Inglis eyed him in doubt, but did not object, though he winced when Pen rolled up his trouser leg. The limb was impressively empurpled and swollen. The sorcerer hummed tunelessly to himself as he ran his hands up and down it. The rigidity of Inglis's body eased. "Oh," he murmured, sounding surprised. Penric's face was bent over his work, but Oswyl could see his lips twitch up.

"A little ragged crack in one bone, but it's not propagating despite your abuse of it. The rest is pulled muscles and some very unhappy tendons. The usual instruction would be to abandon ambition, put your leg up, and rest for about three weeks."

Inglis snorted. Oswyl frowned.

"Indeed. But I may be able to supply a few more treatments as we go along, to replace some of that." Penric straightened his back. There was no visible difference in the leg, but as Inglis sat up in his bedroll, Oswyl was reminded of those nursery stories where the hero removed a thorn from the wolf's paw and was rewarded with the beast's trust. Did Penric and Inglis know those tales, too? From the wry cast to Inglis's face as he watched the sorcerer, Oswyl thought he might.

Penric added casually, "Did the Old Weald shamans have much in the way of healing arts or practices, do you know?"

"It is believed so." Inglis shrugged. "They were largely lost with the rest of their histories. Most shamanic teaching was by word of mouth, mentor to aspirant, and died with its possessors. What little was written, the Darthacans burned, if they could find it. What was hidden fell to the worm and rot and lack of understanding. One of the tasks that the fellowship of the royal shamans has set itself is to try to recover those skills."

"Are they making any more progress, in this new generation?"

"Mm, it seems the women tribal shamans worked the bulk of healing practices. They either wrote less, or were less recopied, as most of what survives tends to tales of spirit warriors and battle magic, and the rites surrounding the hallow kingship."

Penric—or was it Desdemona?—vented an ironic snort. "No surprise there."

"The hints are maddening, cast-away remarks in the midst of accounts about greater matters. There is a small cadre of royal shamans working to try to recreate the skills, relying less on old tales and more on new practices. The skills must have been developed in the first place by such trial and error, after all. Except that error . . . is a problem for an Easthome city shaman in a way it could not have been in the old forest tribes." Inglis had straightened up during this recitation, growing more animated, as if briefly forgetful of his woes. "A couple of the senior shamans have attempted healings of animals, to try to get around that. Some of their recent results have been very exciting."

It came to Oswyl that the reason Inglis had possessed such luck passing for a poor scholar at those inns was that he *was* one. Well, perhaps not poor. And Learned Penric was another, officially even. *Two of them. Dear gods, help me.*

"Is the Mother's Order taking an interest in the work?" asked Penric.

"Some, yes."

"Helpful, or hostile?"

Inglis's lips twitched in dark appreciation. "Some of each, but since the fellowship hit upon the idea of becoming physicians to animals, their oversight has grown more favorable."

"Does this work interest you?"

Inglis slumped again. "What does it matter now? I *can't*."

"Back when you could," said Penric, blithely ignoring this burst of despair, "how did you go about it? How *do* you go into your shamanic trance? Meditation, medication, smokes, bells, smells . . . ? Songs, prayers, twirling . . . ?"

Something not quite a laugh puffed Inglis's lips. "All of that, or any. My teachers said they are training aids, to form habits, and so, arbitrary. Nothing *forces* it. Or works like a machine, without fail. The more senior shamans make do with less and less, and some without any. Slipping in and out of the plane of symbolic action as silently as a fish swimming, and seemingly with as little effort." His sigh sounded suspiciously like envy. Or loss, perhaps.

"So how were you taught? Exactly? I have a professional interest in such things, you know."

Oswyl wasn't sure what Penric was about with this line of inquiry—

the divine was proving more slippery than he'd seemed at first—but Inglis appeared to accept this at face value. Which said something about Inglis, right enough. But the shaman was going on.

"We always began each training session with a short prayer."

"To invoke the gods, or to placate the Temple?"

Inglis stared at him. "Invoke? Scarcely."

"Yes, everyone talks to the gods, no one expects them to answer . . . Almost no one. Then what?"

"After some experimenting, we settled on a chant for my doorway. It seemed to me the most portable possible aid. And it could never be lost, like objects, or not be around when I needed it. Master Firthwyth first taught me in call and response, like two bards sharing the lines of a long poem back and forth. Except mine was short, just a quatrain. We sat across from each other, with a candle burning between us for me to stare at, and just repeated it over and over. And over and over and *over*, till my mind grew calm, or at least so bored I could scarcely bear it. We went through nearly a box of good wax candles. I worried about the waste. I can't imagine how Firthwyth endured.

"After several days of this, one afternoon when I'd been at it so long we both were hoarse, I . . . broke through. To the plane. Just for a few moments. But it was a revelation. This, *this* is what I, my wolf-within and I, had been straining for all this time. All the descriptions in *words* I'd been given weren't . . . weren't false. But it was like nothing I'd imagined from them. No wonder I'd been unable to reach it.

"After that, it quickly grew easier. We dispensed with the candle flame. It took less and less time to break through, and then I began reciting it all by myself. I was working on doing so silently when . . ." Inglis broke off. He added lamely, "My teacher said I was good."

"So what's it like for you? To be in this spiritual space."

Inglis's lips parted, closed, thinned. He turned his hands palm-out. "I can give you words, but they won't teach you any more than they did me. I don't know if you can *understand*."

"Inglis." For such a gentled tone, it was oddly implacable. "From the strangest hour of my life, on a roadside four years ago, I have been sharing my mind with a two-hundred-year-old demon with twelve personalities speaking six languages, and an underlying yen to destroy everything in her path, and I expect to go on doing so till the hour of my death. *Try* me."

Inglis recoiled slightly. And Oswyl wondered at what inattentive point on this journey Penric had started seeming *normal* to him.

Penric sighed and came about to another tack. "Is it intrinsically pleasurable, this trance state?"

"It is a place of wonders." Inglis hesitated. "Some find it fearful."

"And you?"

"I was exhilarated. Maybe too much so." Inglis frowned. "The material world does not vanish from my perceptions, but it is overlain, set aside. Non-material things appear as material ones, symbols of themselves, but not just hallucinations, because in my wolf-form—I appear there as a wolf, or sometimes a hybrid between wolf and man— because I can grasp them. Manipulate them. Arrange them to my will. And in the material world, they are made so.

"This does not move matter in the world, not the way chaos demons can, only things of the mind and spirit, yet mind and spirit can have strong influences on the body that bears them. The mind that moves the matter is the mind that is *affected*. A shaman can convince a person to perform an act, or bind two minds together, so that one person knows where the other is. Persuade a body to heal faster, sometimes. Give visions to another shaman, share thought. At full strength, move a sacrificed animal spirit to another body, bind it to that body's nourishment. Animal to animal, to build up a Great Beast. Or animal to . . . to a person, to share its fierceness . . . " He faltered. "Making a spirit warrior was considered the most challenging of all rites, apart from the transfer of the hallow kingship itself, and is presently forbidden."

So, it wasn't just the Father's Order who would be wanting a word with this young man when Oswyl returned him to Easthome. It sounded as though his assorted authorities were going to have to get in a line.

"At the sty, for the first time, I made the entry-chant work unvoiced. I was so excited, I almost lost the way again. Since I take the form of a wolf, things usually come to me in a sort of, of symbolic wolf-language. The spirit of the sacrificed boar and the spirit of a kin Boarford were already in sympathy. I chased them like a hunt even as Tollin was struggling to get his knife in, till they superimposed and became one. And then I came down and then . . . oh gods . . . " Inglis buried his face in his hands. Arrow whined and licked at him, and Blood rolled over and rested his head mournfully on his knee. Automatically, Inglis reached down to stroke the silky fur.

"Enough of that," said Penric firmly. Inglis gulped and looked up. Penric wrapped his arms around his knees and regarded the shaman through narrowed eyes. "Maybe what you need . . . "

Inglis and Oswyl glowered at him in equal bewilderment.

"Is sleep," Penric finished. "Yes. Definitely that. Go to *bed*, Penric." He uncoiled and picked his way to the trundle, blowing out the smelly candles on the way.

That was Ruchia, Oswyl thought. He recognized her pithy style, and then was a little appalled that he could now do so. But the advice was certainly sound.

"We need to talk," Oswyl murmured to Penric as he settled down just below him in the darkness.

"Yes, but not now. Tomorrow morning. I need to think." Penric pulled up his covers. "And, the white god help me, compose. Only Mira of Adria was a poetess, and she spoke no Wealdean, apart from some rude phrases she learned from her customers. She was a famous courtesan, did I ever mention that? Now, there are your bedtime stories. Although not ones for the nursery. Well, we shall contrive." He flopped over, and whether he closed his eyes, Oswyl could not make out.

Inglis, Oswyl decided, could not get out without tripping over a dog. The darkness pressing upon him like a blanket, he, too, slept.

XI

IN THE GRAY DAWN, a bleary Inglis sat up in his bedroll and begged Penric, "Let me blood my knife."

Pen eyed him dubiously. "You've done this every day? All through your flight?"

"Yes."

Was this necessary? Tollin's ghost was surely still lingering, if in an odd form, wrapped around the knife like fine wool on a woman's distaff. And no more faded than Scuolla's spirit, sitting sadly on its rock. *And no less faded, either.* Penric was extremely curious to witness the inner working of this shamanic rite. *Opinions, Des?*

I am out of my reckoning, here. Ruchia's shaman never demonstrated more than the weirding voice in front of us, small help though it was to him. His other enthralling skills were entirely human. If, perhaps, informed by a superior perception . . .

Pen cut off what promised to be a lengthy, if ribald, reminiscence. It seemed he was on his own for this judgment. "Very well, then."

Oswyl, halfway through shaving at the basin, turned around, folded his razor and stuck it in his trouser pocket, caught up his short sword from where it had stood propped by the head of his bed, grabbed Pen by the arm, stepped around a dog, and hauled him out into the narrow hallway, shutting the door firmly behind them. He drew Pen along to the head of the staircase, where he whispered in a furious undervoice, "Are you mad? You want to hand him back a weapon, *that* weapon? Which is also vital evidence, may I remind you."

"It's more vital than that. He's not lying about the knife. It does anchor Tollin's spirit." And an uncomfortable itch in Pen's perceptions it was, Tollin's not-quite-yet-sundered soul held so close to his heart. "Once I watch him through this, I'll be sure of a lot more."

Oswyl's glare heated. "*Scholars,*" he said in a voice of loathing. "You would dangle your arm in a bucket of adders, just to see if it was true that they bit."

Pen's grin flicked, quickly suppressed. "*Once* I've seen, I'll know if it's true he must do this daily to sustain Tollin. In which case you're going to have to let him do it every morning all the way back to Easthome, as routine as washing his face or shaving."

"I'm not letting him have a razor, either."

Pen sobered. "That, I would agree with. Nevertheless, I would ask you to stand prepared for any sudden moves."

"Quite. Sorcerers aren't immune to steel, I understand."

"Actually, Des has a clever trick for that, though I still don't understand how she can equate steel to wood." And this was one knife he most certainly couldn't let her change into a puff of rust in a heartbeat. "But I think Inglis is more likely to turn the knife on himself." As Oswyl's scowl failed to shift, he added, "I can't think you'd be any happier explaining the suicide of your prisoner than you would his escape."

"Much less," Oswyl bit out.

"There's more. If we lose him, through escape or escape into death, I suspect Tollin can't be sustained, and any hope for Scuolla is lost as well. And Inglis's soul hangs in the same balance. They are like three men roped together on a glacier. If the last man can't hold the other two, all will perish in the crevasse together."

Oswyl, the lather drying on half his face, thought this over. "I don't see how Inglis can rescue anyone if he doesn't have his powers."

"Neither does he, but I have an idea or two in that direction."

"Five gods, you don't imagine to restore them?" said Oswyl, exasperated. "That would be worse than handing him knife, razor, and dogs together. Why not a saddled horse and a purse of gold, while you are about it?"

"Haven't got a purse of gold," Pen said primly, and was rewarded with the sight of the half-shaved Grayjay baring his teeth. "Besides, in any country so well supplied with precipices as this one, a man doesn't need special tools to end his woes." By his expression, this, too, was a picture Oswyl would have preferred to live without. "As for those dogs . . . I'm still thinking about those dogs."

Stiff with reluctance, Oswyl followed Pen back into the bedchamber.

"All right," said Pen, dropping down cross-legged on the bedroll in front of Inglis. He reached back and untied the thongs, sleep-snarled with his queue. After pulling out a few fine hairs, he fished the sheath from his shirt, laid it in his lap, and drew the blade. It was a lovely piece of the armorer's art, all lethal curves, capped with old gold and blood-red gems. He held it out hilt-forward to Inglis. "Do what you must."

Inglis took it gingerly, as if he expected Pen to snatch it back like some child's cruel game of keep-away. The dogs on their bellies crept up to either side of him, like furry buttresses. His hand spasmed as it closed on the ivory hilt, and Oswyl, standing over them all with his sword drawn, twitched. But Inglis only rolled back his sleeves and surveyed his arms.

Pen stared too. There was scarcely a patch of skin unmarred by red scars, brown scabs, or sticky red lines, with angry pink welts of flesh puffing up between. Double that for the trip back to Easthome, and the man would be flayed. Inglis found a bare spot and lined up the edge, and Penric thought, *Des, lend me Sight.*

The trembling blade sliced, skin split red, and Pen's teeth twinged in sympathetic echo. The view was not much different from his unaided vision, except that Inglis's welling blood bore a strange silver sheen, like moonlight rippling off a wolf's pelt. He stropped the knife up and down, coating every inch. The spirit-wool moved with it, trailing smoke that circled back and settled on the blood. Pen tried not to think of flies swarming on carrion. But the spirit did, indeed, seem to draw nourishment from the strange feast, its density thickening as the blood dried and the silver sheen died.

No, indeed. I don't think our blood would serve the same, murmured Des. As Inglis's fingers started to clench again, Pen leaned forward and wrapped his hand around the shaman's. "I'll just be having that back now. For safekeeping."

After a brief moment of tension, Inglis let his fingers grow slack, and Pen pried the hilt out of his grip. Oswyl waited sword in hand, not yet standing down.

Inglis choked out, "Don't sheathe it till the blood is fully dry. It won't take long. The brown rubs right off with a cloth."

"Right," said Pen, and waited. The trailing smoke seemed to withdraw into the main body of the bound spirit. The sticky turned to crumbly, a few passes on the thighs of Penric's trousers brushed it away, and he slid the gleaming steel out of sight again. Des let the vision of Tollin's ghost disappear, a debatable relief.

Breakfast was a quieter meal, as the house's children had not yet returned, although the servant girl had. The six guests, or five guests and one prisoner, were fed on oat porridge with butter, cheese, barley bread, and autumn apples. The dogs loitered lazily by the doors, not enticed by the meatless repast. Conversation was desultory and practical. But Gallin and Gossa seemed very *aware* of Inglis, and not as a criminal.

Penric had to agree, Inglis had made a terrible criminal. His heart wasn't in it at all. Whatever visions of heroic capture of a villain had beguiled Pen on the ride here, the event had been sadly disappointing. *Though if stupid panic is what's wanted, there's your man,* muttered Des.

I doubt I would have done much better, if I'd killed my best friend by mistake with my new powers, Pen thought back.

*I wouldn't have let you. Nothing remotely like that has happened to
a rider of mine . . .* Des seemed to hesitate. *For a very, very long time.*

Your argument nibbles its own tail, I think?

Humph. But she settled again.

The guard sergeant asked Oswyl, "Should we prepare for the road,
sir? We need to see to securing an extra horse."

Oswyl set down his spoon and sat back. "If we can do nothing more
here, we should depart, yes."

"You are most welcome to stay longer," put in Acolyte Gallin, with
studied emphasis. "A day or so more will not matter."

"Thank you, Acolyte, but I must disagree. Every day we linger risks
us being caught by the next snow."

Pen disagreed with both. Might a day or two more here make all the
difference, to some?

Gallin bit his lip. "Learned Penric, I would like to speak to you
apart. About some Temple matters that concern me."

As a Grayjay, Oswyl was just as much a servant of the Temple as
Penric or Gallin, but he permitted Pen to be abstracted from the table
with no more than a dry glance Pen's way. The guards looked alarmed
to be thus deprived of whatever magical protection they imagined Pen
to be providing them, but even if Inglis, Pen didn't know what . . .
weirded them all to sleep and hobbled off, he wouldn't even be able to
get as far as the stable before Pen caught him again.

Gallin took Pen to his parlor-study and closed the door, gesturing
Pen to sit. When they were knee to knee, he lowered his voice and said
directly, "I prayed for help. Are you it?"

Pen sighed unease. "If so, no One has told me. I do not suffer
prophetic dreams." He would add, *Thank the gods*, but that seemed to
fall under the heading of what his mother had used to call *coaxing
lumps.*

"Still, the gods are parsimonious, they say."

"I understand your drift, I suppose. A Grayjay who hates to be late
has arrived at the last hour, bringing me, just in time to intersect a
shaman who was running away. One need not be delusory to think
something is expected of us." If Inglis had been in command of his
powers, the shaman's role would be obvious, but then, if he'd been in
command of his powers, he could have cleansed Tollin's soul on the
spot back at Easthome, and be doing, well, who knew what who knew

where by now. Pen's own role so far reminded him of those caravan guards mustered in a mass not to fight off bandits, but to dissuade them from attacking in the first place. Which, he had to admit, was by far the best imaginable use of a force of arms.

"Are Inglis's powers truly broken, as he claimed?"

Penric hesitated. "His powers appear to me to be intact. Only his guilt and distraught mind seem to be blocking his full access to them."

"Can you do something about that? With your powers?"

"The natural directions of my skills are to mar, not to mend. And they work on things, not minds. Mainly." And Inglis's worked on minds, not things. A peculiar reciprocity, now that Pen considered it.

Gallin's fingers pulled at each other. "Then perhaps it's not your skills as a sorcerer that are wanted, but your skills as a divine. Perhaps you are the one meant to give him spiritual counsel?"

Penric was taken aback. "That . . . wasn't a subject I spent much time on at seminary. It's a rather horrible joke, if so."

Gallin half-laughed. "That's no proof it wasn't from *your* god. More the reverse."

And so the facetious brag he'd made to Oswyl, about being a divine five-fold, curled back to bite him now. Of all the tasks he'd imagined undertaking on the Grayjay's wolf-hunt, whether as sorcerer or bowman-hero, *sage counselor* wasn't even on the list.

So, murmured Des. *Now we see why you are so quick to leave your braids in your saddlebags.*

That wasn't it! he began to argue back, and stopped. He raised his face to Gallin's, again. "You've served here for many years. You knew Scuolla, as a friend and as a shaman. Surely you must be better fitted for such a task?"

Gallin shook his head. "Friend, yes, I hope so. But I can't say as I ever understood what he did with his dogs, except to observe that there seemed no malice in it, or in him. But you and Inglis kin Wolfcliff, you are both brothers in the uncanny. You see things veiled from me. Maybe you can see the way out of this tangle, too."

Penric cleared his throat, embarrassed. "I admit, I had an idea or two. But it was just for things to try. Not any kind of *wisdom.* Oswyl thought it high foolishness, in fact."

"Locator Oswyl wants to leave, I gather. Can you not overrule him?"

"The princess-archdivine assigned me to him, not him to me. The task was his to start with before it grew"—Pen hesitated—"so complicated."

"Could he hold Inglis without your aid?"

"Well . . . " Penric reflected on the possibilities inherent in that weirding voice, were it to be deployed without restraint. Not to mention the other shamanic skills. "No."

"It seems you are the linchpin in this wheel, then. If you elect to stay, he cannot take Inglis and go."

"That . . . would seem to be the case, yes."

"Then I beg you to stay. And apply your ideas. Or counsel. Or wisdom, or unwisdom, or whatever you may dub it." Gallin drew breath. "You have to *try*, at least."

Pen imagined a prayer, or a holy whine—to the white god, either would do—*If You don't like it, give me something better.*

The silence in his head was profound. Even Des did not chaff or chatter.

Penric managed a nod. Trying not to let his doubts show, he returned to the breakfast table to shepherd Inglis—and the two dogs—back to their bedchamber.

They settled cross-legged facing each other on the bedroll once more. Blood flopped down across the doorway and sighed; Arrow sat up beside Inglis and appeared to watch with more than canine interest.

"All right." Penric took a breath. "What I'm going to do here is give you a clean new chant to gate your entry into your spirit space."

Inglis shot him a stare of surprise and offense. "What makes you think you can do the first thing about it? Sorcerer."

"I'm the one who's here. That seems to be the most vital point at present." Refusing to wilt under Inglis's frown, Penric forged on, "My call shall be, 'Father, Mother, Sister, Brother, Other.' And your response shall be, 'Bless this work and let me serve another.' "

"Is that supposed to be the blessing?"

"No, that's your chant. I thought I'd combine the two and save steps."

Inglis met his bright smile with a deepening glower. "It's a stupid rhyme."

"I'm a sorcerer, not a poet."

"Evidently. It's not even a quatrain."

"Repeat it, and it will turn into a quatrain."

Inglis looked ready to rebel. Or at least to refuse to cooperate. And what Penric would do then, he had no idea.

Des muscled into brief control of his mouth, and said in honeyed tones, "Or you could pray, 'Other, Mother, Father, Brother, Sister. Thwack my head and make me less a blister.' " Pen failed to control the upward crook of his lips as she fell back.

After a long, black silence Inglis said, "Use the first one."

"Good," said Pen. And a firm, *No more interruptions now*, to Des. She settled back, falsely demure. "I'll begin. Father, Mother, Sister, Brother, Other . . . "

They began to repeat the call and response much as Inglis and his possibly-not-that-long-ago mentor had. The mindful if simple (*or simple-minded*, Des put in) prayer really did grow boring after enough repetitions. A while after that, the syllables began to lose any meaning or connection at all, a steady, soothing double drone. Pen did not let up until both their tongues started stumbling, when he called a break.

Nothing had happened. Well, he hadn't expected it to, Pen lied to himself. All right, he'd been *hopeful*.

"How often did your shamanic master repeat your practice sessions?" asked Pen.

"It varied, depending on his duties and mine. Sometimes, once or twice a day. Sometimes dozens."

"And how long did you drill at a time?"

"Much as now, till our tongues grew too tired to fruitfully go on. That, too, varied."

"Hm." Penric slapped his knees and stood up. "Rest your tongue, then. And your leg."

Inglis at least did not argue with this injunction.

Pen found one of their guards seated at the top of the staircase. "Where is Oswyl?"

"He walked over to the temple, I think, sir."

"Thank you." Penric threaded his way through the house and turned onto the street. The temple stood as quiet and dim as yesterday when they'd surprised Inglis inside. Once again, the hall held only one supplicant. Oswyl sat upon his knees before the altar dedicated to the

Father, tucked up against its one-fifth portion of the wooden walls. His head turned at the sound of Penric's steps.

"Oh. It's you."

"Don't let me interrupt," said Pen. And then, incurably curious, asked, "What do you pray for?"

Oswyl's lips thinned. "Guidance."

"Oh? I thought everything we've encountered here shouts our course at us. Or are you just angling for a different answer?"

Oswyl turned back toward his chosen god's altar once more, the very set of his shoulders sturdily ignoring Pen.

Pen walked to the hall's opposite side and studied his god's niche. The shrines here had a profusion of woodcarvings, common in country temples in this region. On the lintel, the carver had placed a well-observed flight of crows; in a lower corner, some earnest-looking rats. The Daughter's shrine, to Penric's right, was decorated with an explosion of wooden flowers and young animals, painted in their proper colors, a muted glow in the shadows. A supplicant prayed *before* a shrine, Penric's teachers had made clear, not *to* it. He lowered himself to his knees. Emptying his mind was not an option, but he didn't need to badger the gods, either. He waited.

After a while, Oswyl's voice came from across the hall: "Did you get anywhere with your tutoring?"

Not turning, Pen answered, "Not yet."

A wordless grunt.

After a little, Pen said, "He's not really a murderer, you know."

A pause: then, "My task is to bring a fugitive to justice. Not to judge him."

"Yet you must use your judgment. You followed your own line on the Crow Road."

A considering silence.

"I have another trial in mind," Penric continued. "I want to take Inglis out to the rockfall, and see what he can make of old Scuolla." And what Scuolla would make of him?

A mere pained sigh was all that this elicited. What, was he finally wearing Oswyl down? It occurred to Penric that Oswyl was not so rigidly rules-bound as his stiff jaw suggested; only doubt need pray for guidance. He hoped Oswyl would get his answer. Penric went on speaking to his own wall: "Inglis is in less pain than yesterday. Calmer, if not less bleak. I expect I should take Gallin. And the dogs. We'll need one of the guardsmen's horses. Do you wish to come? Given you've no hand in the uncanny."

Oswyl's voice returned, distantly, "Having spent this long and come this far to find him, I'm not losing sight of him again."

"Well, then." Penric bowed his head and signed the tally, and they both rose together.

XII

INGLIS, TO HIS CHAGRIN, had to be helped onto his horse by two guardsmen and an upturned stump by the stable door. His stick presented another puzzle. He finally set its butt upright atop his foot, which also had to be fitted into his stirrup by a guard, and held it like a banner pole. That and his reins seemed to give his hands too many things to do. The sorcerer almost floated up into his saddle, although Inglis put it down to his wiry build and horsemanship, not magic. Acolyte Gallin availed himself of the stump, however. Given the acolyte's age, that was small consolation. Locator Oswyl frowned down from his mount at Arrow and Blood, swirling amiably around Inglis's horse; the horse, which Inglis judged something of a slug, took only mild exception.

Gallin led the mounted party out past his temple into the street, where Learned Penric held up a staying hand. "Let us go to the bridge, first," said Penric to him. "And over it. I want to see something."

Gallin shrugged and turned his mount left instead of right. The rest of them followed in a gaggle. The dogs, who had darted ahead in the opposite direction, paused and vented puzzled whines. When the riders continued their retreat, they barked a few times, then ran after.

As Penric made to lead them all across the wooden span, Arrow and Blood rushed ahead, turned, and set up a furious barking. The horses shied.

"Calm them," Penric advised Inglis.

"Hush!" Inglis tried, and then, "Sit!" The apparently-maddened dogs continued to hold the party at bay. **"Hush!"** Inglis tried again, more forcefully. **"Settle down!"**

The two dogs recoiled as if blown by a gust of gale, but then remustered their battle line and took up their din again, standing four-legged and braced, the fur rising in a ridge along their backs.

"Enough!" cried Penric, laughing for no reason that Inglis could discern, and made a twirling motion with his fingers. Gallin, staring back and forth between the dogs and him, reined his horse around to lead back up the vale once more. A few villagers arrested by the uproar who had come to their garden gates nodded at their acolyte, frowned impartially at his visitors, and turned back to their interrupted tasks.

The two guardsmen fell in at either side of Inglis, albeit not too close, scowling at him in distrust. Oswyl nudged his horse up beside the sorcerer's, and asked, "Did you do something, back there?"

"No," said Penric, airily, "not at all. Very carefully not at all, in fact."

"So what was all that in aid of?"

"I had three theories about what drives those dogs. This knocks out one of them. Two to go." He nodded in satisfaction, and pushed his horse into a trot after Gallin. Oswyl seemed as baffled by this as Inglis, for he made an exasperated face at the sorcerer's retreating back. What, did the locator find the blond man as irritating as Inglis did?

A little while later Penric reined back beside Inglis, displacing one of the guards, who looked more grateful than otherwise for being relieved of his post. "Well," said Penric cheerily, "shall we beguile the ride with a bit more practice?"

"*No*," said Inglis, mortified. And if a **No!** would have worked on the man, he'd have followed up with one. "Do you want us both to look fools?"

"That still concerns you, at this stage in your career?" Penric inquired. Entirely too dryly. "Though I have to allow, working for my god tends to knock that worry out of a person fairly swiftly." The dryness melted to an even more excoriating look of sympathy.

"I don't know what you're planning, but it's not going to work."

"If you don't know the first, how do you know the second?" Penric shot back. "Although I'm afraid *planning* may be too grandiose a term for it. Testing, perhaps. Like at the bridge."

Inglis hunched his shoulders. Penric eyed him a moment more and then, to his relief, gave up.

The day was gray, the air damp, the mountains veiled, but the wind was light, not spitting rain or snow at them. Inglis studied the vale as they rode up the right-hand branch of the Chillbeck. The high peaks that headed it, and to the east, led only to more peaks. One would have to circle back several miles to find any western trail with even a chance of leading to a high pass over to the main Carpagamo road. It was a half-day's ride downriver beyond that to loop south to the same road, the way Inglis had come in. Given his prior disastrous experience with trying to climb out over this valley's walls, that seemed the best bet. If a man had a head start on a fast horse. The notion of trying to retrace his route all the way back to the Crow Road and head east to Saone after all, as winter turned from threat to certainty, was near-heartbreaking.

The riders strung out as Gallin turned off the road and up into the woods. The sorcerer rode right behind Inglis, a thorn in his back; one of the guards went ahead, looking frequently over his shoulder. The woods were difficult but not, Inglis thought, impassible. Centuries of valesmen gathering deadfall and timber from these more accessible lower slopes had left them semi-cleared, although tangled steeper ravines and erupting granite rock faces broke up the area into a maze.

At length, the trail opened out onto a fearsome-looking landslide, much larger than Inglis had been picturing, and the riders pulled up. The two dogs scampered ahead onto the debris.

Penric peered out over the waste after the bounding animals, and asked Inglis, "What do you see?"

"When I am not in my trance, my sight is the same as yours. Er, as any man's." This was not quite true in this moment, Inglis realized. There was a breathless *pressure* in his mind, as if he were plunged deep underwater. A shiver up his spine. Tollin's spirit, wound around the knife under the sorcerer's shirt, was so agitated Inglis could sense its hum from here. "What do you see?"

"When Des lends me her vision, I can see the spirits much, I think, as saints are said to do, matter and spirit superimposed, like seeing both sides of a coin at once. Scuolla seems a colorless image, like a reflection on glass. I see he's changed his rock since yesterday. So he can move about, some. May be a trifle smudgier? Or maybe that's what I expect, or fear, to find." Penric's gaze had alighted where Arrow and Blood circled a boulder, whining. "He's looking over at us. At you? He

perceives us on some level, certainly. If you could—when you could—
achieve your trance, did you see spirits? And could they speak to you,
or were they silent?"

"I'd not encountered many. The old ones were always silent. I'd not
evoked a new one yet."

"Tollin."

Inglis winced. "Tollin is bound to the knife, and does not speak. To
me. In my normal mind. I don't know if . . . " He trailed off, confused.
If he could have ascended to the spirit plane, might they have spoken
together despite the binding? Inglis wasn't sure if he would have
raged at Tollin for this disaster, or begged his forgiveness, or what. If
he had lost a friend in more ways than one, or if some peace might
have been salvaged between them, at an hour beyond the last. If
Tollin hated him . . .

Penric, Oswyl, and one of the guardsmen dismounted, the latter
taking the reins of all three horses. All of Gallin's attention was on the
dogs. The second guardsman kicked his feet out of his stirrups,
preparing perhaps to go to Inglis's aid. The sorcerer's bow was still
bundled with his quiver, unstrung, tied to his saddle. For the first time
in weeks, the burden of the knife was taken out of Inglis's hands.

If ever I am to have a chance, it is now, right now.

Inglis threw back his head and **HOWLED**.

Every horse in the party reared in panic and bolted, including his
own. He tossed away his stick, wrenched at his reins, and managed to
get the beast aimed generally uphill. They plunged into the patchy
forest. From behind him, curses and a thump as someone fell off, more
curses fragmenting as a man still mounted was carried away back
down the trail. For a few moments, all Inglis could do was hang on to
his saddle and reins as the animal under him heaved and jinked. He
bent low as slashing branches tried to behead him, sweep him from
his precarious perch.

Uphill and to the left was his goal—circle around the top of the
slide and lose himself in the lower forests, then find his way somehow
back out of this trap of a valley . . . the stolen horse was essential, crutch
to his bad ankle, he couldn't let it break *its* legs here . . . at this pace it
must grow winded soon, and then he would regain control . . .

He had reckoned without the dogs. They gave chase, barking and
baying behind him, weaving faster through the trees than the horse

could. Incredibly soon, he saw a rippling copper flash at the corner of
his vision, and, already *above* him, heard the profound deep barks of
Arrow. They began to drive his horse through the tilted woodland like
a red deer, hunted, and its laboring haunches bunched and surged in
fresh terror—his fault, for filling its dim head with visions of wolves,
echoing and reverberating now from the dogs? But a deer was built
for these hazardous slopes; a horse was not.

A gulf of light opened to his left, and the horse shied wildly, hooves
slipping in the wet loam, almost stumbling over the cliff at the top of
the slide. It jerked back upright.

Inglis kept going, the saddle yanked from under him. The world
whirled wildly around his head. For an instant, the bed of broken
boulders far below him invited him like a bed in truth, an offer of rest
at the end of an impossibly long day. A branch brushed his arm, and
his hand closed convulsively, unwilled. Bark and skin grated each other
off like bits from a blacksmith's file. Wood snapped, he turned again in
air, grasped, arm yanked straight, held, slid, lost it, turned, and
smacked hard on his side. If he'd had any breath left, the last impact
would have knocked it out. His lungs pulsed and red murk flooded
his vision before he was at last able to inhale again.

It was a dozen breaths before he could lift his head and see where
he'd landed. Raw stone blocked his vision a foot from his nose. He
twisted the other way, and looked out over the gray valley. He'd come
to rest on an irregular ledge about halfway up the sheer drop at the
head of the rockslide. It was deeper than a kitchen chair, but only just,
and several paces long, but they were paces that led only out into air
at the ends.

No way to climb back up. No way . . . well, one way down. He eyed
the broken rocks fifty feet below him, and wondered if the half-fall
would be enough to kill him outright. Certain death still held
attraction. Uncertain death, less so. He hurt enough *already*.

The skin of his hands was torn, his shoulder wrenched, his bad
ankle . . . not improved. Spectacular bruises for sure. Amazingly, his
neck and back and bones generally seemed intact.

Fifty feet above him, piteous whines sounded. A few barks, less
labored or frantic than before—more puzzled yaps, really. *Whatever
are you doing down there?* they seemed to say.

Truly, I have no idea. I have no idea about anything anymore.

He lay on his ledge and concentrated on breathing, achievement enough.

After a time, he became conscious of movement below him. He pushed himself a little up and looked over. The drop reminded him of crawling out on the roof of the kin Boarford's Easthome city mansion, five floors above a cobbled street—Tollin had dared him, he recalled. The pale face of the sorcerer looked up at him, head back-tipped. Penric was breathing fast, but otherwise seemed unfairly unruffled.

He shook his head, and called up, "I swear, Inglis, you have a talent for disasters. It's not a *good* talent, mind you. On the other hand, I'd suspected you had help, and now I'm sure of it."

Inglis could go neither up nor down, right nor left. He felt as exposed as a wolf pelt nailed to a stable door, and as empty. He could think of no reply, not that the sorcerer had invited one, exactly.

A hundred paces away across the scree, where the path had been cut off, Gallin cupped his hands around his mouth and shouted, "Baar caught a horse! We're going for ropes!"

Learned Penric waved a casual hand in acknowledgment of this news, a lot less excited than Inglis thought he should be. "That will be some time," he said, half to himself—the over-keen hearing that had come so disconcertingly with his wolf-within had still not deserted Inglis. Penric skinned out of his heavy jacket, turned up the cuffs of his linen shirt, rolled his shoulders, stretched his arms and laced his fingers together, shook them out. "Well, then," he muttered. "I decline to shout spiritual counsel from the bottom of a well, so I guess I'd better be about this."

He flattened himself to the cliff wall and began to climb, barely visible handhold to barely visible foothold.

His mouth opened, and his voice emerged in a strained, sharp cadence Inglis had not yet heard from the man: "Penric! I have many powers, but I can't make us *fly!*"

Penric grinned, fierce in his strain. "Then you'd best keep quiet and not interrupt for the next few minutes, eh?"

At a distance, at first, he seemed to scale the rock face like a spider. As he grew closer the illusion dropped away, and he was clearly a man, taller and heavier than he had quite seemed in his smiling affability; the tendons stood out in his hands and arms as he pulled himself up. As he gained each few feet he wheezed, "I admit . . . it's been . . . a while . . . " When he at last reached the edge of the ledge, he very definitely heaved himself over, scrambling, not like the airy aplomb of vaulting onto his horse. "Thank you, Drovo," he gasped, incomprehensibly, rolling to his knees, shaking out his hands again. "I think."

Slowly, gingerly, Inglis pushed himself upright and scooted back till his spine met the stone. His outstretched feet hung over the abyss. Breathing heavily, Penric plopped himself down beside him and stretched his legs out, too. They might have been two boys seated side-by-side on a log across a stream. Perhaps feeling the same, Penric picked up a loose stone and tossed it over the side, cocking his head as if listening for the splash. The faint crack of its landing was a long time coming.

Pinned crookedly to the left shoulder of his weskit, Inglis saw, where it had lain concealed beneath his coat, the divine sported the Temple braids of his full rank, three loops of interlaced white, cream, and silver, the hanging tails tipped with silver beads. They were stiff and clean, as though seldom worn since Penric had taken his oaths. That could not have been so many months before Inglis had been invested with his own powers. Penric's ceremony had probably had less blood in it.

Although, considering the necessary origin of his demon, not less death, nor a lesser sacrifice. *Hm.*

Oswyl's voice called from the rubble below: "Is he all right? Or were you prophetic about precipices?"

Penric swung around on his belly and hung his head over the edge, a move which made Inglis shudder. He did stretch and crane till he could just make out the locator, standing below looking up as Penric lately had.

Penric waved back. "Seems to be little the worse. Shaken up, though."

"Fools and madmen," Oswyl muttered, and sat down on a handy boulder, heaving an exhausted sigh. A bigger man, he did not seem inspired to hoist himself up what Inglis had taken for a sheer rock wall after the divine. Sorcerer. Whatever he was. He raised his face and voice and added, "Remember what I said about putting him on a horse?"

Penric grinned and called back, "Remember what I said about the luck of such a ride?"

"Huh." Oswyl grimaced like a man sucking vinegar. "Carry on, O Learned One."

"I intend to. Is he not what every Temple divine desires, a captive audience?"

"I still want him back when you're done with your lessons."

"Pray for us, then."

The gesture Oswyl made back at this was not in the least holy. Penric, still grinning, spun around and sat back up, and Inglis's spine sought the reassuring rock again.

The grin faded to a thoughtful look, and Penric began to edge away, then stopped himself. "Scuolla has joined us," he said quietly.

"Is that"—Inglis's hands went to his temples—"why I feel this horrible pressure in my head?"

"Did you hit it, in your fall?" A look of medical concern flitted across Penric's features, and he leaned across the space to lift his palm and press against Inglis's forehead; Inglis flinched.

"Not much," said Inglis, as Penric murmured, "No . . . "

His hand falling back, Penric went on with maddening obscurity, "Then I think it must be your other visitor."

Inglis uncompressed his lips, and said, "What does Scuolla look like? To you?"

Penric stared at the empty space between them. "A plain old mountain man in a sheepskin vest, rudely interrupted when he went out to feed his animals. Not at all what I would have taken as a great-souled one, beloved of the gods. Lesson to me."

"Great-souled? I thought that was kings, and, and generals."

"No, those are merely great men." Penric kept on gazing curiously at nothing. "He is very patient. Well, he would have to be, wouldn't he, to work his art in a medium that takes more than a man's lifetime to complete . . . Another who waits here is not so patient, I think." The pressure in Inglis's head throbbed; the divine made the five-fold tally. "So let us pray, too."

"Pray? Are you serious?"

Penric turned his hands out in a shrug. "It's my job. My other job, I was lately reminded. From my very first oath, three years before these"—he touched his braids—"were tacked on me."

"So what do we pray for, ropes? Pulleys?"

"Such material aids are the purview of men, not gods." He held up his hand and spread out his fingers. "The five theological purposes of prayer, I was taught, are service, supplication, gratitude, divination, and atonement. You could easily go five-for-five up here, I think." He dropped his hand and smiled faintly out over the valley; the dreary view did not seem to rate such approval.

"What do *you* pray for?" Inglis thrust back, growing surly with this elliptical . . . humor, if it was humor. At his expense, of course. He was feeling entirely destitute, just now.

"I try not to bother the gods any more than I can possibly help," returned Penric, unperturbed. "Once, One answered me back. It was an experience to make a man cautious."

"Twice, I think," growled Inglis.

"Hm?"

He leaned his aching skull back against the stone and recited, "Other, Mother, Father, Brother, Sister . . . "

Penric's lips twitched. "Are you feeling, ah, thwacked?"

"If I were any more thwacked right now, I don't think I could sit upright." Inglis sighed. "You go right on being stingy with your prayers, Learned."

"Let us practice yours some more, then."

"Will that be any safer?"

"I trust not. Begin. Father, Mother, Sister, Brother, Other . . . "

Their recent drill made his reluctant response fall inevitably: "Bless this work and help me serve another." He eyed the empty space Penric had left between them. Had the couplet's wording not been so simple and silly as he'd thought?

"Continue on your own."

"Father, Mother, Sister, Brother, Other . . . "

It was foolish. He was a fool. So was Penric. They were all great fools, here. He should just give up and live with the fact. The other choice was the rock bed, which had already killed one shaman, which could cap a lifetime of foolery. Did the gods take fool souls, as well as great ones? No, They couldn't, for the fools ran away. Gods, but he was tired of running away.

As the fifth repetition left his lips, he broke through. As sudden and astonishing as his very first ascent ever, he was *there*. But this time he could hold his place, like a falcon gripping the air and, miraculously, rising without even beating its outstretched wings.

The ledge, the stone behind and the vale in front, the material world, were still present, but barely, as a great undefined space seemed to open out all around him. Undefined, yet seething with potential. But he was not alone in it.

Sitting next to him indeed was an old mountain man in a sheepskin vest, his feather-decked hat pushed back on his head. He wasn't an image on glass, though, but full of color, vastly more intense than the faint gray valley around them. His spirit-density was the very opposite of transparent. The beautiful Great Dog he bore within him had made its home in this kennel for so long, the two were nearly one, intertwined. He smiled in a friendly way at Inglis, with a strange pure kindness unalloyed by irony or judgment. He didn't even seem to say, *You are very laggard*, though Inglis thought he had a right.

Penric sat beyond him, staring head-tilted with concern at Inglis's body. The blond man's solid self was grayed out as well, along with all the other surfaces of the world, but for the first time Inglis saw under the sunny exterior. The sorcerer's *interior* was terrifying, its layered complexity reaching back through time like a cavern passageway descending deep into the earth, dark with secrets. His demon. *And he lives with this? Every day?*

Then he looked up, farther.

A tall figure leaned casually against the ledge wall beyond Penric. It seemed a young huntsman in the poor men's dress of this country, much like the fellows who had brought Inglis in off the trail that first morning, or like Scuolla. A triangular sheepskin cap topped his glowing copper curls, which were the color of Blood's fur. His face was a light much too strong to look at directly, and Inglis shaded his spirit-eyes with his spirit-hands, then clapped them over his face altogether. All else was blocked, but not the burning light. He let his hands fall, and found himself gasping as though he had been running.

He thought the face smiled at him, like the sun through the cool air on a mountain's side, warming, welcome. And far, far more terrifying than the demon.

The figure waved a casual hand. *Go on.*

"How, lord?"

Call it out of him. For you, it will come. It was a very good dog, after all.

It couldn't be that simple. Could it? *Here, it can. This is a simple place, after all.* And Inglis wasn't even sure whose thought that was.

Inglis inhaled the no-air of the plane, held out his hand as if to a strange dog to sniff, and called, **"Come, boy."** Then felt stupid for the trailing endearment, for surely the beast was far older than he was . . .

Stop that, said the figure's voice, amiably, like a man commanding his pet to stop scratching itself. *This is the time for my judgments, not yours.*

The response was slow, like an old dog or an old man getting up, one-half at a time. Stiffly, but obediently, the *shape* flowed out of Scuolla. Slipping through Inglis's hands, like a whisper of fur as a dog wriggled out of his grasp. And gone. Where? Surely not into utter dissolution?

"Will it be well?" Inglis asked timidly.

All will be well, in my hands. But you see now why all hunts, however exciting, must end with respect for the creature hunted. That is your hope, too, after all.

Inglis had no idea what to say to that. In terror lest the figure would vanish again, as if—no, he neither summoned nor dismissed this like some mere apparition, but he blurted, "Lord, there is one other."

I do not forget. But that is your task, now.

At some point, Penric had drawn the knife from its sheath and held it ready on his lap. He squinted in concern at Inglis's body, still sitting up against the rock wall: more motionless than sleep, too tense for death. With a huge effort, Inglis flopped out its hand, open. Cautiously, Penric laid the knife on its palm. The hand convulsed around the ivory hilt; Penric quietly lifted hand and knife back into Inglis's lap.

For the first time, Inglis realized he had appeared on the plane in his human form—not as wolf, or even as man-with-wolf's-head. It might be a good thing. The stretched-out boar spirit was, he saw now through its ferocity, quite frightened enough. This time, he coaxed it out softly, gently. He had hated it for what it had done to Tollin, and through Tollin to himself, but it was one of the Son's creatures with the rest. He handed it off to the waiting god, and bowed his head in respect, and spread his fingers wide over his heart in His sign.

Tollin unwound from the knife and stood up, looking dizzied and bewildered. His colors were ragged, paler than Scuolla's, who sat taking it all in like a satisfied onlooker to some beloved campfire tale. Tollin's mouth opened as he saw Inglis, though no sound came out, but then his face rose to the figure by the wall, and he stood stunned.

For a moment, to Inglis's horror, Tollin held back. Guilt, grief? Fear of not being good *enough*, strong *enough* . . . it had not just been youthful arrogance that had led him to beg for the boar spirit, after all. A mixture of motives not savory, but so, so understandable to Inglis now. Tollin stood silent, and small, and ashamed.

The Son of Autumn held out His hand, close but not touching. Tollin's face turned away, suffused with misery, but his hand jerked out, once, twice. On the second, his hand was grasped, and all anguish fled from his features, because the astonished awe left no room for it.

And then he was gone.

The Hunter turned then, bent, and extended his hand to Scuolla. Who, to Inglis's surprise, spoke, and in the affectionate voice of a man to a long-time comrade: "But will there be good beer?"

The Hunter's voice returned, in like humor: "If there is beer, it will be very good. If there is not, it will be because there's something better. It's not a wager you *can* lose. Come on, old man."

As the Hunter heaved Scuolla up, the old man said, "You took your time, getting here."

"I did My best with what I had," the god answered him back.

"Seems so." Scuolla looked warmly down at Inglis. "Take good care of my dogs, lad."

Inglis nodded, breathless. "I will, sir."

Scuolla dipped his chin in pleased acceptance. "*Now* I can go."

"About time," his Friend murmured, amused. "Who is dawdling now?"

Inglis found himself on his knees, holding up both hands palm-out, fingers spread. He hardly knew what he meant to say. *Is that all, am I done?* Instead it came out, "Will we meet again?"

The Hunter smiled. ***Once, for certain.***

And then Inglis let go, and he was falling, falling, back into the world, laughing so hard he was crying, or crying so hard he was laughing, or some other reaction much too large for any human frame to hold.

Fortunately, Learned Penric was waiting to catch him before he rolled off the ledge that he'd forgotten was before him.

"There, there . . . " Penric clutched his shaking body and patted his back as if calming a hysterical child, prudently dragging him over to the wall again. "You've seen a god, I know, I know," he soothed. "You'll be drunk on it for days. No doubt Oswyl will be highly offended, which will be entertaining in its own way . . . "

Gasping, Inglis rolled over in his lap and grabbed up at his collar. "*What*, what did you see? Just now?"

Penric gently undid his clenching fingers before he tore the fabric. "I saw you go into your trance. It was a bit alarming. Might have been taken for a stroke—you should warn your companions about that. Your nose bled. I saw when Tollin came unbound, and when he went off. Scuolla, too. It was hard to get much more, because Des went into retreat. Since she has nowhere to go but inward, this results in her curling up into this sort of impenetrable, *useless* ball—" his voice rose on this last, not, apparently, to Inglis's address, for he added aside to Inglis, "Gods terrify demons. They are the one power that can destroy them. Understandable." Inglis wasn't sure who was supposed to understand what, but Penric hesitated for a long moment. He held up his hand, fingers spreading as if miming a man pressing on a glass, except that it also recalled his five kinds of prayers. *Supplication*, Inglis thought. "Otherwise . . . otherwise, it was like standing outside a window in the rain, looking in on some harvest party, to which I knew I was not invited."

"Oh," said Inglis, stupidly. And at an echo in his mind of *Stop that*, grinned uncontrollably despite it all. He rubbed at his upper lip, and his hand came away sticky and red, but the bleed seemed to have stopped on its own.

Penric held his hair aside and peered down into his face with a curiosity . . . medical? theological? magical? or just the inquisitive scholar? Voices and barking echoed from below, and Penric craned his neck. ". . . Right. So, here comes Gallin, and a lot of excited men with ropes. I hope they brought enough. Arrow and Blood are running over to greet them, or maybe hurry them along. Or trip them and break their legs, hard to tell with dogs. Are you going to give us any *more* trouble?"

"I am in your hands," Inglis said, limply. And truthfully. And thankfully.

Rescue. I am rescued. Of all men to be lost in these mountains, he had to have been the most lost, and the most rescued. Such rescues had been Scuolla's calling, had they not? Him and his brave band of dogs. The shaman's last rescue, and the shaman rescued, hand to hand to hand to hand in a long, long chain of help beyond hope. Reaching how far back?

... And how far forward?

XIII

GETTING THE TWO MEN off the ledge took over an hour. Like the injured shaman, the sorcerer waited to ride the rope net down; unlike the shaman, he stepped out of it with the panache of a prince descending a palace stair. When taxed by Oswyl, Penric claimed that it was much harder to climb down than up, because he couldn't well see where he was putting his hands and feet. No mountaineer, Oswyl had to take him at his word. It was hardly a thing to balk at, considering what all *else* of the uncanny events he was forced to take the sorcerer-divine's testimony for. The eager Acolyte Gallin ate up their wild tale like a starving man, and asked for seconds. The guards and the valemen grew wide-eyed. In all, it was rising dark before they made it back to Linkbeck once more.

Inglis, certainly, seemed a man profoundly changed, unless the fall had struck him mad. Madder. When they'd cleaned up, and Penric in his third guise as physician had seen to their prisoner's new bruises, they all went down to dinner, where Gallin and Gossa were slavishly grateful—to *Inglis*. For Gossa, this took the form of trying to stuff him like a feast-day goose, and feeding his dogs like people. Penric beguiled his own neglect by telling the servant girl, who turned out to be the daughter of the village wet-nurse, all about the fine opportunities for an energetic young woman in the silk industry at Martensbridge, under the princess-archdivine's careful eye.

Oswyl finally broke it up by announcing an early start in the morning. As they mounted the staircase, he said to Inglis, "You are still my prisoner. Still under arrest. And we are still going back to Easthome."

"Oh, yes," said Inglis, pensively. "It's all very good now. And if it is not, there will be something better."

For his part, Oswyl predicted a blizzard with the dawn.

In the blackest hour of the night, Oswyl dreamed.

A deep, slow voice, which seemed to reverberate to the ends of the world, said judiciously: **"You were not too late. Well done, child."** After a thoughtful pause it added, in a far less grave tone, "No snow tomorrow. But do not linger three days."

Oswyl, scrambling to sit up, came awake with a cry. He didn't know if the sound was night-terror or joy, but it was *loud*.

Dogs yipped, covers were thrown back, and Penric's voice out of the shadows called, "Des, lights, lights!" He then cried in fear, "He'll burn my eyes!" and replied to himself, "You haven't got eyes. I do and they're just fine. Or they would be if there were any *light* in here. *Thank you*," he added, as upon the washstand the two tallow candles sprang into flame all by themselves.

Oswyl, clutching his blankets, gasped, "He . . . He . . . "

"Are you all right?" asked Penric, concerned. "You sound like a horse with the heaves."

"Nothing. Nothing," Oswyl managed, trying to catch his stolen breath. "Pardon."

"Judging from Des's reaction, it was not *nothing.*" He added, "You can come out now. I think it's over." He twisted around to Inglis, who was sinking sleepily back into his bedroll and coaxing the dog Blood to lie down to be clutched like another pillow. "Did you sense anything, just now?"

"No . . . I don't think it was meant for me." He cuddled the dog, which slowly gave up its alert mien and put its head on its paws once more. Arrow stepped over, and on, Penric in his trundle— provoking an, "Oof, you enormous beast! Paws off!"—and stretched his damp black nose to sniff curiously at Oswyl.

"It was just a dream," said Oswyl. "Maybe, maybe a little hallucination. It's been a long day." And a long, strange chase.

"A bad dream?"

Oswyl hardly knew, except the corners of his mouth kept crooking up, unaccustomed and unwilled. "No . . . It was . . . a different kind of frightening." He added, "How can you tell? Discern a true voice from, from a mere dream?"

"If you need to ask, it was a mere dream. The other is rare but, hm, not as rare as you'd think. Our daytime minds, I'm told, are too full of ourselves to let Them in. Well, and mine's too full all the time. At night our gates come sometimes ajar, just enough."

Oswyl's brows drew down. "That's . . . unhelpful."

"What was your message?"

He wasn't embarrassed, exactly. But . . . "I'd rather not say. It would sound too absurd."

Penric, propped up on one elbow, studied him thoughtfully. He finally said, "A bit of free theological advice. Do not deny the gods. And they will not deny you."

As Oswyl stared at him, he went on, "Dangerous habit, mind you. Once you start to let Them in through that first crack, They're worse than mice."

Oswyl, thoroughly bemused by now, protested, "How can you speak of the gods so irreverently? And you a full-braid divine?"

Penric shrugged a half-apology. "Sorry. Seminary joke, there. We had a hundred of them. Needful at times of stress. One of my masters said, For all that we trust the gods, I think we can trust them to know the difference between humor and blasphemy."

"Not so sure about *your* god," Inglis's voice came from his bedroll.

"Hey. Yours is no better. A god whose harvest of souls includes all whose last words were, 'Ho, lads! Hold my ale and watch this!' . . . Seminary joke," he added aside to Oswyl, who hardly needed the gloss.

Inglis snickered into his dog, and then mused, "That would be funnier if it weren't so true."

"If it were not true, it wouldn't be funny at all."

The two young scholars seemed willing to debate the theology of humor, or the humor of theology, till dawn. Oswyl said loudly, "You can snuff the candles back out, now. I'm all right."

Penric smiled at him, eyes narrowing. "Ye-es. I expect you are."

"Want to borrow a dog?" Inglis offered. "They're very soothing."

"In my bed? No, thank you."

Arrow, snuffling over the edge of Oswyl's blankets, heaved a disappointed sigh, as if finding that the source of some delicious scent had gone.

"What," said Penric, "they don't have fleas—don't everyone rush to praise me. And Gossa made her children wash their paws."

"You are welcome to him," said Oswyl, shoving the beast back into the trundle. "You, go sit on your master." Giving up on his riotous company, Oswyl struggled from his bedclothes and went to blow out the candles himself.

The heavy snow did not close in till after they'd reached the safety and warmth of Martensbridge, three days later.

XIV

AT THE KNOCK on his workroom door, Pen looked up from his calligraphy and said, "Come."

The door swung open cautiously, and a palace page entered. "The Temple courier has brought you some letters, Learned."

Pen set his quill in its jar and turned to accept them. "Thank you."

The girl ducked her head and, after a last curious look around, went out again.

Penric examined his take. The thinner missive was marked with a Temple stamp from the Father's Order in Easthome; the larger, wrapped in a piece of old cloth and waxed against wet, had been franked by the Wealdean royal court chancellery. He opened it first, to find a letter and an unbound book, freshly copied and pristine. Both from Inglis, ah.

It had been over a month since Oswyl and his prisoner, and his prisoner's vigorous pets, had departed for Easthome. Penric had managed to evade being taken along by virtue of the week they'd all spent snowbound in Martensbridge, which had allowed him to scribble out a full deposition of the late events in Chillbeck Vale, heavily slanted in Inglis's favor. Normally a trip to the Wealdean royal capital at the Temple's expense would have been a high treat, but—not in midwinter, despite Oswyl's descriptions of the fine Father's Day festival put on there at the solstice. *Not my season.*

Nor mine, sighed Des. *Did I ever tell you about the sun on the sea around Cedonia?*

Several times. He'd never seen a sea, warm or cold. Could a demon be homesick? wondered Pen, and broke the seal on Inglis's letter.

Inglis thanked him for his deposition, which had done the trick—the shaman did not appear to be writing from a condemned prisoner's cell, certainly. *You were right that the god-drunk wears off,* Inglis wrote, *for I was very sober when we reached Easthome. I have been strongly reprimanded by the Royal Fellowship, and put on probation, whatever that means, but not dis-invested. I am not sure anyone can actually do that, or at least, no records of such a skill have surfaced in the ancient annals. It seems the old method of execution for bad shamans was to hang them upside down and drain them of blood, which no one in the Fellowship has suggested even for the experiment.*

The Father's judges after much debate finally ordered me to pay a fine to Tollin's family, in the old style, by way of weregild. My parents had to borrow some of it from our kin lord, which did not please anyone very much, but I trust they'd have been less pleased to see me feet-up with my throat cut. Oswyl says I should just give up on Tolla, but I am not so sure. She did listen to my tale and mark my scars. Tollin's second funeral was a comfort to his family, I think, though redundant, as I saw very well which god took him up, and told them so. I'm not sure some believed me until their local temple's holy animal signed Autumn at his graveside.

I had a copy made for you of the Fellowship's writings on shamanic practices that you wanted to read, at least as they are understood so far. I hope we'll need a second volume in a few more years. It seems small thanks, but it was what I could do. You should find it under seal with this letter.

He signed it with a flourishing *Inglis kin Wolfcliff, Fellow of the Royal Society of Shamans (on probation).* And added, as a cramped postscript at the bottom of the sheet, *The dogs are well, and settling into their new home. We maintain a bit of a menagerie here, so they fit right in. They like Tolla.*

Penric's fingers itched to dive for the new volume, but he opened the thinner letter instead. As he'd hoped, it was from Oswyl.

You may be pleased to learn that your affidavit was accepted by the court, though immediately afterward seized upon by some theologians and carried off. From the legal side of things, there is no sign that anyone wants you brought here in person after all. The other I cannot speak to. Inglis got off lightly, but I do not feel there was injustice done.

My former sorcerer and his party arrived back at Easthome about two weeks after we did, frostbitten, footsore, and empty-handed. Happily, their official complaints of me were stopped by word of my success. Their private ones, I feel no need to attend to.

I set an offering on your god's altar the other day, in Temple.

His signature was neat and square, *Oswyl, Senior Locator, the Father's Order at Easthome.*

He, too, added a cramped last word: *I am not sure how demons feel about blessings, so please just give my best wishes to Desdemona.*

Des was so astonished, she was momentarily silent.

Penric smiled and reached for his new book.

PENRIC'S
FOX

PENRIC'S FOX

"NO, you can't make a Great Earthworm!" said Inglis, sounding indignant. Although not indignant enough to rise from his comfortable recline on the mossy bank, fishing pole propped on his bare toes.

"I just did. See?" Penric held out the rosy writhing creature, flecked with moist soil, on his palm. "Isn't he cute?"

"No," said Inglis, grumpily.

The shaman's grimace failed to honor, Penric thought, the loveliest morning to escape all duties and go fishing that Pen could imagine. The quiet pool in the hills above Easthome was everything Inglis had promised his visitor: cool, tree-shaded, gilded with sun ripples. Possibly a little short of fish, but as the hazy day warmed, very inviting for a man to strip and swim. Penric had plans.

"Anyway," said Inglis, craning his neck to peer at the worm in Penric's hand, "how do you know it's a he? It might be a she."

Penric wrinkled his nose in doubt. "I've heard earthworms are both in one body."

"Oh, just like you, then," murmured Inglis, smirking.

Good to see the glum boy's not above getting his own back, commented Desdemona, amused. The Temple demon who lived inside of Penric and gave him the powers of a sorcerer was decidedly female, after all, which as he came to know Pen better had been a cause of increasing bemusement to Inglis. *Inglis kin Wolfcliff, Fellow of the Royal Society of Shamans (on probation)* as he signed his correspondence, though he hoped to be rid of the unfortunate postscript soon.

Penric tried to return a suitable sneer, but the country light was too fine to allow him to sustain the effort; it came out a grin.

Inglis shook his head. "I can't believe you mastered the technique just from watching that one sacrifice in the menagerie yard yesterday."

"That, atop reading the book you sent, your letters, talking to your Royal Fellowship and you over the past two weeks, examining, well, a few other works, half of which turn out to be rubbish. Always a problem with written sources, which frequently tell you far more about the person who wrote them than the subject addressed."

"You are a more bookish scholar than me," Inglis granted. "It seems unfair that . . . never mind. All right, I can see it is indeed on its way to being a Great Earthworm"—a finger reached out to dubiously prod the creature—"two souls, if you can call them that in a worm, piled into one body, but it won't arrive, and anyway, where is the point? No one would wish to be invested with a worm-spirit, and the powers it might grant wouldn't persuade a flea to jump onto a dog."

"Practice for the student shaman," Penric returned promptly. "Or student sorcerer, anyway. Earthworms are theologically neutral creatures, as far as I know. Tomorrow, I might try mice, if their tiny souls prove not too heavy for me to shift. They're vermin of the Bastard—as a learned divine of the white god I should be able to make free with them."

"Brother forfend," sighed Inglis. "Anyway, such tricks have been tried before, by people with more time than sense. After a few iterations, such lowly creatures cannot accept the overload of spirit, and die of the attempt to do so."

"Really?" said Penric, fascinated. "I must test that."

"Of course you must," muttered Inglis, with a defeated air. But he set his pole aside and sat up to watch all the same.

Pen pulled half-a-dozen more earthworms out of their bait pail and strove to get them lined up in a row on a flat stone. They resisted this fate, squirming about in a disordered manner that Pen's god the Bastard might approve, but a brief tap of uphill magic stilled them into a more military rank, temporarily. He set his first attempt at the end of the row, and rather regretfully sacrificed it into the next, persuading his conscience that it couldn't be a worse death for a worm than being impaled on a hook and tossed into deep water to drown. Four more worms down the row, Inglis was proved right, as the recipient of all this effort more-or-less ruptured when Penric tried to tip the accumulating life-magic into it. "Oh," he said, sadly. "There's a shame."

Inglis rolled his eyes.

Penric abandoned his first semi-successful effort at mastering whatever of shamanic magics he could—given that his possession of a demon of disorder would block a Great Beast of any species from ever being sacrificed into him to give him the powers of a shaman proper. Raising his rod, he squinted at his dangling hook, which seemed to have lost its bait. He sniffed and tipped the pole up to swing the line back to him, rebaiting it with one of his late sacrifices, taking consolation that the humble deaths occasioned by his imitation-shamanic efforts would not be totally wasted. He plopped his line back into the pool beside Inglis's.

After a few minutes, he observed, "We are both Temple mages, though of different sorts. Why are we fishing in such an inefficient manner?"

"Because if we applied our magics, we'd be done before the wine gets cold," said Inglis, amiably gesturing at the glazed jugs set to bathe in the rippling shallows.

"Point," agreed Penric.

"Refill?"

Securing his pole with a couple of stones, Pen rose to retrieve a jug. He topped up both their beakers, tapping out the last drops into his host's cup, then rummaged in the basket for a bite more of that good bread to go with it. The purpose of going fishing was not, after all, only to catch fish.

After a little still-fishless silence, beguiled by the local wine that lay like liquid gold upon their tongues, Inglis mused, "I wonder if such limits apply to demons as well? Is there an upper range of accumulating lives, or souls, that a demon can take up and transfer along with it, as it is handed off from rider to rider at the ends of their lives?"

Penric blinked. "Good question. Although it is not souls, exactly, that a demon accumulates from its successive sorcerers. Or not usually, unless the transfer goes badly and rips the dying person's soul apart. Because any number of sorcerers and sorceresses are signed at their funeral rites as being taken up by our god just like anyone else. Not sundered from Him, certainly, or the creation of Temple sorcerers would be the blackest sacrilege. I prefer to think of my demon's personalities as images of my predecessors, like printed pages pulled off an inked plate and bound into a codex, except . . . more so. Else my head would be very haunted."

Inglis turned toward Penric, cleared his throat, and came out with, "Desdemona, do you know?"

It was rare that Inglis attempted to talk to Des directly, like another person, and Pen smiled in approval. He'd get the shaman trained yet. He yielded control of his voice to his permanent passenger, quite as interested in the answer as Inglis.

Des was quiet for so long Pen began to think she would not reply, but at last she spoke, necessarily through Penric's mouth. "You children ask the most bizarre questions. There is a steady attrition of demons in the world, either hurried out of it by certain Temple rites while a young elemental, barely formed, or removed with more difficulty by a saint should they ascend and go rogue when they grow older and stronger. In over two hundred years, I have shared twelve lives with my riders, ten of them human—"

"Twelve half-lives, really," Penric glossed for Inglis's benefit, "since you have never jumped to an infant or child."

"Jumping to an infant would be a recipe for disaster," opined Des. "Instant ascendance, since the mewling creature would not have the developed will and knowledge to control its demon. Very bad choice. Anyway, as I was about to say before you interrupted me—"

"Sorry."

She nodded with Pen's head. "I have not met a demon older than myself for a long time."

"That would make sense," said Inglis, trying to follow this. "The older anyone gets, the more people are junior, and the fewer senior." He frowned. "It must be strange to be oldest, to outlive all one's generation. Yet some person in the world must be that one, at every moment. Do you think you could be eldest among demons, Desdemona?"

"Certainly not!" she said tartly. But Pen sensed an unspoken hesitance in her.

"So what happens to the eldest demons?" pursued Inglis, logically. "Do you suppose they reach a point where no head can hold them, and they jump one time too many, and, ah . . . " His finger pointed to the exploded earthworm.

"Eeeww," said Penric and Desdemona together. "Really, wolf-boy!" said Des, and Pen went on, "I should think if that were the case, the Temple would know of the hazard, and it would have been part of my training in seminary."

"I suppose so," said Inglis, giving up his horrifying hypothesis with apparent reluctance. He took another swallow of wine, then jiggled his pole.

I would place a bet, murmured Des, *which of you gives up first and starts using your magics to cheat the fish, but I've no one to bet with.*

What, you have your whole sisterhood in there, Pen returned. *You could start a pool.*

There's a thought . . . but she broke off and glanced at Inglis, who had sat up and turned his head, listening intently. Penric discerned nothing but the pleasant summer sounds of the woodland and stream, but he knew Inglis's Great Wolf gave him preternatural hearing. Soon enough, the thump of trotting hooves sounded from the rutted road where they'd left their hired cart. The hoofbeats stopped, a low voice soothed the animal, and then quick footsteps approached on the path to the pool.

"Ah. There you are." Locator Oswyl's voice sounded strained as Pen twisted around to wave. "Five gods be thanked."

"Oswyl!" Inglis greeted his unlikely friend as well. "You made it after all!"

The senior locator from the Father's Order had been invited to make the third of their fishing party this morning, but he'd sent a note at the last minute saying that he'd been called out on an urgent new inquiry, and not to expect him. He still wore the gray vest with the brass buttons that caused Easthome inquirers to be dubbed *Grayjays*, but it hung open over his sweat-damp shirt. Done for the day, or just surrendering to the heat?

"Did you wrap things up so soon?" asked Penric cheerily.

Oswyl made his way to the streambank, planted his fists on his hips, and sighed. "No. Unfortunately. Quite the opposite. I am in urgent need of a Temple sensitive, a sorcerer even more, and you two are the closest. I am sorry, but I must conscript you."

"No time to even take a cup?" Pen asked, looking with regret at the second jug cooling in the stream.

"No time for anything. Not six miles from here, I have a dead sorceress on my hands. Murdered, I think. Sometime late yesterday or last night."

Pen, startled, stood up. "That," he said slowly, "would be a very hard trick to bring off. Speaking from personal experience."

"Someone did. One arrow through a person could be a hunting accident. Not two. And I don't think she could have shot the shafts into her own back, not even with sorcery."

"Ah." Penric gulped, and called to Inglis, "I'll harness the carthorse, then, while you gather up things?"

Inglis nodded, already bringing in their poles. It was the best division of labor, since despite his excellent horsemanship Inglis's wolf-within tended to make even such slugs as the livery nag nervous.

Oswyl, jittering with impatience, followed Pen out to the narrow hill road where his own sweating mount was tied to a sapling. "I will give it this. The scene is fresh. Usually, help from the Father's Order is called in days late, after the local authorities have strangled all sense in a mess of their own making. This improves the chances of you or Inglis sensing something useful, yes?"

Pen had no idea. But as he strode over to untether their hired horse and back it into the shafts, his most alarmed question was not who had killed a sorceress, or how, or even why, but rather, *Where is her demon?*

Oswyl's six miles cross-country turned out to be closer to nine back, by the time they'd retraced their cart track, cut across some farm ways, and found a better road leading up toward a hill village. They turned aside before they reached it, then were forced to leave their cart when the side track into the steep woods dwindled to a path. But only a few hundred panting paces along it the trees opened up into a clearing.

It was a pleasant enough glade, the by-now early afternoon light filtering down green-gold through the leaves. Less pleasant was the slumped, muddled figure toward the far edge, and the buzzing of the flies being waved off by the anxious junior locator left on guard. She was using a long, leaf-tipped branch to do so, leaning back as far as possible. Not due to any rotting reek yet, Pen thought as they drew closer; she was more likely spooked by the triple braid in white, cream and silver pinned to the figure's shoulder marking a sorceress.

"My assistant, Junior Locator Thala." Oswyl gestured, by way of introduction, and asked her, "Anything occur since I left you?"

"No, sir," said the guard, rising with obvious relief. She was much younger than Oswyl's thirty or so years, looking even more fresh-faced than Pen.

"Where's that dedicat?"

"He went home to fetch us both something to eat. He should be back soon."

"The body was found early this morning by a lay dedicat from the temple at the village of Weir," Oswyl explained over his shoulder to Pen and Inglis, "sent out into the woods to check snares. This tract belongs to Baron kin Pikepool, they tell me, but he grants the temple-folk gathering rights to deadfall and small game in it, by way of quarter-day dues."

Penric squatted in the place the young locator gladly yielded to him, and peered.

The woman lay on one side, as if sleeping. Her coils of brown hair were fallen loose, a beaded cloth cap snagged awry among them. Neither fat nor thin, tall nor short, comely nor ugly; she might be in her early forties. Whatever mind had enlivened her face—and the divine's braids testified it must have been a keen one—was gone now, leaving her features bland, waxy and still. Enigmatic.

She was not dressed in formal robes, but rather, everyday garb, an ordinary dress with a thin blue coat thrown atop, to which her braids were pinned. It had not protected her clothing from the flood of blood that had soaked it and dried brown. Almost as much had gushed around the arrowhead that protruded from her stomach as from the two fletched shafts standing in her back. By the blood trail on the ground, she had fallen only a few feet from where she had been shot. *A quick death. That, at least,* thought Pen, trying to control his dismay. No sign that she had been otherwise molested.

Inglis looked over Pen's shoulder, his nostrils flaring, possibly at the disturbing smell of the blood. Thick enough for Pen to discern, it was likely overwhelming to Inglis's wolf-within, or at least his face had gone a little rigid.

Oswyl cleared his throat, pointedly, and Pen, rising to look around, thought, *Des, Sight, please.*

Pen half-hoped to find the woman's ghost still lingering, fresh enough to still appear much as she had in life; a sudden and violent death was very apt to produce that effect. Most ghosts could not speak, but a sufficiently distressed one, still reverberating from its abrupt separation from its sustaining body, might sometimes grant to a sighted sensitive a sort of dumb-show. It was a very dangerous liminal state, as the soul could slip into a permanent sundering from its waiting god that was unwilled by either party. So Pen also half-hoped not, for the woman's sake. More usually, soul and god found each other at once, and the only function of a funeral rite was to confirm the destination.

The living souls in the clearing were all vivid enough, congruent with their bodies. Inglis's bore the added spiritual density of his Great Wolf, unsettling if one didn't know what it was. Or maybe even if one did. Penric slowly turned, scanning with sight and second sight together, but found no convenient miming ghosts. Lost souls usually attached themselves to a place, rarely to their own bodies; the strange shamanic practice of carrying away the ghost of a slain spirit-warrior bound to a sacred object did not apply here. Nor was there any sign of the stray demon, not that Pen expected it. Demons could not, after all, jump to trees, which were the only other living things about. The demon must have been carried off by its new host. And *there* was a pressing question or five.

Pen signed himself in the tally of the gods, let his Sight fade, and turned to Oswyl. "No ghost. No demon. No help. Sorry."

Oswyl huffed the sigh of a man perpetually unsurprised that his luck was not in. "Worth checking."

"Very much so."

"Can you tell anything else?"

Inglis's hand tracked the line from the arrow shafts into the woods, seeking the archer's vantage, but then he shook his head. "No saying how much she turned as she fell."

Pen crossed his arms and stared down at the woman. "A few things. She's young, to start with."

Oswyl cocked his head. "Surely not. Middle years."

"I mean young for a Temple sorceress. The Bastard's Order does not usually invest a trained woman aspirant with a demon until she is done childbearing, or at least is sure she wishes no child. The chaos that demons usually shed"—Pen paused to choose a delicate term— "thwarts conception."

Oswyl's brows twitched up. "For some, that would be a benefit."

"True. But a female sorcerer must be extraordinarily clever, attentive, and experienced to successfully manage a demon and a pregnancy both at once. Some few have done it, but it's not a recommended path. So the greater likelihood is this woman has not borne her demon long."

"I don't see any spent arrows," noted Inglis, craning his neck. "Two shots, two hits. Suggests an expert bowman."

"Or bow-woman," murmured the listening assistant, almost inaudibly.

"Or he collected them after," said Oswyl.

"Mm."

Pen eyed the arrows' penetration. "He was either close, or had a bow with a really strong draw. If the latter, probably a man. I think not the former." He cast the junior locator an apologetic nod.

"Why not?" asked Oswyl—intent, not skeptical.

"One reason to murder a sorcerer that leaps to my mind"—Penric cleared his throat—"is to steal their demon."

Inglis's head turned at this. "People really try that?"

"Yes," sighed Pen.

"It wouldn't work with a Great Beast!"

"Lucky for shamans. But if the killer was after the demon, he'd want to be as close to the sorcerer as possible. A knife, not a bow, would be the weapon of choice. About the only way one could get more distance is by that Roknari trick of a throwing the sorcerer into the sea with a leaking cushion and sailing away as fast as possible. A bow suggests a murderer who very much did not want to be lumbered with his victim's demon."

Oswyl frowned. "What's the range that a demon can jump?"

"It," Pen began, but then realized he didn't have to offer a guess. "Desdemona, can you speak to that?"

"It varies with the strength of the demon," said Des, "but a long bowshot would certainly stretch it to its limits."

Oswyl's eyes narrowed as he stared back and forth from the body to the encircling woods. "Or there were two. The bowman at a distance, the other close up." He did not look as if the thought pleased him.

It wasn't an impossible scenario, and it did account for the demon, Pen had to grant.

"It had to have happened before dark last night," suggested Inglis, "to make that shot—twice—at that range."

"Unless she bore a lantern," said Oswyl. Everyone looked around. No lantern lay broken or rolled away, but it might have been carried off like spent arrows.

"A sorcerer can see in the dark," Pen pointed out. "She might not have needed one."

"A bowman can't," said Inglis, clearly still taken with his own theory.

"Unless he's another sorcerer," put in Pen. "Although in that case, he wouldn't need to keep his distance."

Oswyl groaned. "Anything else you can tell me?"

"A sorcerer is very hard to kill," Penric began, rather in the teeth of the evidence before them.

"Sorcerers with experienced demons are very hard to kill," Desdemona corrected this, "if their demons wish to protect them. A young demon will be less adept. But if any demon wishes to throw off an unwanted rider, it's not any great challenge."

Three people stared at him oddly. Penric went on in a louder voice, "What I was *about* to say is, that suggests this sorceress was taken by surprise, by ambush, and so was her demon."

Oswyl rubbed his toe into the dirt, his expression growing distant with this visualization. "Or the murderer was someone she trusted. Or murderers, gah."

Penric grimaced, a little sickened at the picture of the woman, or anyone, really, lured out and so betrayed. "I suppose so."

Oswyl's head tilted as he studied the body. "I suppose she really was a sorceress? Speaking of complications. Because anyone could throw on a coat with a braid pinned to it. Or pin one on somebody."

She'd certainly been wearing the coat when she'd died, by the blood soaking it. Penric knelt and fingered the braid, which was stiff and clean, comparable to his own after less than its first year's use. *Des...?*

Oh, yes. There is ... an emptiness, here in this husk. Hard to describe, but distinctive enough. As if the place where the soul had resided is stretched larger than usual.

Huh. Pen said aloud, "Yes, she was. Which means that the chapterhouse of the Bastard's Order in Easthome should house a bailiff of sorcerers who is her master, and who can identify her. I expect a great many of our questions may be answered there."

He tested her hand for rigor, something that Oswyl had doubtless already done, and had more practice at than Pen, too. The stiffness might be starting to pass off, but then, the day was warm. *Amberein? Helvia?* he called on the two sorceress-physicians numbered among Des's prior riders. *Can you add anything?*

Helvia answered, *Not really. Too many variables. Late yesterday or last night may be as close as you can come.*

Pen blew out his breath and stood up. "I do wonder why she was just left like this. Surely the murderer could have delayed discovery, perhaps indefinitely, by digging some shallow grave. He'd had time. Or hadn't he, and in that case, why not?"

"Add the question to the list," said Oswyl. "I promise it won't be the last. Meanwhile, spread out and see if there is any more this clearing has to say. Mute things may sometimes give more telling testimony than witnesses. And then we'll take this poor woman home."

Pen walked about, looking, and Des looked through his eyes. He mostly found a great deal of nothing. No lantern, no footprints, no dropped objects. No demon. Oswyl's dual-murderers idea seemed ever more plausible. "Or," he commented to Oswyl aloud, "it could have been one murderer, of either sex, and one hired mercenary with a bow. Such ruined men will kill for surprisingly little money."

Oswyl grunted. "I hate those instances. With no connection to the dead person, men like that are hard to trace."

Circling the body once more, Penric mulled, "I have to . . . not take it back, exactly, but—a sufficiently expert bowman might put two shafts in the air at once, possibly before he realized that shape in the gloaming was a woman and not a deer. And then, horrified at his deed, run off. Accounts for everything." *Except the demon.*

"How likely is this?"

City-bred Oswyl was no archer, Pen recalled, despite his other skills. "I could have, when I was in practice. Well, I hope not the part about mistaking a woman for a deer."

"That's a very tempting simplification." Oswyl didn't look like a man tempted. He looked like a man who had just bitten into something with a bad taste. Again. "I won't dismiss it from the list just yet. But it needs verification. *Everything* needs verification."

The lay dedicat from the village arrived, carrying a basket and leading an older woman. She turned out to be the Weir temple's divine, the one who had sent so directly to the Father's Order when her lad had come gasping back to her at dawn with news of his find. The assistant locator accepted the basket gratefully, diving into it for the food, some of which she pressed on Oswyl. Oswyl munched standing—from his prior knowledge of the man, Pen was fairly sure he hadn't yet stopped to eat today.

The local divine solemnly examined the dead woman, and agreed with her dedicat that the corpse was no one they'd ever seen before, no member of her village flock or from the farms round about. *A stranger up from Easthome*, her tone implying the Hallow King's seat was a dangerous sort of fleshpot where one might find murderers or worse on any corner. It made Des snicker. *You could fit five of Easthome in the capital of Darthaca, and ten in old Imperial Thasalon. She has no idea what a fleshpot is. Pretty city, though, I'll grant it that.*

Inglis, who had gone off to take a wider circuit through the woods, still looking for the bowman's stand, came back then with a third arrow in his hand. Thala watched him curiously.

"Aye, same fletching," Inglis muttered, comparing it to the shafts in the corpse's back. "It was just standing in the soil"—he pointed into the trees where the slope fell toward a distant secluded stream—"but there was a bit of this stuck to it."

He offered up a tuft of coarse ruddy hair. Pen took it and sniffed. "Fox."

"So I make it," agreed Inglis.

Everyone stared at the scrap, doubtless all trying to fit it into the multiplicity of scenes they'd imagined to account for the abandoned body. Oswyl finally shook his head and took charge of the shaft, and Inglis pocketed the fur. And then they all joined in the task of carrying the woman's body to their cart. The local divine signed a melancholy blessing upon it as they arranged it in the limited space as decently as possible.

Pen turned the cart around to head back downhill, swinging aboard as Inglis took up the reins and urged their tired horse into motion once more. The two locators mounted and fell in behind, making a rudimentary sort of cortege.

Pen hoped they'd learn the woman's name soon. He was uncomfortable thinking of her as just *the corpse*, not that every person wouldn't share that demotion in time. They turned onto a wider road, and the carthorse, perhaps recognizing the way home, began pulling less dispiritedly. Oswyl rode up beside Pen.

"We really have to find that demon," Pen told him.

Oswyl shrugged. "Bastard's Order business; I yield it to you. The problem of justice for this dead woman presses more on me than concern for a creature who by its nature cannot die."

"Well, then, you might also reflect that the demon was the closest possible witness to the murder."

Oswyl's brows flew up. "Can a demon be a reliable witness? How in the world could it be called to take oath and testify?"

"It would depend on the demon. Desdemona could."

Oswyl took this in, nonplussed, then shook his head, muttering, "Magic dogs. Demons. I swear to the Father, my inquiries never used to be this strange." Distancing himself temporarily from the tangle, he pushed his horse ahead.

Easthome, lying along the river Stork, was already outgrowing the city walls rebuilt just a generation ago. The crude hearse and its escort circled through the outlying houses to the south gate, which put them closest to the heights dubbed Templetown, overlooking the red-roofed spread of Kingstown below. Penric and Inglis dismounted from the cart to give the balky horse less load to pull uphill, and also to keep it moving along through the more crowded streets. Passersby stared at the body inadequately wrapped in the picnic cloth, eyed the two Grayjays riding behind, swallowed any urge to call questions, and signed themselves.

The chapterhouse of the Bastard's Order lay two streets behind the great stone bulk of the city's, and the Weald's, main temple. The old wooden merchant's mansion that had formerly housed the servants of the white god had burned down twenty years ago, and been replaced with a fine new edifice, built more to the purpose, in the cut yellow stone of this country. As the chief chapterhouse of the realm, and in close competition with its sibling Orders for the other four gods, its architecture was high, balanced, and austere, not nearly as makeshift as the more provincial chapterhouses Pen was used to. It made him feel rather provincial himself.

Thala went to pound on the door and summon the porter. Despite the heat of the late afternoon—early evening by now in the long summer light—Oswyl paused to reorder his shirt and button up his vest before turning to help the other two shift the body out of the cart. The porter emerged, straight-backed in his tabard with its emblem of two white hands, fingers curled and thumbs out, pointing both up and down. He opened his mouth to demand the visitors' business, but it stayed open in dismay as he took in their burden. "Oh, no," he breathed. The recognition was instant; clearly, they'd chosen the right destination for the dead woman.

"First," said Oswyl to him, "let us get her off the open street."

"Aye, sir." The porter gave way at once, admitting them to a spacious stone-paved hallway where they lowered their sad freight to the floor.

"Her braids declared her one of yours, and gave her rank and calling," said Oswyl, "but told us nothing else. Can you give us her name?"

"Aye, sir. That's Learned Magal. She's been missing all day, and her bed was not slept in, but we thought she'd just gone to visit one of her children."

"Do you know when she last left the house? Or when you last saw her do so?"

"She was in and out several times yesterday. I don't really remember if, if they don't match up. The night porter might have more to add. He comes on in an hour."

Oswyl nodded. "I understand she has an overseer of sorcerers here. He or she should probably be the first informed."

"That would be Learned Hamo. I'll fetch him down at once, Locator." He stared, still shocked, at the form at their feet. "Where did you find her?"

"In a wooded tract in the hills, about ten miles out of Easthome," said Oswyl, watching the porter's face.

It crimped in confusion. "Whatever was she doing there?"

"Not a place she usually frequents, then?"

"Not as far as I know, sir. Here, I'll get the Learned." The shaken man hurried away up the stairway.

He came scuffing back down very soon followed by an older man, gray-haired, in the workaday robes of a divine. It didn't take the silver cord in the braids pinned to his left shoulder to tell Pen what he was, and Desdemona controlled a slight stiffness.

Will you be all right with another demon this close? Pen asked her in worry.

Oh, aye. At this rank, we are both tame Temple demons. Think of it like two people's spouses who can't abide each other, but feign civility for their mates' sakes.

Hamo's mouth, too, fell open in a huff of dismay at what lay in his hall. "No mistake, then."

"The locators brought her in, sir, and, um . . . these gentlemen," the porter supplied. That last was probably meant as a politeness, given Pen's and Inglis's grubby day-in-the-country garb, but he left his superiors to sort themselves out, stepping back. Though not very far.

Hamo knelt to touch the woman's face, then signed himself, lips moving in some short prayer. His jaw clenched as he took in the blood and the stubs of the arrows. He rose and turned to Oswyl, face more deeply lined than a moment ago. "What happened?"

"Her body was found by a lay dedicat of the village temple . . . " Oswyl went on to summarize the early morning's events, how he came to be called out on the inquiry, and what he'd first found in the clearing. "I could see at once I wanted a Temple sensitive, and I knew Shaman Inglis and Learned Penric to be fishing not far from there, so I conscripted them to my aid."

A look of relief came over Hamo's face, as the uncanniness he could very well sense about the two strangers was slotted into a settled place. He might not know Inglis, but he obviously was well-up on his colleagues and rivals in magics across town at the Royal Fellowship, for he merely nodded and said, "Shaman Inglis. You bear a Great Wolf, I think?"

"Yes, Learned," said Inglis, returning the nod in like kind.

"Shaman Inglis has some prior experience in my inquiries," added Oswyl on his behalf. Of course, he didn't say on which *side*. Inglis controlled his wince.

"And, Learned Penric . . . ?" Hamo's face held the usual doubt, given the way the claimed rank clashed with Penric's apparent youth.

"Learned Penric of Martensbridge"—Penric favored him with a short bow—"court sorcerer to Princess-Archdivine Llewen of Martensbridge. I followed in Her Grace's train on her visit for her great-nephew's name-day ceremonies, and some other Temple business here in Easthome she means to accomplish at the same time."

Given that Llewen was aunt to the Hallow King, and the mewling infant in question his newborn heir, Pen, too, left Hamo to sort it out for himself.

"Ah!" Hamo sounded enlightened rather than taken aback. "I believe I have heard something of your story." His eyes narrowed. "You inherited Learned Ruchia's demon, yes? I thought I recognized that extraordinary density."

"You knew Ruchia?" asked Penric, interested. Although now was not the time to follow it up.

"We met once or twice." Also recognizing the diversion, he waved it aside for a much more urgent concern. "You saw where Magal lay? Her soul was not"—he swallowed—"astray or sundered, I trust?"

"Seemingly not."

Hamo's shoulders slumped in relief. "That, at least," he muttered, and tapped his lips in a brief prayer of gratitude to their mutual god.

There followed some time devoted to physical necessities: carrying the sorceress's body to a decent temporary rest in a sort of infirmary at the far end of the house, sending for the female physician Oswyl recommended as working often with his Order's unhappy (Penric read it *gruesome*) inquiries, requisitioning a dedicat to take the locators' horses back to their mews and the carthorse back to its livery. Junior Locator Thala, perhaps expecting to be sent off on this lowly task, brightened at being allowed to stay by Oswyl's side.

They eventually fetched up at what was clearly Hamo's working office on the third floor: crowded shelves, writing table piled high with papers, not quite enough chairs, a lapse Hamo repaired by stealing one from a neighboring chamber.

As soon as they were seated—not settled, Pen gauged *unsettled* was closer to describing the mood in the room—Oswyl began in what must be practiced formality.

"I am sorry for the loss of your colleague—and friend?"

"Both, I hope," said Hamo.

"But I must ask a great many questions."

"Please do," sighed Hamo. "This is . . . this is horrible. Mags is lying downstairs, while some sundered fool is out there . . . Whatever you require, Locator." And Pen didn't need second sight to read the sincerity in his voice. Thala removed a little notebook and a lead stylus from her vest, and sat back looking attentive.

"First, I must know Learned Magal's kin. The porter mentioned children?"

"Yes, two, a daughter and a son. Her daughter lately made a very good marriage to a silversmith, and her son is apprenticed to an instrument maker. Both here in Easthome. Oh gods, I must send someone to tell them, or, no, I should go—"

"I will undertake that task next, Learned. It's in my mandate for such tragedies, and such close kin should not be told second-hand."

Hamo looked relieved, and gave up the names and addresses of the two, which the assistant jotted down.

"And a husband?" Oswyl asked. Given that Magal was a member of the Bastard's Order, the presence of children did not necessarily imply the presence of a husband, howsoever it required a father.

Hamo shook his head. "She was widowed a few years ago. Earlier in her career she served as the divine of a temple in Oxmeade"—a large town a half-day's ride from Easthome, Pen recalled—"and he was the long-time choirmaster there. A very devoted couple, from all I've been able to gather. But her single state was one of her many qualities that made her a good candidate to become a sorceress."

"Did the widow have any new suitors? Or, pardon but I must ask, lovers?"

Hamo blinked, perhaps realizing for the first time that the locator was collecting a list of suspects. "None that I know. She did not seem to wish for one."

"Would you know?" asked Oswyl. By sorcerous means, Pen gathered he meant.

"Yes," said Hamo, more certainly. Oswyl cast a look at Pen, who gave him a brief nod.

Penric then offered a question he wasn't sure would occur to Oswyl: "How long ago did she receive her demon?"

"Not long. Just three months. I thought they were settling in so well together." He rubbed his forehead and burst out, "This makes no *sense*. She was level-headed, amiable, experienced—a decade serving all sorts of people as a temple divine will certainly disclose one's character—are you sure it couldn't have been some terrible accident or mistake?"

"I haven't ruled out anything yet. Not even that."

Penric could almost see Oswyl struggling not to say aloud, *But it just doesn't smell right.* The locator had earned Pen's respect last winter. Only now was he beginning to garner Pen's pity as well. Pen was increasingly glad this grim task was Oswyl's calling, and not his own.

Oswyl went on, "Any other kin? Or in-laws?"

"Not here in town. Mags has—had none living, and her late husband's family are all back in Oxmeade."

"Friends and colleagues here in Easthome?"

"Many of both. She was well-liked."

"Any of special note?"

Hamo tossed off a few names, which the assistant dutifully jotted down.

"Were any of these colleagues rival candidates to receive a demon?"

Was Oswyl imagining professional jealousy, to add to jealousy in love? Pen supposed he had to cover every aspect.

"Well, Learned Basum is also waiting for the next opportunity, but I wouldn't call him a rival."

"Why not?"

Pen put in, "Temple demons are almost always handed down to riders of the same sex." At Oswyl's questioning glance, he added, "My case was unusual, as Learned Ruchia had her fatal seizure of the heart unexpectedly, on the road near Greenwell as I was passing by. Her demon was supposed to have been handed off to a female physician-aspirant, waiting at her deathbed."

"And that's another thing," Hamo burst out. "I thought Mags might become my successor, in some few years, and at the end of her life have a demon tamed enough to grant to a physician. It's . . . the waste goes on and on. Utter *waste.*" Hamo increasingly had the look of a man who needed to go apart to cry, or rave, or both, as the enormity of the loss to both himself and the Temple sunk in.

Oswyl, with a list of people to tax growing longer than his arm, looked as though he wanted to let him. But Hamo himself turned to Penric.

"And you found no sign at all of where her demon went?"

The missing demon was as much Hamo's task to manage and regulate as the late woman; in its own way, it, too, had a Temple career. Pen wasn't sure if Oswyl quite grasped this yet, though Inglis, with his experience of Great Beasts cultivated over decades, surely did. Inglis had been very silent throughout this interview, possibly daunted by glimpsing what his own disastrous misadventure must have been like for the people trying to follow after him.

"None, sir," said Pen. "It was very disquieting."

"It could not have got far on its own without seizing on some being of matter to sustain it," said Hamo.

"Yes. A person, either accidently or on purpose, or an animal, likewise—"

"An animal," faltered Hamo, "would have its own dire consequences to such a developed demon."

"Yes, sir, I am very aware. Or the third possibility." They both grimaced.

"Which is what?" prodded Oswyl.

Hamo answered, "If there is no creature whatsoever in range capable of absorbing a demon when its host-creature dies, even a small bird, it . . . I suppose you could say dissipates. Returns to its elemental chaos, losing all the knowledge it used to hold. Even the ability to be an elemental capable of starting over with the next animal along. Just . . . gone."

"It sounds a lot like sundering," said Oswyl, his eyes narrowing as he tried to picture this.

"Very like," agreed Pen. "Only faster." Within him, Desdemona shuddered.

Hamo regarded Pen intently. "Did you have any sense of that, in that clearing?"

Pen hesitated. "It's not something I've ever encountered before, so as to immediately recognize some trace." *Nor I,* Des conceded. *Such instances are, by their nature, never witnessed.*

"Our stray demon must be sought, and I can't leave here with all the rites to arrange for Mags," said Hamo, with an agitated swipe of his hand through his hair. "My own people are scattered, or unsuitable." He glanced across at Oswyl, who held up his palms in a fending gesture, and Pen tried unsuccessfully to remember the name of that Easthome sorcerer Oswyl had so definitely clashed with last winter. He, too, must be one of Hamo's flock. Hamo's gaze circled back to Pen. "Learned Penric . . . "

Penric, seizing the hint, nodded. "I'd be very pleased to assist you in this matter, if I can beg leave of my superior the princess-archdivine." Which he likely could. Inglis shifted, but said nothing. Yet.

Oswyl looked very relieved. "I'd be pleased to accept your assistance." He glanced more hesitantly at Inglis. "And yours, Shaman . . . ?"

"I'd like to take another look at that clearing," said Inglis slowly. "Before it has a chance to rain. There were—I'd just like some more time to cast a wider search." For what, he did not say, but Pen recalled that mysterious third arrow, and the bit of fox-fluff it had caught. And wondered what tracking abilities Inglis's wolf-within might lend him, even beyond the hunting skills of Pen's canton-mountain youth.

"Wherever Magal's demon is now," said Penric, "it had to have started out from that point. We should go together. Tomorrow morning."

"Early," agreed Inglis, earning an approving nod from Oswyl.

Oswyl went on to Hamo, "Does—did—Learned Magal keep a chamber here, or live elsewhere?"

"Yes, she lived in."

"I'll need to look through her things, if you can undertake to keep her room undisturbed till I get back. Probably also tomorrow morning. We must go to the next-of-kin tonight, before it gets any later." He added a bit wearily, "And then report to my own superiors."

Everyone present having a hundred new chores pressing down upon them, Oswyl extracted his party with more condolences, assuring Hamo that this tragedy would have his inquiry office's utmost attention.

By the time Pen had made it back to the Temple guest house reserved for the princess-archdivine and her train, hastily washed up, donned his best and cleanest white robes, and dashed down to the courtyard, he was running very late, as well as just running. Well, more of an awkward skipping, as he tried to blend the dignity due from a learned divine with his need for speed. But his superior was still being loaded into her sedan chair when he came puffing up.

"Ah, Penric," she greeted him. "And Desdemona, of course." The smile on her aging lips was dry, but not actually annoyed. "At last. I was preparing to send you to bed without any supper at all, if you missed this one." Llewen kin Stagthorne was dressed tonight as princess and royal aunt, not Temple functionary, though her gown showed off silks of Martensbridge manufacture, one of the more lucrative enterprises of the Daughter's Order that she oversaw there.

"My apologies for my tardiness, Your Grace," he replied, bending to kiss her archdivine's ring held forgivingly out to him. The hand went on to flick at her bearers, who hoisted up her chair and began to cart her along downhill towards Kingstown.

"Walk beside me, then," she said serenely, "and tell me all about your day off. I take it the fish were either very good or very bad?"

"Neither, as it turned out. Locator Oswyl was called out on an inquiry in the early morning—"

"Oh, that's a pity. I know you were looking forward to a visit. I quite liked him, during his brief sojourn in Martensbridge last winter. And your shaman friend was . . . interesting." She paused to consider this. "So good he wasn't hanged."

"I must agree. It would have been a pointless waste. Among other things. But we spent the day with Oswyl despite all, because he came to ask us both to help with his inquiry. And so some innocent fish were spared."

Her glance aside was sharp. "Really. And thereby hangs a tale?"

"Yes, Your Grace, but not one for the street." The bearers allowed the honor of transporting her, sturdy dedicats in the blue and white of their goddess and hers, were not the only prick-eared listeners within range.

Her eyelids lowered in understanding. "After, then. I am too old to stay out late, even for the sake of my Stagthorne kin."

"And I've undertaken to go out early tomorrow, so our steps will match on that."

"Hm." She digested this, then set aside her curiosity for dessert. "In any case, you will gratify me tonight by introducing yourself as Learned Lord Penric kin Jurald of Martensbridge, instead of your usual contraction."

"Too wordy, Your Grace. It offends my sense of literary economy."

She sniffed. "There are places where a pious humility is a suitable thing. Tonight's venue is not one of them. You are my sorcerer; your status reflects on my own."

His conceding nod was undercut by his grimace. "Jurald Court is little more than a fortified farmhouse in an obscure mountain valley, and I am its portionless younger son, as you and I both know."

"But no one else here will, and you are in no wise obliged to inform them. The world is not always so friendly a place that you can afford to squander your advantages on a pointless conceit."

"I much prefer the meaningful title I earned to the empty one I inherited."

"So, not modesty at all, but sly pride? Your scholarship is a delight to me, Penric, but of the many things you learned in seminary, I doubt court polish was one."

"Recalling our meals in the student refectory, I'm afraid you're right," he granted ruefully.

"Think of this visit as an opportunity for a different kind of learning, then. Another day will put some other plate on your table, more to your taste, but do not waste the food in front of you."

"Yes, Your Grace," he said meekly.

Their conversation broke off as her guards and bearers, and the second sedan chair porting her inseparable secretary, negotiated the long flights of steps crisscrossing down the bluff. Pen fell behind as the lanes narrowed and twisted, then strode up beside Llewen again as they came to the wider street fronted by the mansion of the royal relative hosting tonight's festivities. When the chair grounded beside the entrance, he was granted the privilege of raising her to her silk-slippered feet and offering her his arm, which she took with a rather smug smile.

The official naming ceremony for the blobby scrap of humanity Penric had been assured was a prince had gone off smoothly, the gods be thanked, three days ago. So he supposed the worst was over. Since the Archdivine of Easthome had officiated, Penric was not sure what his own superior's Temple task had been, besides swelling an already impressive procession. Good fairy, perhaps? Penric's function had seemed to be to stand around, look decorative, and try desperately to guard his best white robes against the detritus of a busy city. Tonight was shaping to be a reprise.

He even spotted some of the same faces, here in the hall of the elderly lord who was husband to Llewen's even-more-aged sister Princess Llewanna—Llewen released her hold on Pen to embrace this sibling. Really, it didn't seem all that different from some of the princess-archdivine's god's-day banquets back in Martensbridge. Well, more lords, fewer merchants. Fewer Temple folk, for that matter; Pen didn't spot that many other robes. More highborn relatives, though the influx of the aristocracy into town was already starting to thin. More expensive clothes and jewels. Ambassadors from far countries, not near counties, all right, that was a novelty—perhaps he'd have a chance to practice his languages before the evening was over. Men whose mistakes could kill more people, faster; but still, just men.

The candlelit banquet chamber was excessively warm in the summer evening. Pen sat by Llewen's left hand and was painfully polite to the few people who spoke to him and not her, smiling but not too much, since she'd once chided him for the latter. Was *court polish* a euphemism for being very bored while being stuffed very full?

It wasn't until the tables were being cleared away for the doubtless sedate dancing that he spotted an object of interest, or at least another person under fifty years old. The young fellow was even skinnier than Pen, managing to look less like a lord and more like a very well-dressed scarecrow. His most prominent feature was a pair of the thickest glass spectacles Pen had ever seen on a person's face.

They drifted together next to a wall wainscoted in gilded leather. "Is that not Martensbridge lens-craft?" Pen inquired, as pleased as if he'd run across an unexpected old acquaintance from his home village.

"Ah!" The young man's hand flew to his gold-decked temple. "You know the work?"

"Yes, very well. And the workman, I daresay. The artisan in Lower Linden Street, yes? I've heard several of my more aged colleagues pour blessings upon his head. And his hands."

The fellow's chest swelled as much as it could. "You understand!" He peered more questioningly at Pen. "Do you?"

"As I can think of no greater nightmare than to lose my ability to read, yes."

The bespectacled lordling smiled gratefully. "I was fourteen before I even found mine. Everyone just thought I was a clumsy fool when I was younger."

"Oh, that's unfortunate."

He nodded. "Because I could see shapes and colors and light and movement just fine, I didn't think myself blind, didn't realize others saw so much more than me. And neither did they. It was a Temple divine who'd been trying to tutor me, and who wore them himself, who first suspected my malady, and took me to Martensbridge to have me fitted. It was a revelation. Trees had *leaves*. And letters were not elusive fur-bearing creatures hiding coyly behind each other. I wasn't stupid, I just couldn't *see*." He was a little breathless, getting this all out at once to a rare sympathetic listener. "When I graduated Rosehall with second honors, it was the proudest day of my life, and no one understood why I was weeping till I nearly couldn't see again. Except Yvaina." He nodded sharply at this mysterious codicil.

"I attended the white god's seminary at Rosehall," Pen returned, quite willing to be cheerful for a fellow bookman's miracle. "I wonder if we could have been there at the same time?" Or not; Pen would certainly have remembered the spectacles, however unprepossessing their owner. Although the great university at Rosehall did host some six thousand students at a time. "I took my braids and oaths a year ago this spring."

"I left four years back," the young man said. "So maybe?"

"Mm, no. That would have been just about the time I arrived."

His brows crimped in puzzlement over the arithmetic; a divine's training normally took six years, not three. But he shrugged this off.

Pen asked, "What was your study?"

"Mathematics, mostly. I'd hoped to find a place in the Father's Order, perhaps rising to comptroller, at which point I thought I could afford to marry. I even began there as a lay dedicat. But, uh, other things happened first."

A young woman approached them, nearly as lanky and scrawny as the man apart from the distinctive pregnant bulge about her middle, like a plum on a stick. Pen had thought Des had fallen asleep, as he'd wished he could do, but she put in, *The word you are groping for, young Pen, is* willowy. *Far more flattering, thus safer. Trust me.*

Her clothes, though rich, hung on her almost as tentatively as the fellow's, but at the sight of her, his face lit as though the sun had come out behind his winking lenses.

"Ah. Allow me to introduce my wife. Baroness Yvaina kin Pikepool. And, oh, you are, learned sir . . . ?"

Pikepool was not one of the major Wealdean kin houses, or Llewen would have made Pen con it before now. Possibly not as obscure, however, as his own. Pen bowed. "Lord Penric kin Jurald, presently of Martensbridge."

"Ah, that's why you were sitting with the Princess Llewen at the high table. You looked a very daunting guardian."

Yvaina's rather thick brows knotted. "Is that not a Darthacan name?"

"Saonese, courtesy of a younger son with a short-lived dower and a last canton kin land-heiress. Then you would be Baron . . . ?"

The fellow opened his hands as if in embarrassment. "Wegae kin Pikepool. Though only lord for the last two years. The inheritance was quite unexpected."

The name might be obscure, but it was memorable. "You wouldn't happen to own a large tract of wooded hills about ten miles east of here?"

Wegae blinked in surprise. "It's part of the old family seat. That and that dreadful falling-down fortress. It's only good for a hunting lodge anymore, if I had the least interest in hunting." He made an excusing gesture at his face. "That was another skill no one could beat into me as a lad, along with reading."

He had not betrayed the slightest flinch at the question. Possibly no one had informed him yet of what had been found this morning in his woods? Oswyl, with all those closer relatives and colleagues of Magal's to work through, might not get to him till tomorrow. Pen decided he'd better not step on the locator's lines, contenting himself with, "Very pretty countryside."

Wegae shrugged. "We prefer the house in town, traitorous to my forest-tribe ancestors though it may be to admit it." His lady smiled and wrapped his arm in hers, comfortingly.

Penric tried to think of a subtle way to ask, *Where were you last night?* "Have you been much taken up with this royal launching?" A circling hand-wave indicated the past two weeks of name-day festivities.

Wegae shook his head. "Only to route around, mostly. But my mother insisted we come tonight. I think my inheritance gratified her almost more than me."

"Well, mothers," Penric offered in prudently vague sympathy. Both his auditors nodded in unison.

The princess-archdivine's lady secretary found Pen then, to murmur, "Her Grace is ready to leave now."

Pen was forced to make polite introductions and farewells in the same breath. He let the secretary guide him past the hazards of thanks to their highborn hosts, and, safely outside, took his place beside the sedan chair once more. Uphill, there was less breath for gossip, at least on his part, and the same problem with listening ears. So it wasn't until Llewen invited him to her rooms that, seated between the two women in the candlelight, he was able to recount his day's experiences. Despite his weariness, he tried to make it all sound as interesting as possible.

He must have succeeded, for his superior finally said, mildly, "I did have other plans for you tomorrow."

Did have not *do*, right. "So did I, Your Grace"—though probably not the same ones—"but I'd like to help Oswyl find justice for that poor sorceress if I can. And no one else is speaking for the lost demon. It was a victim, too, in my view."

She gave a conceding wave of her beringed hand. "Report to me again tomorrow night, then."

Playing on her curiosity had worked, good. Relieved, he signed himself, managed not to yawn in her face, and made his way to his own chamber.

By the time Penric and Inglis rode out from Easthome at dawn, made arrangements to leave their horses in the hill-village temple's paddock, discouraged the lay dedicat from tagging along, and returned to the clearing, it was not as early as either had hoped. At least the light was good.

Beginning from the dried blood patch, infested now by only a few green flies, Penric walked out in a slow spiral, all his senses deployed. No ghosts today, either, and at length he conceded that any chill of unease was being supplied by his own imagination.

Inglis went off to look for telltale horse droppings or cart tracks, and found some, but, given all the animals and people that had been in and out of here yesterday, they failed to be definitive. Yet another search for where the bowman must have stood to make his killing shots found no special clues. Inglis came back to the center of the clearing, held out an arm toward the stream, and squinted along it. "He shot the woman from somewhere in that arc of woods. But he shot at the fox from here near the body."

"If the body was even there yet. I'll grant you the shot."

Inglis shrugged and led some forty paces through the brush to the spot where he'd found the third arrow. The gouge in the ground where it had landed was barely visible. No sign of blood or the struggles of a dying animal.

"Can you, ah, smell a trail?" Pen asked him.

"Not exactly. My nose is no keener than any man's. It's just something I attend to more closely."

As his second sight was granting him nothing, Pen was content to follow Inglis's first nose. They wandered generally toward the hidden stream, eyes on the ground. The shaman, too, had hunted in his youth; the Raven Range from which his kin hailed was not as breathlessly high as the mountains in the cantons, but they'd been rugged enough. So Pen was not too surprised when Inglis stopped at the streambank, pointed down, and said "Ah," in a tone of satisfaction.

Fox prints dappled the mud, though only a few. More useful were a couple of human dents, one of which lay half-atop a pawprint, plus a deep round pock that might have been from a walking stick. "Someone gave chase. Or tracked," said Inglis.

Pen tried matching the prints with his own, off to the side, and examined the results. The original footprint was a touch longer, quite a bit wider, and deeper. "Long stride, or running. A heavier man than me."

"Most men are, surely." But Inglis made a similar test on the other side, and allowed, "Heavier than me, as well."

"The arrow was undamaged, but he didn't stop to pick it up," Pen noted.

"Might have been dark by then."

"Not so dark he didn't take a long shot at a fast-moving fox. And nearly hit it."

"Hm."

They picked up the tracks on the other side of the stream. The fox's were quickly lost, the man's soon after, although a few broken branches or ambiguous scrapes in the soil led them onward. After about two miles of thrashing through the steep and treacherous undergrowth, Inglis, huffing, plunked down on a fallen log and said, "That's it for me."

Penric joined him, catching his breath and staring around. This tract measured some six or seven miles on a side, giving something like forty or fifty square miles of precipitous green woods. They needed a better plan than blundering around at random.

Inglis scratched his sweating chin. "So, I gather you are thinking this fox might have picked up your missing demon?"

Penric opened his hands in doubt. "Not an impossibility. Although any human, no matter how unsavory, would have been a first choice for it. A fox before a bird or squirrel, though."

"You once told me that demons always try to jump higher, to a larger or more powerful animal, or person to a more powerful person."

"If they can."

"What happens if one can't? If it is forced downward?"

Penric sighed. "What do you think would happen to you, if someone tried to force your body into a box half its size?"

Inglis's brows twitched up. "Nothing very pleasant. Crushed, I suppose. Maybe bits cut off."

"Something like that, I gather. Except happening to a mind instead of a body."

"But a demon isn't a material thing. Shouldn't it be more . . . foldable?"

"'Spirit cannot exist in the world without matter to sustain it,'" Penric quoted. "Maybe it's more like . . . being forced to exist on half the food and water and air you require. Or a shrub transplanted with nine-tenths of its roots amputated. Or I-don't-know what material metaphor. But this demon, if I understand Hamo aright, contained imprints of at least three human minds and lives including, now, Magal's, together with any animals that went before. That's not a small demon."

"So . . . somewhere out there is a very smart fox?" He added meticulously, "Assuming the fox."

"Smart, mentally mutilated, and insane. Or worse."

"Wait. The woman who was murdered is now in the fox?" Inglis considered this. "You might want to add *angry* to that list."

"Angry, bewildered, terrified, the Bastard knows what." Well, He probably did, at that. Pen hoped the soul of Magal had found deep comfort in His care. The image of Magal . . . required another caretaker. And Penric was horribly afraid he could guess just who the god had tapped for the task.

Time to earn your keep, O Learned Divine? said Des, amused. *As I recall the Saint of Idau once gave us a warning about that.*

Mm. Pen sighed, not happily. *Any suggestions, Des?*

An impression of a shrug. *Such manly sports as fox hunts were never ours. Well, Aulia hawked as a girl in Brajar. Sugane set snares, though her most notable weapon was a rusty spear. Rogaska killed more chickens than any fox, but she didn't need to hunt them farther than her father's farmyard. Still . . .* She turned Pen's head. *Try over that way.*

"Let's take a cast up there." Pen pointed, and with a shrug Inglis rose to follow him. They pulled their way upslope from sapling to sapling, then came out onto a stretch of flatter, less obstructed ground. Penric, for a moment, tried to control his busy mind and just let himself drift, or be drawn.

"Oh," said Inglis, and his stride lengthened. After a few more paces Pen could hear it too, a muffled whine.

Near the base of an oak tree, they found the pit-trap, sprung and occupied. Inglis knelt to clear away the disordered concealing branches, and they both peered down. A smell of dubious fish, elderly pork fat, and the sharp reek of fox wafted out to greet them. The trap's resident cowered and bared its teeth up at them, growling.

"A fox," said Pen, "but not our fox."

"I can sense that. Hm."

The pit did not seem to be freshly dug, but it had been freshly straightened and, of course, freshly baited. And not, evidently, with poisoned bait.

"Why trap a fox alive?" Pen mused.

"Keeping the pelt intact?"

"Fall or winter is the season for good pelts."

"Any season will do for farmers warring on vermin," Inglis noted.

"Then why not use a snare or an iron trap?"

They both stood back and frowned down at this new puzzle.

"Hoy! You there!" a brusque voice yelled.

Pen's gaze jerked up to find a man in huntsman's leathers approaching them, his bow drawn. He scowled more fiercely than the fox. But he hesitated as his auditors failed to run away like surprised poachers.

Despite this check, he gathered his resolve and went on, "What are you doing trespassing on Pikepool lands? I'll see you off!"

Penric, his eyes on the bent bow and trying to make out the fletching on the nocked arrow, scrambled over the blank in his mind and came out with, "Ah, you must be Baron kin Pikepool's forester! I met Wegae and his willowy wife last night at Princess Llewanna's dinner. He recommended his woods to my attention. Permit me to introduce myself." Penric managed a short, polite nod, aristocrat to servant. "Lord Penric kin Jurald." He elbowed Inglis.

"Inglis kin Wolfcliff," Inglis came through, though he cast Pen an eyebrow-lift. That high kin name, certainly, would be recognized by any Wealding. Pen let the notion that they were here by some lordly invitation stand implied.

"Aye . . . " The bow lowered, thankfully, although the suspicious glower remained. Arrows that he could see *coming* were no threat to a sorcerer, but Pen decided he'd rather not reveal his calling just yet. "I'm the baron's man."

"Oh, very good!" said Penric, with a cheer he hoped did not sound too desperate. "Then you can tell us about this trap."

The man stared at him anew. "It's a pit trap. As any foo—man can see."

"I see, well, smell you baited it for foxes. Got one, too, very good."

"Aye . . . ?"

"Have foxes been a particular problem around here lately?"

"Vermin's always a problem." Slowly, the man eased the bowstring, un-nocked his arrow, and returned it to his quiver. "We clear them out from time to time."

Penric smiled and rubbed his neck. "How many foxes might live in these woods, d'you think, Inglis?"

By his expression, Inglis was not following this start, but he shrugged. "You might find one to three on a square mile, usually, for land like this. More this time of year, when the new pups take to the field."

"So . . . anywhere from fifty to a couple of hundred? My word. That's a lot of foxes," Pen marveled, trying for an air of city enthusiasm. The bowman winced, though whether at Pen's tone or his arithmetic was unclear. "I had no idea. You certainly have your work cut out for you, forester! And what would your name be?"

The man gave it up reluctantly: "Treuch."

Penric backed up from the pit and waved as though inviting the man to partake of a repast. "Well, don't let us impede your work. Carry on, Treuch!"

On the way, Pen managed a closer look at the fletching bristling from the quiver. Similar to the arrows they'd found yesterday, but not obviously identical. Unhelpful.

Do you make anything of him, Des?

Seems very tense. But he would be, encountering trespassers who outnumber him, and younger men at that.

Treuch might be any age from his mid-thirties to his mid-forties—a forester's life was no easy one. He seemed about Inglis's height and weight, if more bowed. But he donned a pair of thick leather gauntlets and lowered himself into the pit with considerable agility, first trapping the animal between his knees and muzzling its bite with a swift wrapping of rawhide cord, then binding its feet and lifting it out. Inglis, unasked, bent to help in this task. The fox, which had snarled at the huntsman, shrank from the wolf-shaman and whimpered.

Treuch managed a gruff, "Thankee," as he clambered back out. He rebaited the trap with some offal from his pack, then arranged the concealing branches and leaves once more. Slinging the squirming animal over his shoulder, he stood and regarded his unwanted visitors.

"Best you see yourselves out of the woods, and watch your step when you do. I've some snares set about as well. But Dorra, the alewife up at Weir village, makes a good brew. If you go out that way, likely you can quench a gentlemanly thirst there speedily enough."

"Good advice," said Pen, "on both counts. Shall we wend our way to Dorra, Inglis?"

"If you say so," said Inglis.

"Good hunting," Pen called over his shoulder as they tromped off in the opposite direction to the fox-burdened forester.

They kept walking, carefully, only until the man was out of earshot before stopping in mutual accord.

"You want to follow that fellow?" asked Inglis quietly.

"Absolutely."

They turned and retraced their steps, much more silently.

Treuch made his way through more of the trackless stretch, then turned onto a trail and strode faster. Penric and Inglis kept just out of sight behind him, although they almost came to grief when he turned aside to check a snare. They hunkered down until he returned to the path. After about two miles, he came to an open area. Pen and Inglis stopped at the shaded verge, concealing themselves in an overgrown copse.

An old stone building, half castle, half farmhouse, rose tall and brown on the far side of the wide cleared area. Some thatch-roofed houses of wattle-and-daub in various states of disrepair clustered at its feet, along with a stable set in an L around its own courtyard. Wood fences pastured a pair of oxen and a few horses. A better-mended fence set off a large kitchen garden.

The forester disappeared around the side of the stable, then returned in a few minutes, foxless. He trudged off to the stone house and let himself in through a heavy oak door. The yard fell silent.

The sheer face of the manor house boasted very few eyes, its windows small, deep set, and, as nearly as Pen could tell at this distance, very dirty. "Do you sense anyone else about?"

Inglis nodded toward a chimney in one of the daub houses, venting smoke from a cooking fire. "Likely people in there."

"Hm. Well, they'll be busy about their tasks. Let's see what he did with that fox."

Inglis shrugged but followed behind Penric, his curiosity, too, overcoming his prudence.

The stable had once been meant for more horses, judging by the number and generous proportions of the stalls. All its current residents seemed to be out in the pasture, leaving several doors hanging open or half open. Only one stall had both the top and bottom halves of its door latched.

Gently, trying to make no squeak, Pen unlatched the top and swung it part open. He blinked to try to adjust his eyes to the shadows, then gave up and thought, *Des, light.*

Some half-a-dozen, no, seven unhappy foxes were imprisoned within. Some lay in the straw panting in apparent exhaustion, others crouched as far from their fellows as they could get, growling. Several were bleeding from fox fights. The hostile atmosphere, Pen thought, was much the same as one might get by jamming seven sorcerers and their demons into a similar space.

"That," Inglis muttered, "is a decidedly odd thing to do with foxes."

"Really. If that fellow spoke the truth about thinning the local vermin, they should all be pelts tacked to the stable wall by now, waiting for the women servants to get around to scraping them."

"So what's next? I might add, my probationary status with the Fellowship would not be helped by my being either arrested for trespassing, or for getting into a fight trying to avoid being arrested for trespassing."

"Yet . . . hm. You have a valid point. We need Oswyl up here in order to go much further."

"For what? It's not against the law to trap foxes. Especially by a forester on his own lord's land."

"All right. That's a problem, too." Convincing the somewhat rigid Oswyl of . . . what? Even Pen wasn't sure.

Inglis snorted softly. "It does look like, if you were craving to survey all the foxes on this land, someone seems to be doing it for you. Might be easier to stand off and wait."

"Except there is one fox out there I'd rather no one catch but me."

"I wonder if anyone *could* catch it but you?"

"Hm." Which led directly to the uncomfortable question of the state of mind of the lost demon, trapped in a lower animal that could not support it. It might (if indeed in a fox, not yet proved) make a very shrewd fox indeed. Or it might make for a drowning agony of confusion and despair. Easily mistaken for a sick fox by anyone, and thereby hung a whole host of other hazards.

"I'd want to find out what Oswyl has uncovered today, first," said Inglis. "Before . . . "

He didn't complete the thought, but the heartening implication seemed to be that if Pen wanted to try something chancy in aid of all this, he might not have to do it alone. Pen bit his lip, trying to think. They were supposed to meet Oswyl in town for dinner, and there relate the events of each of their days. The light was leveling. By the time they made it back to the hill village of Weir, collected their horses, and rode down into Easthome, it would be well on toward evening.

"I think," said Pen slowly, "we'd better withdraw for tonight, before someone catches us skulking around. Come back tomorrow in better force."

Inglis nodded agreement, and they turned to slip away into the woods. At the last moment Pen stepped back, unlatched the lower door to the stall, and edged it open. Inglis raised his brows but did not comment until they had reached the cover of the copse once more. As they paused to look back, they saw one rusty streak, then another, flit around the corner of the stable and speed for the forest.

"Two hundred foxes," Inglis murmured. "Do you think your god has His thumb in all this?"

"Oh, yes," sighed Pen, signed himself, and tapped his lips twice.

The tavern where they were to rendezvous was a modest place, tucked up in an alley not far from the big chapterhouse of the Father's Order on the Templetown heights. They found Oswyl and his assistant arrived before them, though not by much, in a small upstairs chamber, a compromise between cheap and private. But the pitcher of beer the servant brought was decent, the tureen of stew contained identifiable meat, the bread and butter were abundant, and Penric, by this time, was starving. The servant's presence gave them all a welcome head start on the meal, but at last he decamped, closing the door behind him.

Though town-clean, Oswyl looked even more tired than Pen felt after barging around in the woods all day. Both Oswyl and his assistant Thala, who Penric gathered was also his apprentice, were dressed in their most formal gray uniforms, having just come from Learned Magal's funeral; it being high summer, the ceremony had not been delayed. Penric was relieved to learn that the Easthome sacred animals had plainly signed her soul as taken up by the white god.

"Her service was very well attended," Thala remarked. "Whoever killed her either did not know or did not care how much his deed would have her entire Easthome Order up in arms against him."

"Aye," said Oswyl. "Although I spoke to as many as I could, and their most common response after anger was bewilderment. Kin and colleagues both. Usually by this time in an inquiry I start to have some direction, some odd crack, some . . . unpleasant smell, but not here. She seems to have been the most blameless woman imaginable. I'd feel myself forced back to *shot by mistake for a deer*, except no one had any idea what she was doing out in those woods in the first place. Either she'd told no one of her errand, or at least one person was lying to me." He sighed, as if this latter were an irreducible hazard.

"We made a good start on finding out everything she'd done day before yesterday," said Thala, "right down to what she ate for breakfast, but about the third hour of the afternoon she left the chapterhouse and just never came back."

"Afoot?" said Inglis. "Hard to get all the way up to those woods before dark that way. Livery stables . . . ?"

"We're in process of canvassing them all," said Oswyl. "No luck yet."

"Why shoot a sorceress?" Pen mused. "Why murder anyone, for that matter?" Belatedly self-conscious, he managed not to glance at Inglis. "I mean, in a premeditated way."

Oswyl chased a bite of bread with a long swallow of beer, then sat back. "Some reasons are more common than others."

"Money?" asked Inglis. "An inheritance . . . ?"

"Money to be sure, but inheritances very rarely. Usually murder happens in the course of a robbery. Next most common is some brawl or ambush after losses at play, and after that, debt."

"Her purse was still tied to her belt," observed Thala, "though it didn't hold much, and those little pearl earrings were still in her ears. No ordinary cutpurse would have left either. Stolen demons I can't speak to."

Oswyl nodded at her in a mentor's approval. "Magal was an orphan, she didn't gamble, and she neither owed nor was owed money," he said. "We've checked all that. She owned no property. What she inherited from her late husband went to her daughter's dowry and her son's apprenticeship."

"Temple divines are seldom rich," Penric noted.

"To hear them complain of it, no, yet they seldom go hungry," said Oswyl. Penric considered his dinner of last night, and let this comment go by. Oswyl continued, "But no, I'm . . . let's say I would be surprised if money turns out to be an issue in this.

"Then there's jealousy. And not just rivalries of the bedchamber, in all their customary variations. Siblings. Colleagues, fellow workmen, fellow students. The envy by one with lesser skill or luck of those with greater. Some very corrosive emotions, there. Except I've found nothing of that sort hanging on Learned Magal's robes, either. So far." He drank again, and frowned. "An odd sort of fellow traveler with jealousy and envy is revenge. That one can be tricky. People, and not just the stupid sort, can decide that the most absurd things were an unbearable slight to them. And not necessarily in retaliation for some wrongdoing, or in some cases even right-doing, as we of the Father's Order have sometimes suffered." He grimaced in memory. "Not all who experience justice appreciate it."

"That has possibilities," said Penric. "A sorcerer might easily perform some legitimate act in service of their duties to which some caught-out wrong-doer might take exception. The person to ask in that case would be Learned Hamo."

"If it were obvious, I'd think he should have thought of it sooner than this, and volunteered the information," said Oswyl. "Nonetheless, yes, it does seem worth asking again." He sopped up the last of his stew with a morsel of bread. "So much for our day in town." As exhausting as it had been fruitless, apparently. "What of yours in the woods?"

Penric and Inglis took turns recounting their tale. Oswyl listened intently, his scowl set, till Penric came to his theory of the two hundred foxes, whereupon he looked deeply pained.

Inglis chewed on his knuckle for a moment. "Regarding the fox problem, Pen. I think I might get us some help with that."

"Help how? Ordinary searchers won't be able to tell one fox from another."

"I wasn't thinking of ordinary searchers. But I'll have to ask around before I can make any promises. I'll see what I can find tonight, after this."

Penric wasn't used to thinking of help in Temple matters, given both the solitary nature of demons and the rarity of sorcerers. He wasn't sure whether to give credence to Inglis's words or not, but decided it would be premature to melt with relief.

"Oh," said Penric, "I should add, I met Baron kin Pikepool last night. He and his wife were at a dinner at Princess Llewanna's town mansion."

Oswyl's brows climbed. "Rarified company."

Penric, who had not found it to be all that rarified, shrugged. "He didn't seem to have heard of the murder on his land yet, and I didn't say anything about it. Is he on your list of people to talk to?"

"Very much so. Today, by preference, except that the funeral ran long and I am almost out of today. What did you make of him?"

Penric wondered if he meant, as a suspect? "Young. Bookish. Interesting for that."

"Many men of his rank are skillful sportsmen."

"Not him—bad eyes. Apparently a lifelong affliction. If you are looking for a bowman, he's not it." Not that kin Pikepool couldn't have hired such a mercenary, and easier than most, if his purse was as deep as it had appeared. But why?

Around a last bite, Thala put in, "I was able to speak briefly with one of the kin Pikepool maidservants this morning. She said her lord spent day-before-yesterday at home, and he and his lady wife had friends in for dinner, who stayed late." She mopped her lips, thoughtfully. "He sounded an unexceptionable employer, if not lordly enough to suit some in his household. The main objection seems to be that he routinely feeds a pack of poor hangers-on from his university days."

Which sounded more like people Pen would care to meet than most of last night's company.

"It would be an odd plan," said Inglis, "for a calculating murderer to leave the body to be found on his own land." He hesitated. "Unless it was someone trying to cast suspicion in kin Pikepool's direction."

"More likely," said Oswyl, "is that the body was intended to be better concealed, but that the murderer didn't get back to do so before it was discovered."

"Because he suddenly decided to chase a fox? Through those dire woods, at night? All night?" said Penric. "That's a very distractible murderer. Or a very important fox."

"You are thinking it bore away Magal's demon, yes? And her murderer knew it?" said Oswyl. "It may be so, but why give chase? If it is as you describe, the demon would be crippled, impotent. And, certainly, unable to accuse her killer."

"Which brings me back to the question, why was the kin Pikepool forester hunting foxes today?" said Penric. "And taking care to catch them alive, which is not the usual approach to foxes."

Oswyl sighed. "So I will add the kin Pikepool forester to my list. After the baron."

"Please." Penric nodded. "He might have been physically capable of the act. Still leaves the problem of why."

Oswyl drummed his fingers on the table and frowned. Some more. "This is not the first time that kin Pikepool has come to the attention of justice in Easthome. But I'm not seeing a connection."

"Oh?" said Penric, trying, and failing, to imagine how Wegae and his willowy spouse could possibly have done so. "Was he caught stealing books?"

Oswyl blinked, then said, "Oh. Not the present baron. His predecessor. Uncle, I think. He was accused of pushing his wife down the stairs during some marital spat. Broke her neck in the fall. Two, three years ago. The tribunal was truncated when the accused man fled the realm. But after some legal delays, his title and property were sequestered for the crime, and passed along to the nephew. I suppose they couldn't leave the estate without management. I don't remember if the old baron was rumored to have died abroad. This is hearsay, by the way. I didn't work on the case—given the status of those involved, it was too far above my head."

"I don't suppose this uncle was a burly bowman?"

"No idea. But that he's a thousand miles away, or dead, and has no known history with Learned Magal whatsoever, disinclines me to get too excited."

"That first could be reversed," noted Inglis. "Not the second, I grant."

"Mm." Oswyl glanced across at Penric. "Would you be willing to come along with me to kin Pikepool tonight? I should like to borrow your rank."

"Which one?" said Penric. "Learned divine? Sorcerer?"

"Those as well, but I was thinking of your kin rank. That is"— Oswyl cleared his throat—"you once told me your father was a baron, Penric, but you had not mentioned whether your mother was a baron's wife."

Irregular birth was a common assumption about members of the Bastard's Order, and too often correct for Penric to take offense. "Very much so, although she's a baron's widow now. There were seven of us, my three sisters and three brothers. And then me, the youngest."

Oswyl nodded. "It will serve to get us in the front door. And not the servants' entrance. Kin lords can be, mm, difficult to deal with to those not of the highest echelon of Temple inquirers, themselves with kin bonds."

"I'd have thought your Temple calling was a password for every portal."

"Unfortunately not." Oswyl paused, eyes narrowing in curiosity. "Why, is yours?"

Penric had never thought about it. "I've . . . not tried every portal yet."

Oswyl snorted, and rose. "Well, let us see how you work to open this one."

❖ ❖ ❖

The kin Pikepool townhouse lay farther out from the Hallow King's Hall than the lordly mansion of last night, on a narrower street. The row of dwellings was more modest but more recently built, also of the cut stone so common in the capital replacing, by fire and fiat, so many earlier wooden structures. The young baron was evidently sociable enough to keep two cressets bracketing his entry burning in the early night, with a porter to tend them and the door.

"Learned Lord Penric kin Jurald of Martensbridge to see Baron kin Pikepool, upon an urgent Temple matter," Penric told this functionary, thinking of his princess-archdivine's tutorials. "And colleagues." Alas that he hadn't had time to return to his room and change into his whites with his shoulder braids, which spoke so firmly for him. But the porter, after a wary glance at his grubby person and the tidier Grayjays, gave way at least to the point of leaving them standing in the hall rather than on the step while he went to find out if his master was receiving such odd company. He disappeared into a doorway off the single central hallway, returning soon after.

"This way, Learned," and, entering before them, "Learned Lord Penric, my lord. And party."

They entered a pleasant bookroom, primarily furnished with a writing desk behind which their host-and-quarry sat with papers and ledgers spread out. Oil lamps and wall sconces relieved the evening shadows, warming the room quite enough without a fire in the grate. Wegae's eyes, magnified by his spectacles, widened with interest at the pair Penric trailed. "Ah, yes. It's all right, Jons." He unfolded from his chair and came around his desk, receiving Penric standing, as an equal.

Pen ran through the introductions, with no reaction from Wegae beyond baffled curiosity. They were invited to two cushion-padded benches set across from each other before the dark fireplace. The porter brought around the desk chair to make up the numbers, which Wegae took. Penric politely declined Wegae's offer of refreshments, and the servant went off. Penric and Oswyl glanced across at each other. When Oswyl did not at once take the lead, Penric opened his hand to him; he seemed to take a breath like a swimmer before plunging in.

"Yesterday morning, the lay dedicat from the village temple at Weir was checking snares in your woods nearby, when he came across the body of a woman," Oswyl began. "His divine sent promptly to the

Father's Order. I was dispatched to examine the scene, together with, later, Learned Penric and Shaman Inglis."

"Five gods," said Wegae, and signed himself in reflexive dismay. "Who was she? What had happened to her?"

Oswyl's narrow look at this first reaction evidently found nothing to pause for—Pen wasn't sure if he was disappointed—for he went on to summarize the scene much as he had for Learned Hamo. "She proved to be an Easthome Temple sorceress, Learned Magal. Do you know the woman? Ever meet or see her?"

Wegae, wide-eyed, shook his head from side to side. "I direct my devotions to the Father's Order these days. I've not had much to do with the house of the white god. They'd always seemed rather strange and secretive, over there. Um." He looked briefly as if he'd like to swallow back that last remark, considering present company, but it was too late and he forged on. "I'd not even met a sorcerer to talk to before Learned Lord Penric last night. Wait." He blinked, turning his head to Pen. "Did you know about this then? Is that why you spoke to me?"

There seemed no reason to dissimulate. "Yes, and yes."

"Why didn't you say anything?"

"At Princess Llewanna's party?" Pen countered, dodging the question nimbly.

Wegae seemed to accept this: "Oh, of course." He scrubbed his hand through his hair, but his stare at Pen remained round. Maybe it was just the spectacles? "Why would anyone do such a heinous thing?"

"That is my puzzle to solve," said Oswyl, "and it's proving peculiar. How she was killed was clear enough. Why is still unknown. It was not theft. The only treasure she bore was her Temple demon, which seems to have, ah, escaped. Perhaps you could speak to that, Penric?"

Penric cleared his throat. "Our present best guess was that when Magal died, her demon jumped to a passing fox, which ran off into your woods. The murderer seems to have given it chase, futilely. Learned Hamo, Magal's Temple superior, has passed me the mandate to locate and secure the lost demon, which we think is still somewhere on your lands."

"Oh," said Wegae. "Did you wish permission to search my woods? Certainly you may."

"Thank you," said Penric, wondering if this was an opportune opening for a confession. *If you're going to, yes,* opined Des. Ah, so she was listening in, good. "In fact, Shaman Inglis and I took a preliminary look up that way earlier today."

"What did you find?" Wegae asked, his interest in the tragedy clearly overshadowing any concern about trespassers on land he never visited. He could have chosen to be sticky about that.

"Not the fox we were looking for, unfortunately. But we did encounter your forester, Treuch, who was very busy about the woods— trapping foxes. He'd secured seven of them alive, so far. I will say, he did his job for you by inviting us to leave."

"Treuch." Wegae grimaced. "He quite frightened me as a boy, when I was dragged up there to try to teach me the sports of a nobleman. I was only my uncle's heir presumptive at that point, his poor wife not yet having proved barren, so eventually my complete ineptitude frustrated them into desisting. Thankfully."

"You could dismiss him now, if you don't like him," Pen noted.

"Oh, I couldn't do that! He's been a kin Pikepool retainer for ages and ages. He knows no other life."

"But you may see," said Oswyl, "why I also wish to obtain your permission to question your people."

"Oh," said Wegae again, more thoughtfully. "Do you think Treuch could have had something to do with it? I mean, he's a hardy man, but he's not . . . I could picture him killing someone in a drunken brawl, except that he doesn't brawl. Or drink that much."

"Either he has something to do, or knows something about it," suggested Oswyl.

Pen considered yet again his theory of a man killing a woman by mistake for a deer. "If he shot someone in error, thinking them an animal or a poacher, would he run off, or report it?"

"I should think report it, although . . . a Temple sorceress would be a very alarming victim for the man." He added after a moment, "For any man."

"Do you think he would be physically capable of such an act? Putting two arrows through a person at that distance?" asked Oswyl.

"Well, yes, but . . . " Wegae shrugged unhappily. "Many men might have that skill. My late uncle, for one."

And himself, for another, Pen reflected. *Could* wasn't *would*. *Necessary but not sufficient*, as his mentors had tagged arguments in seminary.

Wegae went on, "Uncle Halber was a passionate hunter, and skilled in all the usual manly sports. Riding, wrestling, you name it."

"What exactly happened to him?" asked Oswyl.

Wegae looked surprised. "Do you not know? I thought everybody did."

"Only in broad outline. His was not my case, and those inquirers and justiciars most closely involved were obliged not to gossip about it."

Bet they do anyway, murmured Des, *in the halls of their house. Even the Father's devotees are not so inhumanly rigid.*

Hsh, thought Pen back, though he privately agreed.

"I'm not sure I know that much more myself," said Wegae. "I was working as a lay dedicat for the Father's Order at Shallowford at the time, and only had letters from my mother and sister about the matter, and from the lawyers, until the legal issues were settled and I was sent for. My mother was following things more closely here in Easthome, on my behalf. You might ask her. It was all so very disturbing. Although it did involve a Temple sorceress, come to think."

"Who?" Oswyl and Penric both asked at once.

"Not Magal. What was her name?" He knuckled his forehead. "Sverda. Or Svedra, one of those."

Pen came off-point, letting his breath back out. "Locator Oswyl has likely heard more of the tale than I have. Could you begin at the beginning?"

"Insofar as I know it. My aunt was found dead at the bottom of the main staircase of the old manor house, assumed to have broken her neck in an accidental fall, unwitnessed. It would have passed quietly as a private tragedy, but at her funeral no sacred animal signed her soul as taken up. At my mother's insistence, a Temple sensitive was dispatched at once to look for her ghost, lest her soul be sundered. That was this Learned, um, Svedra. She testified to have found my aunt's shade, repeatedly acting out a different tale on the stairs. She would have it that she was pushed down by her husband, presumably in the midst of one of their many disputes—I have to admit, she was a notable shrew—"

"Not normally a capital crime," Thala muttered almost inaudibly into her notebook, where she'd been industriously jotting.

"Although any woman married to my uncle, well, never mind. And then, apparently, he descended after her to twist her neck to be sure. It might have started as an accident, but it didn't seem to have finished as one, or so it was charged. Anyway, Uncle Halber was arrested on the suspicion, and somewhere in the proceedings seems to have gone over the line from protests to self-justifications. Confession of a sort, I suppose, although not repentance."

"What happened to your aunt?" asked Penric. "Was she sundered?"

"At the very last, no. She'd resisted the prayers performed at the stairs to send her on her way until her husband was finally arrested, but then she consented to go to her goddess. The Daughter, in the end, by her second rites. I hope she found some comfort there. She'd had little enough in life."

The assistant glanced up from her notebook, and asked curiously, "Can ghosts lie?"

Oswyl gave her query an approving nod. "I would never take such testimony as definitive on its own without some cross-check. Or several cross-checks, by preference. At most, it is a pointer, one more scent to follow up."

Good question, Des, Pen thought. Can *ghosts lie?*

Well, they're not usually any smarter *than they were in life . . . Although they can be mistaken, or still in the grip of the passions that are forcing them to linger. Your friend Oswyl is wise not to take them at face value. As their sundering proceeds, all that fades away, of course.*

"The whole case drew in any number of inquirers and divines and lawyers and judges before it was done," Wegae allowed, "because of my uncle's status. If there was any stone left unturned, it wasn't for lack of trying. I was surprised there was any of the estate left by the time they were all done."

Oswyl dipped his chin in rueful understanding of this.

"How did he come to escape?" asked Pen.

"He was too lightly guarded, I suppose. He was being kept at Magpie House, not the municipal prison, although he was supposed to be moved there once he was sentenced. He must have had help, and a horse, from somewhere."

"How do you know he's dead?" asked Oswyl.

"We had a letter from some mercenary captain in Ibra, addressed to kin Pikepool generally in Easthome, a sort of to-whom-it-may-concern missive—I suspect those captains have practice at the task."

The news about Penric's brother Drovo dying in that mercenary camp in Adria had come from such a captain, although additionally from a friend, Pen was reminded.

"Could it have been forged?" asked Oswyl.

"I've no idea, really." Wegae paused in brief reflection. "On the whole, I hope not. We gave it to the lawyer to keep with the other estate documents—he should still have it, if you wish to examine it."

"Maybe later," said Oswyl, "should it prove in any way pertinent. We've more immediate concerns. May we go up on your lands tomorrow?"

"Yes, certainly. Would you like me to go with you, to smooth things over? The people there don't take well to city strangers, and it's been too long since I visited. I'm supposed to be overseeing it responsibly. The lawyers were very firm on that point." He pushed up his spectacles and vented a small sigh. "The old manor neither produces nor consumes much, but it can't be farmed, the timber is hard to extract, and it has no known minerals. I suppose a hunting preserve remains its best use."

"That might be helpful," allowed Oswyl.

They spent a few minutes arranging a rendezvous for the expedition in the early morning. Wegae himself saw his three visitors to his door, student fashion. Penric wondered if he had not grasped, or just didn't believe in, the much stiffer public manners of most older men of his rank. (The private manners of barons Penric had no illusions about.) Oswyl seemed something between impressed by this extraordinary courtesy and suspicious. Since the latter was his usual mode, Pen gave more weight to the former. The long summer twilight had faded into full dark; the porter lent them a lantern, to be returned on the morrow, which Thala dutifully took charge of.

As they were making their way back through the shadowed streets of Kingstown, Oswyl said, "That went more easily than most of my encounters with kin lords. I should keep you around, Penric."

"Mm, I don't think it was all my doing. Wegae seems a man who'd rather be back in his university life, except without the poverty. No one misses the poverty. And he probably wouldn't be willing to give up his marriage for it, either."

"Understandable."

They were climbing the Templetown stairs when Penric, noting the private moment, thought to ask, "Whatever happened to Inglis's heartthrob, Tolla kin Boarford? His letters stopped mentioning her, and he's not said anything to me since I've been here."

Thala gave a slight twitch, as though she wanted to bring out her notebook, but continued climbing ahead of Oswyl, lantern lifted and eyes resolutely forward.

Oswyl's lips twisted, half grimace, half amused. "She became betrothed to someone else. He's been glum ever since."

Pen reflected on this. "How can you tell the difference?"

Oswyl barked a short laugh. "Glummer, then. I was relieved for him, myself. I did not see how that arrangement could ever prosper, in the long run, after what happened to her poor brother. I thought he should rest content with her forgiveness, which he did surely earn, and not bay for the moon."

"Did you say so?"

"Of course not."

Penric grinned, and saved the rest of his breath for the climb.

Reaching the Templetown heights, they stopped first by what proved to be a sort of boarding house for single female devotees of the Father's Order, where Oswyl scrupulously saw his assistant safely inside. They parted company then, heading toward their respective beds.

Pen was entirely ready for his. He wondered if he might attend on the princess-archdivine in his day dirt and wash after, to speed things up. He didn't want to risk knocking at her chambers after she'd retired. And it wasn't as though he had any definitive news to report, just a mess of miscellaneous information and far too many foxes.

Des commandeered his mouth to speak aloud, breaking through his bleary musings. "Pen."

"What?"

"Ask Learned Hamo what sorceress held Magal's demon before her."

Pen stopped short in the street, his tilting mind seeming to whirl onto a whole new axis. After a blinking moment, he said, "Huh."

"Because there were two victims in that clearing, and Oswyl is only asking after the history of one of them."

"A man would have to be mad . . . "

"Some men are."

"This is a great leap, Des. With not nearly enough evidence to hold it in the air. Oswyl would sniff at my fancies."

"So good you are a member of the white god's order and not the gray's, then. Are not furious fancies in His gift?"

"Along with obscene verse, but yes."

"*Ask*, Pen," she repeated, a little impatiently. "We just need an answer, not an argument."

"Aye." He changed directions and began striding toward the Bastard's chapterhouse, recalculating people's bedtimes and willingness to be visited at them by a grubby, overexcited sorcerer. Within a few paces, he was jogging. He wasn't actually sure if Hamo lived in at the chapterhouse, the way Magal had. Well, the porter would know his address if not. If anyone else besides Pen and Oswyl was likely to be haunting the night over this matter, it was Hamo.

He arrived breathless to be scrutinized by the night porter, whom they'd briefly interviewed yesterday, and who thus recognized and admitted him even without his whites and his braids. The man tried to make Pen wait in the stone-paved hall while he went to inquire if Hamo would receive him, but Pen dogged his heels, and he hadn't quite the nerve to insist. Their first stop was Hamo's work chamber. Pen was not too surprised to see yellow candlelight sifting through the doorway.

Hamo squinted up from his writing desk, his quill paused in air. He was still dressed in his most formal white tunic from the funeral, although his outer robe and braids hung on a peg on the wall. "Ah. Learned Penric. What brings you to me at this—"

Pen blurted, "The sorceress who held Learned Magal's demon before her. Was it a Learned Sverda?"

Hamo's gray brows rose in surprise. "Svedra, but yes. Why do you ask?"

Pen let his shoulders thump against the doorframe. The name felt like a stone thrown into a murky pond, creating agitation but no clarity. "Mention of her came up earlier this evening, in connection with an investigation she once performed as a Temple sensitive."

"She performed many such, in her time," said Hamo. "Why don't you come sit down? You look a little, ah . . . " He did not complete the description, but Pen didn't doubt it. Hamo waved the anxious, and curious, porter back to his post. Deprived of his chance to eavesdrop, the man seemed to depart in some disappointment.

Pen pulled a chair around and sank into it. And then felt at a loss, his thoughts all so newly disarrayed.

"What brought up Svedra?" Hamo prompted him, setting aside his quill and papers.

"I hardly like to say yet. It's all wild supposition."

Hamo's eyes narrowed. "Go on anyway."

"What if—" Penric paused, Oswyl's remarks about not leading a witness dancing in his head. "Do you remember any of her assignments as particularly fraught?"

Hamo leaned back in his chair and tapped his fingers against each other. "Not especially, but I don't know them all. I'd only been her supervisor for five years before she had her fatal stroke a few months ago. She'd held her demon for over three decades. I may have been her appointed Temple bailiff, but she was much my elder in age and experience. She mostly chose her own tasks and went where she pleased. Which tends to be the way of senior sorcerers. Sorceresses even more so." He winced in some memory he did not confide.

This wasn't getting there—fast enough—Pen led anyway. "About three years ago, she was called out to lend her Sight and expertise to a domestic murder inquiry involving Baron Halber kin Pikepool, yes?"

Hamo's attention sharpened. "An unpleasant fellow, by her remarks. Yes, she was in and out on that several times. Trips to the country, and much back and forthing to the Father's Order, the city magistrates, and the Hallow King's court. There were disputes over jurisdictions, which we tried our best to leave to them. The gods having no such boundaries." He hesitated. "But I thought the man was dead. All disposals in the hands of higher Powers now."

"There was a letter. But not a body, nor any eyewitness account of one."

"Mm . . . ?"

"Imagine . . . " When out on thin ice, move fast, had been a lesson of Pen's canton mountain boyhood. Did it apply here? "Picture a proud, hard man who has lost everything, and been brought as low as humanly possible, facing an ignoble death. Who did it to himself, but only blamed others." *Indeed, there's only half a chance his* wife *was the infertile one,* Des put in. "Fled from justice into self-exile, but then, for whatever reason . . . " Yes, why? Pen was having a hard time positing why a fellow who had got away clear would put himself back at such risk. *That's because you don't think like that,* said Des. *Thankfully.* "This is all utter speculation, you understand."

"Go *on*, Learned Penric," said Hamo, more tightly.

"Suppose he came back for revenge on those he blamed and hated for his downfall. And found the sorceress whose accusation had destroyed him beyond his reach, but her Temple demon . . . not." Pen took a gulp of air. "Maybe Magal was no one to him, just a barrier he had to get through to reach his real target."

Hamo gripped the table edge, bent his face down, and swore. Short, horrible, heartfelt words.

Ah. Maybe telling Hamo all this so soon had not been such a good idea. Although witnessing Magal's body had been dismaying, Pen had to admit there had been an element of stimulating intellectual puzzle to it all. For Hamo, this had to be a much more personal outrage.

The more so, Des pointed out, *as Hamo himself put Magal in this harm's way, by choosing her to receive Svedra's demon.*

Ouch, thought Pen weakly. He swallowed, feeling a bit sick.

When Hamo raised his face, it was gray with new tension. "That is a grotesque idea."

"Truly. But it may explain why a woman whom no one disliked . . . "

"Yes." Hamo drew a long breath, letting it out slowly. He lowered his hands from the table edge to his lap, where he clenched them, perhaps to conceal their shaking. After a moment, he said, "Do you really imagine Baron Halber kin Pikepool is still alive? Why?"

"Well . . . One hears of such things. There was such a case in Greenwell Town, when I was a boy. A man came back from the wars after his wife had remarried. It was something of a mess. Or men reported lost at sea, who turn up years later."

"And how many cases where no one came back, making nothing to remark? No tale worth repeating? One hundred to one? Five hundred to one? The exception always gets more attention than the rule. I'm not sure you should race off down this road too quickly."

"I'm not sure I should, either," Pen said frankly. "But I don't think I would have evolved the notion at all without Halber's tale to start the trail of thought." Des sent him an impression of a throat-clearing noise, and he corrected, "We would have," which only caused Hamo to squint at him.

"What does Locator Oswyl think of your theory?"

"I haven't tried it on him yet. I can't imagine it will please him. He prefers firmer evidences."

"I thought you were seeking such, today?"

"Oh." Getting practiced, Pen made short work of describing his and Inglis's day in the woods, the encounter with Treuch, and the elusive scattering of the kin Pikepool foxes. It did not make Hamo look any happier.

"As a suspect, or at least a man engaged in suspicious activities, this forester Treuch does have the advantage of being certainly alive, and present in the area," Hamo pointed out.

"There is that. Baron Wegae didn't seem to see him as a, a plotting sort of fellow, but who knows? Maybe . . . " Pen hesitated. "Would you be able to look back over any records the chapterhouse may maintain of Learned Svedra's assignments, and see if there is anything, mm, overlooked? Other possibilities?"

Hamo grimaced. "Tomorrow. In full light, yes. I will."

"Tomorrow," Pen went on, "we're all going up again to look around the old kin Pikepool manor and forest. If the demon is indeed in a fox, and we find it, maybe . . . it will tell us some more." *How*, Pen couldn't guess.

"If you do find this fox—or Magal's demon howsoever contained— bring it to me unharmed."

"I'll try, sir." Pen hesitated. "What will you do with it?"

Hamo pressed the heels of his hands hard over his eyes, which emerged blinking and reddened. "I have no idea. Yet." He added under his breath, "And here I thought I was finally going to *sleep* tonight . . . "

Penric stretched in his chair, the day's aches catching up with him, his penalty for sitting down. As Hamo did not at once add more, he rose. "I should go. We mean to start out early."

Hamo nodded, waving a weary dismissal. "Yes. Thank you."

"If we find anything more definite, I'll try to let you know as soon as I can."

"Please."

"And if you find anything . . . I'll stop back in tomorrow night after we return?"

"Do, yes."

As Penric reached the door, Hamo spoke again. "Penric . . . "

"Sir?"

"If this mad murderer, whosoever he may prove to be, is still seeking our demon-fox, and you are seeking this same fox . . . Well, just be careful up in those woods, yes?"

"Ah." *There's a thought I should have had sooner.* "Quite so, Learned." Pen touched his thumb to his lips in a parting salute, and took his leave.

Penric, Oswyl, and Thala rendezvoused with Baron Wegae, trailed by his porter-and-groom Jons, in the street before his townhouse while the morning air was still dew-damp. They rode through Kingstown in sleepy silence to the north gate, and out it to the main installation of the Royal Society of Shamans. This had once been a farm beyond the city walls, but the town had grown up around it since, the original wattle-and-daub buildings shouldered aside by more substantial structures. The old rustic fences along the street were replaced by an imposing wooden palisade, shielding the Society's secrets.

They threaded through it all to the menagerie yard, formerly extensive royal stables. Penric had visited here a few days ago at Inglis's invitation to witness the sacrifice of an elderly and tame lynx spirit into a half-grown lynx cub, on its way to making a Great Beast rather more desirable than a worm. The young shaman performing the ritual cuts under the close supervision of his elders had been visibly nervous, but the animal had been strangely serene, and Penric had been put in mind of those tales of people on their deathbeds going gladly to their gods. Except messier, Pen supposed.

No bloody rituals going on this morning, but the last of the short night's cobwebs blew off Penric's brain as he took in the unexpected group that awaited them. Not just Inglis, but three more, yes, shamans were sitting together on the mounting blocks, holding their horses' reins and chatting. All dressed for a day in the country like Pen's party—riding trousers and sturdy boots, with light shirts or sleeveless tunics in anticipation of the day's heat.

Inglis looked up, waved, and rose to make introductions.

"These are my friends Nath"—a big burly fellow, perhaps Oswyl's age—"Kreil"—the bouncy-looking young man in question gave a cheery salute—"and Lunet." The last was a young woman with sandy-red hair and a smattering of freckles across her sharp cheekbones. "They've volunteered to help you hunt for your haunted fox, Penric."

Penric grinned in surprise, instantly envious of the shamanic skills of collaboration, although working alone suited him well for the most part. "Ah, so this is what you went off to find last night. Outstanding idea. Thank you!" Pen took over the task of introducing the Grayjays and Wegae. The shamans, royal pets as they were, seemed not in the least daunted by Wegae's rank, and Wegae in turn appeared openly fascinated by them. He wasn't the only one, although Thala stared more covertly. Lunet eyed her with like interest.

They all mounted up and took the road toward the hills, a substantial cavalcade of nine. A lone murderer, however dangerous, must surely be intimidated by these numbers? Penric hoped so. Readily overcome by his curiosity, Pen turned in his saddle and thought, *Des, Sight.*

Inglis's wolf was its usual more-than-wolfish self. The burly, dark-haired Nath certainly bore a bear, deceptively placid within him. If the eager Kreil didn't house a Great Dog, enthusiastic for this outing, Pen would very surprised. Of them all, only the ruddy Lunet lifted her chin and glanced keenly back at him, poised in stillness, instantly conscious of his more-than-gaze. Great Fox, indeed. That might prove handy.

Penric wondered if their Beasts had been matched to their persons in advance, or if the young shamans had taken on aspects of their possessions after acquiring them. Aspirants worked in the menagerie for some time before being paired with their powers, Inglis had mentioned, so perhaps it was more a matter of the two compatible spirits finding each other. Like a person and their god.

Or their demon, Des put in, slyly.

So what does that reveal about me?

You possess the Bastard's own luck?

Eee. And then wondered how literally true that might be.

Lunet looked as if she might be wondering, too.

Thala rode for a while next to Lunet, the two women quietly talking. At a turn onto a wider road, Thala said, "Well, we have one of each right here. Let's ask," and pushed her horse up between Penric and Inglis. Inglis, after a glance back over his shoulder at his foxy colleague, returned the young Grayjay's look of inquiry.

"I am curious," she said to the air between them, like a woman fairly dividing a cake. "Which came first, sorcerers or shamans?"

"It had to be sorcerers," said Penric.

Inglis's mouth took a noncommittal twist.

Lunet called up, "How can you say? The tradition of shamans in the old forest tribes goes back centuries, maybe millennia, and is lost in the fog of time. The traditions of sorcery can hardly go back farther."

"Do a few thousand years seem like a long time to you?" asked Penric. "I think that must be an eyeblink, in god-sight."

"Then no one can really say either one?" prodded Thala.

"I don't get to it by any historical record, missing or not. I get to it by logic," said Penric.

Oswyl had taken over Thala's stirrup-place beside Lunet: the shamaness looked the senior locator up and down with fresh interest. Amusement tinging his voice, he said, "Logic, Learned? I thought that was my Order's task."

"Task it might be, but not sole dominion. Think about it. Shamans may create other shamans, through the slow building of Great Beasts, but who created the first shaman? Or the first spirit warrior, for that matter, since the simpler creation likely came before, and the more complicated later, probably through some trial and error." Penric reflected on this. Wait, maybe not? There seemed an uncomfortable circularity involved. "The period of error must have been a frustrating time, for those involved. Anyway, the gods, and the gifts of the gods, surely came before people." He hesitated in uncertainty at that last sentence. But this was not the place for the deeper debate on the origins of the gods, in all its subtleties. And heat. He forged on, "Since sorcerers are created by the gift, of sorts, of a demon from the Bastard, those powers must have come first."

"The oldest forest stories would have it that the first shaman was a blessing of the Son of Autumn," said Inglis. "No sorcerer required. Those shamanic practices that sorcerers can replicate, and I'll grant you a few—"

You'd better, thought Pen, recalling his Great Earthworm with, well, not pride exactly, but certainly provisional satisfaction.

"—could as well have been learned the other way around." *As you did*, his eye-glint implied.

"And the Bastard, it is said, was the last of the gods," put in Oswyl, though Penric didn't see how he had a stake in the debate.

Thala frowned. "It's all starting to sound like hearsay evidence to me," she said, eliciting a muffled choke of, possibly, laughter from Oswyl. She did not turn in her saddle to check.

"Welcome to the study of history," said Penric genially.

"And theology?"

A sudden silence fell from all three men.

"Maybe . . . not so much," said Penric at length. Although that was not a conviction based on his seminary studies for a divine. *Nor hearsay.* "But there is no question people can get theology wrong, too."

"People can get almost anything wrong," sighed Oswyl. "Theology cannot be an exception."

"Mm," Penric conceded.

At the next turn, the road narrowed, and the riders strung out and resorted themselves. The early summer sun was making its slow climb into a blue sky, but their shadows still stretched long across the nearby fields, the strokes of the horses' legs sweeping like scissors. From passing farmsteads, cows released from their morning milkings made their clanking way into pastures, and distant voices echoed around the byres and coops and granaries.

Penric took the opportunity to drop back beside Oswyl, displacing Lunet, though not out of earshot, and detailed to him his new theory from last night's inspiration. Well, from Des. He wasn't sure if naming his source would lend weight to his words or not. As Pen had guessed, his argument about the alternate victim elicited more scowls than smiles from the senior locator.

"What did Learned Hamo think of this . . . idea?" asked Oswyl. That last word seemed deliberately neutral, replacing something tarter, but at least he seemed to be turning Pen's words over in his mind rather than spitting them back outright.

"He didn't think it was impossible. I mean, from the point of view of the sorceress—either one—or their demon. The actual identity of the murderer being another matter."

Oswyl mulled as their horses plodded up the steepening road. "It seems almost a distinction without a difference, from where I stand. Magal's murder is the crime that will go to court. Her killer must still be secured. Everything must still be proved."

"It might cut down your list of suspects. Or at least redirect it."

"Oh? It seems to me it just lengthens it." After a little silence, he added, "I'm not sure it even is a crime to injure or kill a demon. I mean, doesn't your Order dispose of them routinely?"

"Technically, they are given back into the hands of the white god, whence they came. The god disposes." *Or sometimes not*, Pen was reminded. Des's displeased silence at this turn in the conversation was palpable. "It is no more nor less routine than when the machineries of justice hang a criminal. Whose soul must also go on to the gods, or be sundered as the case may be. A consequence not controlled by any executioner, else justice would be sacrilege."

It was Oswyl's turn to say, "Mm," although with less concession in it.

After a longer silence, Penric asked, "Oswyl . . . have you ever been only part-way through one of your inquiries and been *sure* you were right?"

"Eh? Certainly."

"You'd push for it, yes?"

"No."

"Why not?"

"Because sometimes, I'm proved wrong. Later."

Pen digested this. "I suppose that's all right."

Oswyl glanced aside at him, looked between his horse's ears, and said, "Not if the accused is hanged first."

Pen opened his mouth, had just the mother-wit not to ask *Has that ever happened to you?* and let his jaw sink closed. As Oswyl's was.

No. He had no envy of Oswyl's calling. He'd be sticking with the white god, thank you.

How fortunate for us all, murmured Des. She might be smirking; might be serious. Or both. Pen rather thought both.

Penric leaned into his stirrups as the road angled up and began to switch back and forth, and the lower edge of the kin Pikepool forest tract closed in around them, casting moist green shadows. He begged Des's Sight again, stretching his senses for foxes, or rather, for one animal that might be much more. The surrounding woods grew glorious, colors seeming brighter, limned with life and movement both swift and subtle, but no foxes as such, though he was briefly distracted by the flash of birds and the musky dusk of a badger. The shamans in the party, too, grew more alert, and he wondered how strangely—or akin—they sensed all this, but no one called an alarm before they finally turned aside into the rutted lane leading to the old kin Pikepool manor house and farm.

Approached from the front, the fortress-like house seemed nearly as brown and blank as when seen from the back. They rode around it to the stable yard before encountering any other people.

As they dismounted, an old man emerged from the house, alarm on his features which faded as he spotted Wegae and Jons. "Oh," he said. Pen thought he might have tugged on his forelock if he hadn't been bald. "Young master." His tone was respectful enough, but . . . ah. *Young master* not *my lord*. Old retainer, then, relict, like the rest of this place, of the prior baron.

"Ah, Losno, good," said Wegae, turning with an air of familiarity. "We will be here for the day. We'll rest the horses in the pasture."

"I'll fetch the lad." The man trudged off to roust out a stable boy, or gardener's assistant, or general young village laborer—it looked as if the one gangling youth held all such posts. He and Jons and the shamans coordinated in setting the tack in a line atop the fence and loosing the beasts. The pasture's current equine occupants looked as dubious about this alien influx as Losno and his lad, although neither of the human hosts bit, squealed, or kicked.

"Losno is the gardener and caretaker," Wegae explained to Penric and the Grayjays, "along with his wife, who sees to the house. As much as it gets, these days. I'll collect them all for you in a moment."

"Please," said Oswyl.

Pen was dismayed to spot five new fox skins tacked to the stable wall, reeking in the sun. A quick check of the stall found it empty, or emptied. Inglis and Lunet joined his examination.

"Can you tell anything by looking at them?" Pen asked anxiously.

"Not . . . especially," said Inglis. "They all seem alike, if that helps any."

If anyone had killed the wanted fox already, they would likely have been jumped-to by its demon, Pen reflected uneasily. Creating a whole new problem, but clearly it had not happened to the old gardener or his lad. Nor, when they came out in a few minutes, his wife or her scullion-girl, who could have been sister to the boy. Or maybe cousin, or both, rural villages being what they were.

Oswyl sat them all down on a bench beside the back door and, reinforced by Wegae's weedy authority, began a systematic inquiry. Penric listened, hanging back as anonymously as he was dressed, although he did carry his braids tucked away in his inner vest pocket. The pattern of questions was starting to become familiar. The news

about the dead sorceress found in the Pikepool woods induced shock
and surprise in the four servants, and some haste to assure everyone
listening that they'd seen or heard nothing of it. Pen had no idea if any
of them were lying, even with a flash of Sight; all he could sense was
agitation, and a certain amount of wriggling gruesome curiosity from
the boy, which did not require magic to discern. He wondered if Oswyl
could tell any more by experience.

No, no one had seen any strangers about the place in the last few
days. Nor in the woods, but you'd have to ask Treuch. Who had gone
off there to continue his fox-thinning project. Was this unusual? No,
not especially. Wouldn't winter be better for pelts? Well, yes. Did
Treuch live in the main house, too? Oh, no, not the forester; he had
his own little cottage, pointed out a double-hundred paces away at
the edge of the woods. It looked more like a hut to Pen, but no
shabbier than the other old wattle-and-daub structures scattered
about the grounds. No, Treuch had no wife nor children, never had.
No skill at courting, when he was younger, though he would have it
that the girls were too picky and proud; the housekeeper sniffed.
Oswyl, rather than cutting off this discursion, led them on to gossip
about the absent man for a bit, but what he made of it Pen could not
guess.

They grew, oddly, less gossipy when asked about the three-year-old
tragedy of the slain baroness. The two youths had not worked here
then, but the old couple had, and had apparently suffered their fill of
interrogation about the crime at the time. In any case, they added
nothing new or startling to the tale already told. Though the
housekeeper sounded grateful to the Temple sensitives who had
removed the ghost from the premises, as if it had been an infestation
of some especially appalling vermin. Wegae's mouth twisted—
remembering his aunt as a person, perhaps.

They were all squirming when Oswyl finally released them back to
their labors. The housekeeper did not look too pleased when he
assigned Thala to look about inside the manse, taking the grounds for
himself. Penric returned to the stable yard where Inglis had been
organizing his squad of shamans for a search of the woods.

"Are you sure you should split up like this?" Pen asked dubiously
upon hearing the plan.

"We'll be able to cover more ground, faster," rumbled Nath.

"I was thinking of the dangers of perhaps surprising a desperate murderer," Pen said. "He could still be about." Something, certainly, had to account for Treuch's out-of-season fox-obsession. Or someone? Oswyl himself had not yet closed off the notion of more than one man—person—being involved.

"Penric," said Inglis patiently, "we're shamans. Would you consider yourself in danger?"

"Er . . . not forewarned, I suppose. But I have certain physical powers that you all do not possess."

"And we have certain mental ones that you don't."

Penric increasingly wanted to do something about that lack before this trip was done, if he could. But that would require some canny negotiating with the princess-archdivine, and was not the meal upon his plate this day. "Well . . . be careful, anyway. If you run across any strange men in the woods, don't approach them. Come back for reinforcements first, eh?"

There was a general, unreassuring *meh* in response to this.

"Oh. And if you encounter the forester Treuch, send him back here. Tell him the baron wants to talk to him, but don't mention the Grayjays yet."

It was decided to begin with the sections to the north and west of the house first, in the general direction of the village of Weir, and all meet back here in about three hours to eat and plan the next cast. Unless someone found the demon, in which case they were to inform Penric in the most expedient way they could. They all fanned out and plunged into the tangled green shade.

Two hours of blundering back and forth through his assigned sector brought Pen no prizes, although he did find and spring an iron leg-hold trap baited with pork fat, and two snares. Might the demon-ridden fox have a more-than-natural wariness of such hazards? Pen hoped so.

Casting around the woods with his Sight fully extended was a strange experience in its own right. He could have used it when hunting as a youth, except . . . it was so overwhelming. It wasn't like ghosting along with his bow trying to pick out one tasty target, disregarding all the rest; rather the reverse. The whole tapestry of the forest's life folded in upon him, its intricacy interlocking in finer and finer stitching, so that the mere perception, after a time, grew exhausting. His range was short, half-a-hundred paces, or this god-sight would be entirely too god-like. What kind of Mind was it that could hold the whole world like this, all at once, all the time? Could the gods ever close their Eyes and rest from it, even for a short while? And what would happen if They did?

Also, if he were ever the-gods-forbid by some accident blinded, could this substitute for his lost eyesight? He was in no hurry to find out.

Aside from that, Des grew replete ingesting the life from more biting insects than Pen thought possible, and bored enough to attempt exploding a scampering shrew, a pastime he caught up with just too late. He stared down with some disgust at the splatter across his boot. "Really, Des. Are you a two-hundred-year-old woman—"

"Women," she corrected, blandly.

"—or an idle village lad? Even *I* never pulled the wings off flies."

"Somehow, I am not surprised, dear Pen."

And he was reminded, again, that beneath the two centuries' accumulation of human experience and knowledge that she shared so generously with him, she *was* a chaos demon. Which made him wonder, again, what must be going on right now with the *other* chaos demon, thrown so violently backward into worse disorder.

Hot, sweaty, and hungry, he turned his steps back toward the kin Pikepool manor. His pace quickened as he found yesterday's path. Perhaps one of the others had come upon something. Perhaps they were impatiently waiting for him.

He found Oswyl and Thala sitting on the bench by the back door, though with no sign of impatience. Inglis and Kreil lounged cross-legged at their feet, sharing around a pitcher of well water and some of the food they'd brought along. Inglis looked glum and Oswyl grim, but since both were their natural expressions, it didn't tell Pen much.

They all looked up as he trod near. "Ah," said Oswyl. "Find anything interesting, Learned?"

Pen sighed and joined the pair on the ground, grateful to be handed down a cup. "Not so far. How about yourselves?"

Inglis and Kreil both shook their heads, but Oswyl confided, "Treuch's hut shows signs of hosting a visitor. There was a bedroll, and maybe a few too many cups and plates scattered about."

Thala put in, "The housekeeper notes he's had a hearty appetite of late. Since he brings in game for the table to keep the other servants in meat, she can't exactly complain, she said. While complaining." Her lips twitched back in a brief rare smile—she seemed to be sopping up the sober demeanor, as well as the tips on their trade, from her mentor. "Since he keeps to himself by habit, and is not of a cheerful disposition to start with, no changes there."

"Huh," said Pen. "He's not come in yet?"

"Not so far," echoed Kreil.

One could not accuse Treuch of lying about seeing strangers lately, since he hadn't yet been asked. It wasn't odd for a man to have a visitor. It was odd to keep his visitor a secret, however. "It couldn't have been a woman, in the hut?"

"No signs of such in the clothing or clutter, no," said Oswyl.

"That's very interesting."

"I'd be willing to call it so," Oswyl conceded. Which, from Oswyl, was something like a large signal flag. Not that he'd admit to such a thing. But Pen bet he'd be keeping an eye on Treuch's hut.

"Where's Wegae gone off to?"

"Looking over household accounts, and inspecting the place," said Thala. "He seemed to think it was expected of him. I'm not sure his servants appreciate his conscientiousness." Inglis snickered, and tore into his bread and cheese. Penric put down his emptied cup and waved a hand, and Thala portioned him out a share.

Oswyl came alert first, Pen following his gaze to find Lunet jogging back to them. Her eyes were merry, her cheeks flushed beneath their smattering of freckles. Pen's breath caught in anticipation.

She fetched up before them and bounced on her toes, all smugness. "Found your fox," she announced. Even Oswyl was surprised into a smile.

"Ah!" Pen nearly sprang to his aching feet; his spine straightened. "Then it *was* a fox, we were right! Where?"

Thala handed over a cup of water, which Lunet drained, smacking her lips. "Thanks, needed that. The den's nearly in the center of this tract, about as deep into the woods as you can go without starting out again. On a steep slope, really tangled. But there's a hitch. It looks like your demon has gone into a vixen with cubs."

Pen was taken aback. Somehow, in all his imaginings, he'd pictured a dog-fox, a bachelor ready to travel, although upon reflection that had only ever been half the chance.

"She seemed very distressed," said Lunet. "It was hard to tell if that was the demon part, the vixen part, or both. I haven't tried to get too close to her yet. I thought maybe I'd better come get you, first."

"Did she see you? Or sense you?"

Lunet nodded. "She gave me rather a frantic look, before she shook the cubs off her teats and sped away to hunt. Not the usual time of day for a fox to hunt, but I can see why she had to. Six babies. Oh, Mother and Brother, they were so *darling*. All fluff and flurry, tumbling over each other and chewing on their siblings' ears and tails. She barked at them, such a strange sound foxes make, you know, and they retreated inside. I left a brace of rabbits just in front of the den as a peace offering, then I hurried to get you."

Pen wondered what shortcuts a shaman might undertake to hunt—barehanded!—and if they were anything like the easy devastation he could now wreak, if he chose.

"We should get back soon," Lunet went on. "She might become afraid and move them."

Pen pondered this unexpected development. If he'd had trouble imagining the damaged demon's state of mind before, the puzzle was redoubled. The vixen certainly had her own present obsession, and the demon had been imprinted by at least one sorceress who'd been a mother herself. How were the two fighting it out in the animal's brain? Or had they achieved some bizarre sort of cooperation? Women did that . . .

Sometimes, agreed Des, seeming as fascinated as he was. And he was reminded that of her twelve previous riders, six had once borne children themselves, if all before they'd joined with the demon. Of Des's two centuries of memories, experiences, and disturbing dream-fragments that Pen did not talk about to *anyone*, those intimacies led the list.

Eight, murmured Des, *counting the lioness and the mare.*

Ah. Yes. Quite. So, maybe one of them had been through something like this before. *Des, help me out, here.*

A rather long pause. Then, slowly, as if feeling her way forward herself, Des offered, *Perhaps we'd better ask the vixen.*

"Huh," said Pen aloud, and then as much to his human companions as to Des, "We can't leave her unguarded, out there. Not with all this unexplained fox-slaughter going on."

There was a general murmur of agreement, and a speeding of the consumption of lunch.

As Pen was chewing down his bread and cheese, Nath lumbered across the yard, the last of their hunting party to report in. He looked his companions over. "Treuch not back yet?" he inquired.

"Did you find him?" asked Oswyl, sitting up.

"I met him in the woods, setting snares. He asked who I was. I said I was a visitor come with his lord, who wanted him to come back to the house. He said he would, as soon as he was done with his task. I drew off and waited till he'd gone, then tripped the snare and followed."

"Then he should have come in ahead of you," said Oswyl.

"Did he seem suspicious of you?" asked Inglis. "Accuse you of poaching or anything?"

"No, our exchange was brief. Civil enough, I suppose. Then he limped off."

". . . Limped?" said Penric. "He didn't have a limp yesterday. Was it a new injury, could you tell?"

Nath waved a thick hand. "Old, I'd say. He walked with a staff. Big fellow, grizzled beard. Well-spoken, though, for the little he said."

Inglis and Penric looked at each other and blinked. "How old was the man?" asked Penric.

"Maybe the near side of fifty?"

"Not . . . around forty, dark-haired, lean, about Inglis's height?" asked Pen.

"No, closer to my size. And shape." Nath shrugged bearish shoulders.

"That wasn't Treuch," said Inglis. "Or . . . it wasn't the man who said he was Treuch yesterday."

"He answered to Treuch, when I called out to him," said Nath.

"What *exactly* did you say to him?" asked Oswyl.

"I said, *Hello there, are you Baron kin Pikepool's forester, Treuch?* and he said . . . well, he actually said, *What's it to you?*"

"Could be Treuch's mystery visitor," said Oswyl.

"Or just some random poacher," said Kreil, though his ears had pricked with interest.

Really, murmured Des, *young Kreil makes me want to throw a stick, just to see what would happen.* Pen ignored that one. Nath's description made him deeply uneasy, but there were, inevitably, any number of benign explanations for the man, as Pen was sure someone senior to himself would point out.

"What was he using to bait his snare?" asked Inglis.

"A very dead fish."

"Not after rabbits, then," said Pen. "Or anything else you'd want to eat."

"I wouldn't say so, no," agreed Nath.

Oswyl drummed his fingers on the bench, but, being Oswyl, added no more.

It was decided Kreil would stay at the manor with the Grayjays, in case Treuch or the mystery man returned, to help or run messages as needed. Once they'd secured the demon-fox, Pen wanted to secure the bearded stranger as well, if only to settle his doubts, assuming he could persuade the tired, hot shamans to search the woods a second time. That odd exchange with Nath *could* have just been a poacher being cleverly evasive. Or, if he'd been an honest man, he might turn up on his own, in which case Oswyl could evaluate him. Oswyl, Pen was sure, would jump to no conclusions.

Pen, Inglis, and Nath followed Lunet into the forest once more.

They'd tramped a good three miles off the path, including laboring in and out of one wrong ravine, before Lunet put a finger to her lips and slowed, her steps becoming stealthy. Pen tracked her pointing hand to a pile of deadfall and wild grapevines on the gully's opposite slope, and unfolded his Sight. The fox family was at home, judging by the warm pile of squirming life he could sense below the thin green screen.

And so was their mother, by the unmistakable density and roil of a chaos demon therein. The roil instantly grew tense and dismayed; for once, Sight ran two ways, instead of Pen's more usual secret spying.

Just as humans were natural enemies of foxes, there was every reason for the demon to presume a Temple sorcerer was an arresting officer come to carry it off to some execution-by-saint, and no savior. That was certainly a grim task both he and Des had carried out before. Des's density tended to daunt lesser demons, and the fact that she was not ascended was apparently no reassurance. Pen did not see how he was to make up for that by any slathering-on of innocent charm to the demon's host this time.

Was this demon ascended? It was the obvious assumption, and yet . . . *Des, what do you make of her? . . . Them.*

Yes, she said slowly, as if herself unsure. *And yet . . . the burden of care seems reversed. Magal's doing, maybe?*

It took Pen a moment to figure out what Des meant by that. *The demon is trying to look out for the vixen? Like . . . like a pet?*

Or a child. Which is what people make of their pets, I suppose. She seemed to consider the cubs, and added, *Children.*

"Lunet," Pen whispered. "Let's you and I try to get closer, without alarming the vixen. Don't want her to bolt. You other two stay here, for now."

"She's already alarmed," Lunet whispered back, swiping a strand of rusty hair off her sticky forehead. "She won't bolt till the very last gasp, though. Because of the cubs."

"Right."

Trying to move quietly, Pen and Lunet made their way to the bottom of the ravine and angled up again until they were just a few paces from the den. Lunet wriggled her finger at the ground, and Pen nodded; they both sank down to sit in the leaf litter, he cross-legged, she on her knees. The silence from under the screen of grape leaves matched their own. The gleam of wary eyes, the faint outline of the furry mask, might almost have seemed a trick of the light and shadows in Pen's sight. But not his Sight.

Can the demon-fox still understand human speech? Pen thought to Des. *You were once a mare. And a lioness. Could you then?*

That was two centuries ago, Pen! In any case, no. Neither one had ever been in a human yet to acquire such skills. Going the other way . . . is not something I've ever done. Thankfully.

Could the fox's brain even process the complexities of human tongues, to pass along to its demon? Pen, who possessed six languages so far, did not underestimate the task. The sounds, presumably, must pass through unimpaired—foxes had keen hearing—but could a demoted demon retain such comprehension? *No spirit can long exist in the world of matter without a being of matter to support it,* the basic Temple dictum ran. Could the skills of a spirit exist piecemeal? Linger for a time, at least?

There seemed no way to find out but to test it.

Oswyl, Pen had noticed, routinely used Thala to speak with any female interrogatees. Possibly another reason for the canny man to value his assistant, which he obviously did. Perhaps the fox shaman could be such an ambassadress?

"Inglis has this weirding voice," he whispered to her. "I've seen him use it to command dogs. And men, though I should warn you it doesn't work on demons. Can you use such to speak to the vixen? Draw her out?"

Lunet frowned, and whispered back, "The voice is more command than enticement. And dogs already have some grasp of speech. Although there are also songs."

Pen didn't think she meant mere Temple hymns; he needed to find out more about that. *Later.* "I've heard there are stronger spells, geases."

She nodded. "Those only last as long as the shaman pours life into them. Or parasitizes some source of life, most handily the subject himself, but that's a more complex and costly compulsion to set."

"Mm." Compulsion in general only lasted as long as it was enforced. Persuasion could linger more usefully. "Try speaking to her, first. Coaxing gently. Keep the message simple."

"What message?"

Any threat to take the vixen to the Bastard's Order, as Hamo had wished, would terrify the demon. With cause. "Offer to take her—and her cubs—to the Royal Fellowship. You have the wherewithal to keep foxes healthy at your menagerie, yes?"

"Of course." Lunet smiled. "Good notion." She walked forward on her knees closer to the shadowed mouth of the den, and crouched again. **"Hey, lady. We mean you no harm. With all these men hunting, we want to take you to a safer den than these woods. My shamans' den. And your children. Will you trust me?"**

The resonance of the weirding voice, though familiar to Pen by now, still made the hairs stir on his arms. The vixen crept forward into the light, wriggling low to the ground, lips drawn back on her white teeth, ears cycling back and forward. Panting in anxiety. Lunet leaned forward to lay her hand up between the two black front paws, and hummed to no tune Pen recognized, faint and eerie.

Slowly, the vixen lowered her muzzle to touch her nose to Lunet's palm.

Communication of some sort achieved, although with the fox, the demon, or both Pen was not sure. Pen thought back to his own immense confusion upon first acquiring Des. He couldn't very well hand the fox a slim volume on sorcery to read up on her new state, despite all the unnatural awareness that seemed to shine from those copper eyes.

"I suppose," Pen murmured, "we must first get them all back to the manor. And then maybe have Wegae lend us a farm cart to take them to town." Or pannier baskets, or something. If he'd been thinking, they might have brought some such transport aids into these woods. "Six cubs. Can they walk that far? Will they follow?"

Lunet seemed to be making inroads with the vixen, her humming becoming a wordless song, the animal relaxing into her moving hands. She stroked the vixen's head, made play with her tufted ears, ran her slim fingers through the ruddy ruff. Half shamanic persuasion, Pen thought, and half simple, honest delight, persuasive in its own right.

Fascinated, Pen crept forward and extended his own hand, only to have the vixen tilt her head and curl her black-edged lip back on a toothy growl. Lunet shot him a look of annoyance, and Pen subsided, feeling weirdly disappointed at his exclusion from this love-fest. *You just want to pet her, too*, Des snickered. The strange communing continued for a few minutes, then Lunet crawled into the den, to return momentarily followed by the half-dozen sleepy and bewildered cubs, who were indeed, as touted, darling. They blinked shoe-button eyes and made a concerted run on their mother's dugs, but the distracted vixen irritably shoved them away. Almost automatically, Pen took a moment to rid them via Des of their fleas and ticks, which drew a sharp look from the vixen—or her demon—but her sudden tension faded again as it was plain the cubs had taken no harm from him.

So, how much of Magal's demon's powers, or control of its powers, did the fox have? Insect eradication was one of the simplest of destructive magics, the first Des had ever shown him back when he'd so inadvertently acquired her. This did suggest the fox-demon might be less dangerous than he'd feared.

Simple, observed Des, *but requiring fine control.*

Magal should have been able to do it, though. And Svedra.

Oh, certainly. The point is, less-fine control is not necessarily less dangerous.

Hm.

"Let's get them all back to the manor," Pen said. Which would give him a bit of time to think. "And then to the Fellowship." Which would give more. This conundrum was going to need it. Because, having coaxed the trust of both fox and demon, betraying same, in any of the many ways it might be required by his Temple duty, was growing unappetizing.

At Pen's beckoning, Inglis and Nath left their vantage and approached curiously. Pen explained the new plan, and the whole party rearranged itself for the trek. Lunet took the lead, the vixen at her heels. The cubs followed with about the orderliness one might expect of any other six toddlers, which was to say, none. Inglis and Penric secured the flanks, shooing their little charges back into line, and Nath brought up the rear. For all that he smiled at them, the cubs, after a first wary glance back at him, seemed intimidated by his bearish aura. At least they didn't fall behind.

Hostages, Pen thought unwillingly, eyeing the barging balls of fluff. It seemed he'd taken hostages. It didn't make him feel as clever as it should have.

You're feeling guilty about lying to a fox? Des asked, amused. *Only you, Pen.*

Or, perhaps, to a demon. Or both. It would depend on how events played out.

Ah. Yes. Periodically, I am reminded why I like you. A hint of smug possessiveness.

He had nothing to say to that, though he was vaguely warmed.

The floundering cubs were starting to whine their displeasure at the trek, and Pen's lips twitched as he imagined them nagging, *Aren't we there yet, Mother?* The peculiar procession scrambled out at last to more level ground, heading for the main path. Less than a mile to go to the manor.

The arrow came out of nowhere, too fast for Pen to respond, almost too fast for Des. She was barely able to flip it so that it hit the side of the fox flat-on instead of point-first. The animal yelped and spun. By the time the next arrow was in flight, Des, unasked, had speeded Pen's perceptions to match her own. He splintered the second shaft and sent the iron point tumbling, even as he whirled just like the fox, seeking the source.

From his point of view, when Des deployed this defense, the world around him slowed. Lunet was turning, Inglis raising his hand, Nath lifting his head, all with the languor of a bead dropping through honey. The cubs, at their mother's cry, were either crouching or scattering. Pen's gaze sought frantically through the woods for the bowman—*there*, in the cover of those upended tree roots. Pen had just the presence of mind to snap the bowstring *before* he started running toward the assassin, so that the third shaft was not aimed at him, but flew wide as the broken ends whipped into the bowman's face, drawing blood.

He jumped over a fallen log, feeling the strain of too much power forced through his legs too fast. Behind him, Inglis yelled, "Look after the foxes!" and pelted in his wake.

And then he was upon his target. Dizzied—he felt as if he'd left his wits blown back along his track. He grabbed the man by his leather jerkin, hoisted him to his feet, and slammed him against the nearest upright tree trunk. The bow clattered to the ground.

It was Treuch, he realized at last, as Des let the world fall back to normal speed and his lungs labored for breath—this unnatural bodily debt did have to be repaid, oh aye, and no extensions. Treuch did not cooperate with his sudden arrest; he punched his clenched hands up through Penric's grip and broke the hold, shoving Pen back. Pen stumbled and came around again.

I could snap his tendons as easily as his bowstring, Des offered. Not quite the theologically forbidden act of murder by magic, but too close for Pen's comfort, too irreversible. The reminder abruptly cooled Pen's heated head just as Inglis, thankfully, arrived.

"You two!" wheezed Treuch. He reached for the hunting knife at his belt and whipped it out before him.

Pen turned the blade to rust, bursting off in a spray of orange flecks as Treuch slashed. Inglis bellowed, "**Stop!**" and the hilt, passing a bare inch from Pen's belly, dropped from nerveless fingers. The forester's mouth fell open in astonishment, and then, as his eyes rose to meet Pen's, fear. "What—!"

The three men fell into a stiff triangle, fists clenched, chests heaving. Pen seized the teetering moment to try to shift the encounter from ill-considered actions to words. Where he, at least, would be on safer ground. Because shooting at a fox, as Thala might remark, was not normally a capital crime.

Oh, I'd see you safe regardless of your ground, Des purred. But she settled in disappointment as the chance for more chaos died away.

Pen yanked his triple-looped braids from his inner vest pocket and brandished them at the forester. "I am Learned Penric of Martensbridge, Temple sorcerer," he declared, then drew a breath he wasn't quite sure what next to do with.

If he'd thrust a live adder in the man's face, Treuch couldn't have recoiled more sharply.

"I am detaining you . . . " In the name of what? Legally, Pen only held higher authority over the demon in this jurisdiction, and that bestowed by Hamo. He skipped over that conundrum and went on, "in suspicion of complicity in a murder."

Treuch pushed away, hovering between fighting and running, although Pen thought the fates of his bow and knife should have taught him better than to try the first again. Inglis growled, "**Surrender**."

The man did not so much surrender as seize up, caught between the conflicting demands of terror and shamanic compulsion. "I didn't shoot her!" he all but squealed.

Pen blinked, going still. "I didn't say who was murdered. Or how."

Treuch froze in a different sort of horror, gaping fish-fashion.

"Oswyl will want this," said Inglis.

"*I* want this," said Pen, his stare at Treuch intensifying. Inglis regarded Pen warily.

They were interrupted by the low growl of a fox. The vixen stalked up to them stiff-legged, the ridge of fur standing up on her spine, ears flattened backward. Her copper eyes were bent on Treuch. For all her vicious air she had not the size to be a lethal-seeming threat, as predators went, but no, it wasn't the *fox* that was the true danger here.

"It seems you are accused," said Inglis dryly. Treuch's terror slumped in a rush sheer bewilderment.

The panic transferred to Pen. He stepped hastily in front of the fox, between her and the forester, and cried, "No, you cannot!"

The animal—no, the demon—crouched away from Des's roiling density, the bolt of damaging chaos gathering to pitch at the man dying away again. *Bastard be praised.* Pen wasn't sure if such a blast of unformed magic could have killed Treuch outright, but he was very sure of the unwanted consequences if it did.

"I don't know yet if I can save you, but I do know I can't if you do this!"

Did either demon or fox understand him? Even if more-than-vulpine comprehension flashed in those copper eyes, that didn't make it *human*.

A bow-shot away, the frightened yips of the cubs being forcibly gathered up distracted the vixen part of this unintended creature. She turned once, turned back, halfway to frenzy from all the conflicting demands.

"We have to get these two separated," gasped Pen to Inglis, gesturing blindly at Treuch who now seemed the least of his troubles. He raised his voice. "Nath! Get over here!"

Nath lumbered across the deadfall, his arms full of protesting fox cubs, and said, "Yes, Learned?"

"You and Inglis take Treuch ahead of us to the manor," Pen said. "Lunet and I will bring the foxes." And the demon, he did not say aloud. Did Treuch have the least notion of how much danger he'd just skirted?

If he'd had his way, that first knife-slash would have disemboweled you, Pen, Des noted dryly. *And then nothing would have saved him.*

And Pen didn't think she meant from the fox-demon. He chose to ignore both this and the belated trembling in his belly. His sweating hand still clenched his Temple braids, he discovered, and he shoved them back into his vest pocket. It was a continuing wonder to him how much less, rather than more, freedom that acquiring a responsible authority gave to one. Not at all how he'd pictured his elders, so seeming-powerful, as a child. As Nath bent to release the cubs, who ran to their distrait mother, Pen also decided it must be a more universal condition than he'd ever imagined.

"You"—Pen turned again to Treuch—"your baron has commanded your immediate attendance, and is awaiting you at the manor." Yes, better not to mention the Grayjays quite yet. If the man did break away from his captors, he'd likely be as hard to find in his woods as a fox.

Treuch jerked, taken aback. "What?" Then, "Oh. Young Master Spectacles."

Pen nodded. "He brought us up for the fox hunt." He met Treuch's surly glare. Indeed, Treuch knew what he'd really been hunting, however poorly the sundered fool understood the ramifications. Pen would be taking this up with him as soon as possible, even if he had to get in line behind Oswyl. He gestured at Inglis and Nath. "Go, quickly!"

The pair of shamans, thankfully, didn't question or argue, but each took one of the forester's arms and marched him off between them. Between Nath's hulking size and both their powers, Pen fancied the arrest would hold till they could deliver Treuch to the Grayjays. Treuch glanced in fear over his shoulder at Penric, clearly unaware that this sorcerer-divine might have just saved his life. Twice. So, was that Pen's good deed for the day, or a regret in prospect?

Pen waved at Lunet, and they both turned to the task, *again*, of calming the vixen and collecting her offspring. Six languages at his fingertips, and this was the hardest communication task he'd ever undertaken. They were making their way onto the beaten path when Lunet muttered something annoyed under her breath, put down her trio of cubs, whipped a handkerchief from her trouser pocket, and clapped it to her nose. Pen was startled to see it soaking with red.

"Are you all right?"

She nodded, moving the cloth off her messy lip to say, "The price of shamanic magic is blood. Did you not know?"

"Mm, yes, but I'm still not clear on the how of it."

She shrugged. "Small magics, small price. Larger magics, larger price. But always the same coin."

Pen thought of the array of gruesome scars on Inglis's forearms, which was why, Pen presumed, he wore long sleeves even in hot weather, and never rolled them up unless among his most intimate friends.

Lunet stopped mopping, frowned at her handkerchief, and folded and pocketed it. She bent and chirped to coax her cubs back; they came readily to her arms, and they started off through the woods once more. She allowed them to reach up and lick her face, which seemed to amuse her vastly. Pen swallowed his *urk*, almost.

"There are less convenient ways to spontaneously bleed, trust me," she tossed aside to him, grinning.

Pen wondered what. Or how many different—

Des, with an air of taking pity on innocence, apprised him: *She's talking about monthlies. I imagine that could make for some confusion, for a shamaness.*

Pen kept his eyes up. He trusted his flush from the heat masked his blush. He was relieved when the nose-drip died away, and Lunet stopped using the cubs for a substitute handkerchief.

I have to learn more about this.

Of course you do, Des echoed Inglis's words of—was it only two days ago? At least her tone was more fond.

As they made their way more quickly along the beaten path, Pen's three cubs were fuzzy weights in his arms, warm and charming, but kept sharply nipping at him. Lunet managed to stay unperforated, which seemed backward, given their respective magics. The vixen still seemed to trust Lunet, and her demon was deeply wary of Des, so by whatever internal truce the two had, the animal's body followed along. Pen calculated how to house them all once they arrived at the manor. Probably a stable stall, again. With the bottom door closed to contain the cubs, and the top open to give the vixen the illusion of freedom. Toss in a couple of rabbits, place a basin of water, and it would with luck hold them till it was time to decamp for Easthome. Would Oswyl arrest Treuch?

I didn't shoot her, Treuch had cried. So who had?

Des, did you sense he was speaking the truth?

A pause. *Not sure. He was distressed, and I was busy.*

Well, it was plain Treuch knew something—far too much—about Magal's death. Pen imagined Oswyl had proven ways of getting such things out of men.

Bet we could find ways to break him open if Oswyl can't, Des suggested slyly.

Pen bet they could, too, but Oswyl needed more than just knowledge—he needed a case. Father's Order business, that. "Best wait till we're asked," he replied aloud, which made Lunet cast him a puzzled glance.

The path opened out into the meadow on the back side of the manor house. Everyone appeared to have gone within, or elsewhere. They circled to the stables, and Lunet sang the foxes into a suitable stall. Pen breathed relief when he was finally able to swing the lower door shut on them.

"I think you'd better stay with them till I find out where Treuch was taken," he told her, shaking out his tooth-pricked arms. Would they count as shamanic coin? "To keep them calm. And, if necessary, protect them." Pen stared a bit doubtfully at Lunet's slender form, but . . . powerful shamaness, he reminded himself. If others underestimated her, so much the better. Or so he had found it in his own case. "And, ah—maybe protect everyone else from the vixen. Keep people away from her, certainly."

Lunet nodded understanding, and Pen made his way around the stable block, heading for the manor house. A movement at the edge of the meadow caught his eye—oh, it was just Wegae. Continuing his diligent inspection of his property, presumably. He followed along behind his elderly gardener-caretaker, Losno, who gestured him in his wake and pointed to, yes, that was Treuch's hut in the distant shaded verge.

They were too far away for Pen to hear what they were saying, but Losno turned back and Wegae went on in. Wait, Treuch couldn't be back home already, could he? Surely he must have been delivered to Oswyl just a short time ago.

Someone's in there, said Des. *Not Treuch, no. Someone new. Someone . . . angry.*

Pen thought the Grayjays had taken inventory of all the manor's servants already. He hesitated, torn between the two curiosities of Oswyl's interrogation of Treuch and this fresh mystery. He took one step each way.

Something's very wrong in that hut, said Des suddenly, and Pen angled toward it, planning to intercept the gardener and ask what was going on. Losno glanced his way and shuffled faster, looking oddly frightened.

Pen. Run!

He didn't think to ask why till he was already in motion. She didn't volunteer his trick of uncanny speed, so maybe the emergency wasn't lethal?

Yet, she said grimly.

Pen sped up on his own, the meadow grass slapping around his legs like thin green fingers trying to delay him.

Thumps echoed from the hut. He bounded up the porch and yanked open the door on murky dimness. Shapes moved within it. *Des, light!* His vision brightened and he saw a small table toppled over, Wegae lying on the plank floor, his hands flung up across his bleeding face. His spectacles spun aside, just out of his reach. A heavyset older man with a staff in his hand heaved forward, stamping down a booted foot; the glass crunched horribly, and Wegae cried out as though he himself had been struck.

"Eh?" The bearded face of the stranger jerked up at the light from the door and Pen's awkward entry.

Was this the not-Treuch that Nath had encountered in the woods a few hours ago? It seemed they wouldn't have to hunt him down after all. Lucky chance? Pen had barely opened his mouth to demand explanations, or say he knew-not-what, when the man lunged toward him and the staff whipped around at his head. *Ah. Bastard's luck.*

Pen's duck this time was with demonic haste, or he'd have won a fractured skull. But the miss did not impede the attack; the man shifted his thick hands and the staff's other end followed up near-instantly. If Des had managed to burst it into splinters just before, and not just after, it smacked into Pen's forearm, that would have been quite helpful. As it was, he yowled and jolted back, arm throbbing and just short of broken.

Singlestick fighter. Trained and dangerous. And possibly berserk, because shattering half of his weapon didn't even slow him down. He just reversed it, the sharp, jagged end Pen had inadvertently supplied now turned into a short spear; it jabbed savagely. Battlefield reflexes? Pen squawked and burst the whole thing into blazing sawdust in the man's hands.

That finally got through to him, or at least his eyes widened in astonishment. It still didn't give him pause: he kept on coming, hands widening out through the cloud of smoke and flames, seizing Pen's neck. Which was what Pen was due, he supposed, for so rudely interrupting a murder in progress. Wegae yelped and scrambled to his feet, blindly feeling around for some sort of weapon or shield. Pen hoped he'd find something. Meanwhile, he was on his own.

Not quite, said Des. And reached out to snap the bones inside their assailant's hands. The muffled sound, so close to Pen's ears, was sickening. Fair payment for the spectacles?

The strangling grip weakened; a last attempt to wrench his neck fell away in what Pen hoped was excruciating pain. For someone besides himself. Choking, he fell back, trying desperately to open some distance between himself and this murderous madman. Because even a sorcerer needed a moment to plan his attack, or defense.

Not this fellow, apparently. Every movement he'd made since Pen had broken in upon him had felt mindless. Practiced? Because in the middle of a such a fight, there was hardly time to think. Maybe Pen should have trained like that. But, sunder it, a divine entrusted with a demon was *obligated* to think before he acted. He was sure that was in his Temple oaths somewhere, by implication at least.

"It's Uncle Halber!" Wegae shrieked from the side.

"Figured that out!" Pen wheezed back.

"Quit fighting, you fool!" Wegae shouted. Oh—not at Pen, for he followed up with, "He's a sorcerer!"

Halber had seemingly not quite realized it yet, or else he was beyond reason, but the result was likely not the quelling one Wegae had envisioned. He plunged at Pen with sudden and renewed ferocity, eyes wide and glaring. Pen barely evaded a thunderous kick. Then Halber actually tried to grip his belt knife in his swelling hands. And *succeeded*, Bastard's tears.

Having a few moments longer this time as he was chased around the small room, Pen varied his defense by heating the hilt. *Pen*, Des chided, *this is not the time for showing off.* It had actually started to glow before Halber finally dropped it clattering to the planks. He bellowed in pain.

We have to stop this, Pen thought. *Before I get killed and you end up in Wegae.*

Mm . . . Des hummed.

His demon, Pen decided, wasn't so much brave as *vicious. Are you playing with him?* Only his speed allowed him to dodge a few more fierce kicks.

Wegae had finally located an iron frying pan. He managed one good whack—not hard enough—before he was punched aside again. The pan flew away with a clang. That Halber bent over his fists in agony after was small consolation.

Try to get your hand on his lower back, said Des. *Just for an instant. This is going to take some precision.*

Bastard's tears! Well, give me all the speed you can, then.

For the first time, Pen went on the attack, or something vaguely resembling attack. He spun around to face Halber as the man closed the distance trying for another mighty booted kick. *Left, right, under, over?* The world slowed to its utmost, and Pen, tapping his lips with his thumb, crouched to make springs of his legs. He bolted off the floor and into the air, one hand bracing on Halber's shoulder, curling his knees to avoid slamming his feet into the low ceiling beams. He swung his other hand, still tingling from the singlestick blow, down to flatten his palm against the man's lower spine. His touch was quite soft.

The bone-crack this time was sudden, sodden, and final.

Halber's nerveless legs splayed out, and he dropped like a bludgeoned ox. "*Eh?*"

Pen's feet kissed the planks, and his legs bent double to absorb the shock of his landing. He came up and staggered a few steps before finding his balance. His body was dangerously, boilingly hot from the rapid deployment of his magics, even as the pace of the world came back to itself once more. He stood gasping, sweat running down his face, netting in his eyebrows, dripping from his chin. Bending, he tore off his boots and socks, vest and shirt, in a desperate bid to cool.

On the floor, Halber snarled filthy curses and threats and struggled to stand. Futilely, as his body from the waist down had gone as flaccid and helpless as a sack of custard.

Wegae recovered his pan and, holding it like a shield in one hand with the other out before him to feel his way, blundered fearfully to Pen's side. "He said he was going to *kill* me," he choked. "I mean, I always knew he despised me, but I didn't know he hated me that much!"

"—and that bitch your mother—!" Halber picked up his diatribe; his violence, blocked from physical expression, finding its outlet in words. Venting. Spewing. The targets of his obscene wrath seemed to include Wegae, Wegae's mother, Penric—not by name, but Pen presumed that *you bloodless blond Bastard's tit* meant him—all Temple sorcerers, the demonic fox, and Easthome judges. And his baroness and his brother, both of whom were long dead as far as Pen knew.

Penric steered Wegae to the door. "Run to the house. Find Oswyl. Find everyone. Bring aid."

Wegae needed help determining which brown blur in the distance was the manor house, but once Penric gripped his head and got him aimed, he stumbled off in the right direction.

Penric turned back to the hut, trying to figure out what in the gods' names had just happened here. Deposed Baron Halber come back for revenge, obviously, but never before had Pen found the proof of one of his theories to be so appalling.

Deprived of an audience, Halber had fallen silent. Pen could believe he really had fought in a mercenary company, after he'd fled Easthome three years ago. Would Penric's brother Drovo have turned into something this brutal, if he'd survived his camp fever? Pen shuddered.

Halber's broken hands must hurt, for he was curled around them, but Pen supposed he wasn't feeling further pain, or anything else, from his lower body. *Is that right, Helvia?* he asked tentatively. Because the knowledge of exactly what injury to devise and how must have come from her, or Amberein.

More or less. She didn't sound happy. Although not nearly as distraught as Pen. He'd never before inflicted a magical wound so intimate and calculated.

But controlled, put in Des. *Consider that.*

Deep bruises were starting on Pen's forearm and neck. Any number of pulled muscles were already rioting in protest. He bent to collect his shirt, shrugging it on. He wasn't ready for the rest yet, but he did don his Temple braids, pinning them crookedly to his left shoulder. He had to be the least dignified divine ever, bloodied and sweat-soaked, blond queue gone wildly askew, judging from the hair hanging in his face. He retied it while trying to collect his scattered wits, staring down in bafflement at his abrupt victim, who stared up in loathing.

Pen cleared his throat. "Do you normally try to murder people you've just met?" Although that was what a soldier did, he supposed.

More cursing, if wearier and not so loud.

Pen worried. If the man died later from this injury that Pen had done him, would it count as death by demonic magic? Could he still lose Des to the Bastard's peculiar justice, which had nothing to do with the vagaries of any human court?

Had Des, if not outright sacrificed herself for him, certainly risked such a fate?

I wouldn't fret, she said coolly. *He's bound to be hanged first.*

A dubious hope.

Pen was sure he needed Oswyl here, with Thala and her notebook, before he started interrogating suspects, but he had to know. "*Did* you shoot Learned Magal in the woods three days ago?"

Halber glowered at him from his thatch of hair and hatred. "That stupid Temple woman? It was the only way to get that hag Svedra's demon out of her to destroy it. If it hadn't jumped to that accursed fox, I would have been half done."

"Half . . . ?"

"And then there was that bitch my brother's wife. And her whelp Wegae. It was all her doing from the start. Trying to take what was mine—for *that* weed."

"Surely . . . you didn't imagine that if you could murder all those people, you could get everything back? Your rank, your property, your place?"

Halber snorted contempt. "If I can't have it, let no one do. Especially not *them*." He turned his head away, spat, and added, "Didn't have much more time. He's *spawning*."

Pen blinked. "Er . . . shouldn't it have been a greater concern how you are to present your soul to your god?" Although *Which god?* was a good question. The Father of Justice was right out. The Mother and the Daughter likewise. The Bastard, god of all leftovers, seemed unlikely after Magal, although there was no telling. The Brother was a god of vast mercy, as Pen had reason to know, but . . .

"Curse the gods. Curse the world. Curse . . . everybody."

Comprehensive, murmured Des.

"So . . . so you went through all this effort, perpetrated all this pointless cruelty, just to make yourself *feel better*?"

A wordless snarl.

Pen's voice went dry; he couldn't help it. "Is it working?"

Halber's arms flailed in helpless rage, but he couldn't reach Pen. He tried to the last, though.

Pen went back out to the porch and sank down on the wooden steps. The late afternoon was still bright and sunny. Perfect picnic weather, or to go fishing. After that abysmal bout of Halber, it felt as though it ought to have been midnight, and raining.

Pen ached. And felt ill. "Well. That was ugly."

"You foresaw it," said Des. Comfort? Cold comfort?

"It's one thing to foresee. Another to see. It turns out."

She was kindly silent.

He looked up to find Oswyl tromping toward them across the meadow, followed by a mob. Thala and her notebook, half-blind Baron

Wegae being led by the hand of Jons his servant, Nath and Kreil bracketing Treuch between them. Inglis. Pen was relieved to see Inglis. They'd need a couple of men to get the helpless Halber back to the house.

Oswyl shot Pen a look of sharp inquiry as he neared.

"Your prisoner"—Pen gestured over his shoulder—"is restrained. Have at him."

"Baron kin Pikepool says you saved his life."

"Mm, probably. His lunatic uncle was just warming up to beat him to death, I think."

"You coming in?"

"Rather not. I've had enough for now."

"Hm." Oswyl frowned in concern at him, but led the party inside.

He left the door open, though, and Pen, despite himself, ended up listening shamelessly.

After some noises indicating them getting Halber sitting up, Oswyl began with what were by now familiar preliminaries, with no cooperation from his surly suspect. But Oswyl shortly managed to get Halber and Treuch started in on each other, which perhaps explained why he'd dragged Treuch out here. The exchanges of blame and recrimination were better than any interrogation an inquirer could have devised, with or without red-hot irons. Oswyl only prodded them a little when they started to slow down.

"It wasn't my fault!" Treuch declaimed. "He didn't tell me *why* he needed me to get the Learned up there!"

Halber snorted contempt. Thala's stylus scratched busily.

"He told me to tell her there was a badger I thought was possessed by an elemental. That I needed her to see if it was so, and take it away to her Order."

Certainly a routine task for a Temple sorcerer, if important. A shrewd draw. If Halber had known little of sorcery before his first arrest, he'd likely had an opportunity to learn after.

Which was why Halber had pressed his old lackey Treuch to be his stalking-horse, of course. He'd been afraid Svedra's former demon might have recognized him. Possible, that.

"I didn't even see! He told me to just bring her and leave her. Tell her I was going to check if the creature was still in its den. I didn't see anything!" Treuch somewhat spoiled this impassioned defense by adding, "He should have hidden her right then, not gone fooling off after that fox all by himself. It wasn't my fault!"

"That will be for the judges to decide," Oswyl sighed.

After Thala collected signatures from the listening witnesses, the men collaborated on devising a makeshift litter for Halber to be lugged away to the manor house. He'd be put on a cart to the Easthome magistrates as soon as a horse could be harnessed. Treuch whined horribly at the news that he was to be taken along tied to the rail. Oswyl was plainly unmoved by his protests. By nightfall, they would both be someone else's problem, though Pen was certain the senior locator would have reports to write.

Oswyl came out on the porch as Nath and Jons maneuvered the litter down the stairs and marched away with it. Treuch followed with the dolor of a mourner in a cortege, Thala keeping a close watch on him. Kreil guided Wegae like a loyal dog. Oswyl lingered a moment to stare oddly down at Pen.

"Restrained? His spine is broken. Did you realize?"

"Oh," Pen sighed, "yes."

"How did that happen?"

"In the fight," Pen answered, although that likely wasn't exactly what Oswyl was asking. "Wegae witnessed it, I believe." How much the poor fellow could *see* being an open question.

"Hm, yes, his description was dramatic, if confused. He sounds wildly grateful to you."

"I don't believe he could have succeeded in defending himself from Halber. The man was terrifying."

"And yet you are standing, and Halber is . . . not."

Not ever again. "I'm sitting," Pen pointed out.

Oswyl puffed something not nearly a laugh. "Baron Wegae is coming with us to lay his deposition and accusation. What about you?"

Pen gestured to Inglis, leaning against the porch post and glummer than ever. "The shamans and I will be taking the foxes to their menagerie, for now. Best to keep them well separated from Halber and Treuch. I'm not sure I could control the fox's demon if she sees them."

"Ah." Oswyl frowned uneasily. "You would know best, I suppose. We'll need a deposition from you, too, in due course."

"I won't be hard to find. I imagine I'll be splitting my attendance between the menagerie and the princess-archdivine, for now. And

Hamo. I promised to call on Hamo tonight. I didn't expect to have this much news for him." Pen wondered if he'd need to apologize for sending Hamo on a blind search through his records all day.

"Oh. Yes. I had better speak to him myself. Although the next-of-kin may need to come first. Tell him to look for me tomorrow." Oswyl blew out his breath. "I hope he will be pleased with our success."

"Ah. Hm." Pen wasn't sure if he should speak this thought aloud. "Best you keep Hamo separated from Halber and Treuch, too. For a few days, till he calms down."

Oswyl's brows flicked up. "Really?"

"Hamo's a smart man. I suspect the stupidity of this entire revenge escapade is going to enrage him beyond measure."

". . . How far beyond?"

"He's a man with responsible authority." *And a chaos demon.* "Just don't . . . bait him. Tempt him."

Oswyl took this in, thoughtfully. After a moment, he murmured, "I am advised."

"Thank you."

Tilting his head, Oswyl asked, "And how tempted were you?"

"Less than Hamo would have been, I'm sure. But there were difficult parts."

Oswyl glanced after the retreating litter. "I shall like to hear more about that. When there is time. But Penric . . . "

"Hm?"

"Subduing a criminal who violently resists always has elements of risk. For everyone. It comes with the task. Things can happen too fast, and no one is in control. It's understood, in my Order."

"Some risks"—Pen scratched absently at the drying scabs on his arms, palpated the throbbing bruise—"are different than others." He looked up. "Are all your cases this awful?"

"No. Well, some." Oswyl's gaze at him was less than reassured. "We'll talk later," he promised, and hurried after his charges.

"So." Pen looked up to Inglis. "We have a lost demon to shepherd."

"Aye."

Sometimes, Inglis's gloomy silences could be quite soothing. They walked together toward the stable.

The fox family was loaded into pannier baskets, one pair carried over the haunches of Pen's horse and the second on Lunet's. The young passengers whined for a time, restrained under closed lids, but then settled down to sleep. The vixen was granted the courtesy of being allowed to ride behind Lunet in her own basket with the top fastened open. Pen tried to persuade himself that her cynical expression, as she was trundled along, was merely the usual one for a fox. It was nearly dark by the time they'd transported their furry charges to the menagerie of the Royal Fellowship.

A spare stall was swiftly readied, the animals bedded down for the night with small protest. Pen made promises to the vixen to return on the morrow, with as little assurance that they were understood as that he could keep them. The tired shamans could at last depart to find their own beds, with Pen's repeated thanks.

And Pen could crawl atop his horse one more time—he used the mounting block—and make his way up through Kingstown to Templetown and the chapterhouse of the Bastard's Order, for what he prayed would not be too difficult a report.

The night porter, recognizing Penric, let him in without demur despite his bedraggled appearance. Pen found his own way to Hamo's workroom. The candles were burning late as before, although Hamo had put down his quill and sat with his elbows on his writing table, his face resting in his hands. He jerked up at Pen's knock on the doorjamb, blinked reddened eyes, and said in a blurry voice, "Ah. Good. You're back at last." Had he been waiting up?

Pen fetched his own chair and dropped into it.

Hamo looked him over. "Five gods. Were you dragged by a horse?"

"I feel like it," admitted Pen, running his hand over his grimy face. *Yech.* "Not quite. But let's have your tale first."

Hamo pursed his lips but complied, shoving a thin stack of papers across his table to Pen. "I found four accounts from Svedra that looked promising. As she grew older, they tended to become more laconic, which was not as much help as you'd think, since they required more cross-checking. Her most difficult cases from the past five years, that may have left someone angry but not confirmed dead. I can look back farther if needed."

Pen took them up and squinted through them. He puffed relief at finding Halber's case second in the sheaf. "Locator Oswyl will wish to see all of these. If only for his own reassurance. He means to call on you tomorrow." He forced himself to at least look at the other three, but set them down when he realized that Oswyl would be better able to evaluate them, and that he was just stalling. "But he has former baron Halber kin Pikepool in custody, and his confession."

Hamo went stiff in his chair. Pen could feel his demon stirring from where he sat. Dark, with red flashes like heat lightning.

"Halber had been in hiding up at his old forest manor, where we flushed him out. Not being a man who does things by halves, Halber also tried to murder his nephew Wegae. Crime of opportunity, as nearly as I could tell. Caught in the act, fortunately for both Wegae and for Oswyl's case. He also had a try at me. I don't think we need count me. I'm redundant to need."

Hamo's fists curled into tight balls. "Did he shoot Mags?"

"Yes. Had his thrall lure her with some tale of a badger possessed by an elemental. Up to his home woods, where he laid an ambush. His aim was to destroy her demon. Magal was just . . . in his way. He said."

A little silence, broken by a growl. "Where is he now?"

"I don't actually know," said Pen, glad he could answer, or not-answer, that question honestly. "Wherever the Grayjays usually take dangerous suspects in Easthome." Not that Hamo couldn't find out, but anything to slow him down . . .

As Hamo's tight-lipped silence thickened with menace, Pen went hastily on, "He's not going anywhere. Can't. His back is broken, and both his hands. If your heart wishes him pain, I promise you he has it. If you wish him dead, well, the magistrates of Easthome will accomplish that task for you as well. Magal's family and friends may not even have to endure his trial, if they decide to execute him for the murder of his wife, for which he's already convicted. The wheels of justice will grind him fine, and soon." Pen hesitated. "No need to . . . compromise yourself."

Hamo looked up, the peculiar list of injuries perhaps penetrating whatever red haze his mind was lost in. His voice rough, he asked, "Are you compromised, Penric?"

"Mm . . . " Pen shrugged. "Possibly a little. Oswyl seemed to think that the fact I injured Halber in the course of his resisting arrest would pass unquestioned. That it was by . . . more-than-physical means might not, if it were looked into by a hostile inquiry. I've never done anything like this before. Well, there was that time with the kin Martenden brothers, but I only set them on fire—never mind," Pen ran down before his mouth did him more harm than good.

Hamo unclenched his teeth. "Should anyone ask," and now his voice went soft, which was somehow not less alarming, "you may say you acted under my authority, Learned Penric."

"Thank you," said Pen. He was fairly sure the princess-archdivine's cloak would cover him, but more layers wouldn't hurt, and it gave Hamo a straw of usefulness to clutch. *Useful to us, at least,* Des murmured, a trifle sardonically. Time for the next diversion: "And also, with welcome help from some shamans Inglis brought from the Royal Fellowship, we located Magal's lost demon. It was indeed in a fox."

Hamo sat up, his tension thinning like slate-gray clouds shredding in a wind. Des's attention upon her internal counterpart eased. "Oh! You took it alive? Is it here? What condition—"

"It turned out to have lodged in a vixen with six cubs, which had some strange consequences."

"It is ascended, surely."

"Well, yes, but in an odd mode. It seems to be, I'm not sure how to put it, taking *care* of the vixen. And her children."

Hamo sat back, nonplussed, but then after a moment sighed. "That would be Magal, I suspect. It sounds like her. Svedra was a woman more in the style of your Ruchia. Very . . . forceful."

Pen wondered what less flattering term Hamo had swallowed. Des snickered at him, or possibly at them both.

"I have some ideas of what might be done with her," Pen put forward. "The vixen, that is. Uh, and the demon." Or he would, when he'd had a chance to sleep and recover. Hamo could take this burden of care from him with a word, Pen knew. Half of him was almost weary enough to let him, but . . . "Yesterday, you said you were thinking on it?"

Hamo scrubbed his hands through his hair, grimacing. "There are only two choices. First, have the Saint of Easthome remove the damaged demon to the god."

Of *course* the Bastard's Order at the royal capital would have its own saint at hand. Although not, probably, at call, from what Pen had experienced of saints. Such directly god-touched men and women did not owe their primary allegiances to the *Temple*, after all. Des flinched.

"Or second," Hamo went on, "sacrifice the fox and transfer whatever is left of the demon to a new Temple sorcerer. Salvaging . . . something."

"Do you really think it would be that much different than when an elemental is transferred for the first time from an animal to a sorcerer?"

"I am quite sure it would be different. What I don't know is how dangerous it might be to the recipient to take in such a crippled partner."

Pen almost rose to the defense of the vixen by arguing that Hamo wouldn't be talking of sacrifice if the demon had gone into some random *person*. But of course, if it had gone into a person, they'd be able to speak for themselves, human and demon both. Gods, he was too tired to think straight. "There's a third choice. Leave the vixen with the shamans for a while, let them tame her."

Hamo sat back, startled. "What would be the point of that? They cannot use her demon-spirit for the basis of a Great Beast; the two magics are incompatible. And the longer we wait, the worse the demon's condition may grow. The more of Mags and Svedra to be lost."

"Or what was lost, was lost at the first. Like pouring water into a cup until it overflows, which then remains as full as it can hold. The point is to study a rare situation, at least for a little. The point is, there is time to think about it. The vixen is probably not going anywhere till the cubs are weaned, some weeks at least." Unless the ascendant demon was directly threatened with annihilation. When it surely would try to save itself, and then they'd have a real problem. Well . . . *another* real problem.

Hamo hesitated. "Did you sense it to be so?"

"I've only observed the vixen briefly. It would take more time than that to perceive ongoing changes." He carefully did not say *deterioration*. Not that he had to.

"Fine if she's stabilized. Not if she hasn't."

Pen shrugged in provisional concession. "You should certainly come out to the Fellowship's menagerie and examine her carefully, before making any irrevocable decisions."

Lips twisting in bemusement, Hamo said, "Penric—are you trying to preserve the life of a *fox*?"

"Magal's demon seems to be doing so," Pen defended this. Weakly, he feared.

Hamo rubbed his eyes. "Feh. I can't . . . Let us take this up again out there, then. Tomorrow."

"Good idea, sir." At least the man was not dismissing Penric's words outright. Time for a tactful withdrawal, before he fell off this chair onto that lovely, inviting floor.

Hamo stood up to see him out, another hopeful sign. At the door, he lowered his head and murmured, "I would never have compromised my demon, you know. . . . I'd have used a knife. Or my bare hands."

Pen couldn't very well feign being appalled when he'd run through similar thought-chains himself. "Not needed now." He mustered a sympathetic smile and signed himself, tapping his lips twice with his thumb in farewell.

It was midnight by the time Pen made his weary way back to the Temple guest house. He was trying to mentally compose a note to slip under the princess-archdivine's door, excusing himself from appearing due to the lateness of the hour, when he discovered a paper pinned to his own. It was in her secretary's fine hand, and charged him to call on her before he retired regardless of the time.

He threaded the halls to her chambers and tapped tentatively, waited, and knocked again. He was just turning away when the door swung open, and the secretary beckoned him inside the sitting room. "Ah, Learned Penric, at last. Wait here."

He stood dumbly in his day dirt, feeling every bruise and muscle-pull. At length, Llewen emerged from an inner door, wrapped in a brocade night robe and with her hair in a gray braid down her back. Not an ensemble he'd seen before.

She looked him over. "My, my, my."

Three *mys* tonight, goodness. He usually rated only two. He wondered what he'd have to do to win four.

"My apologies, Archdivine, for waking you at this hour. It's been a long day."

"At my age, I'm never asleep at this hour." She made a dismissive gesture, charitably fending his apology. Her secretary settled her in a cushioned chair, and her wave directed Pen to another.

Fine blue-and-white silk stripes. He stared at it in dismay, considered his reek, and then settled himself cross-legged on the floor at her feet, instead. Her gray brows rose ironically as she looked down at him.

"So, how was your day in the country this time?"

He was grateful for the practice he'd had recounting it already. He didn't have to think as much. She pressed her fingers to her lips a few times, but did not interrupt him apart from a few shrewd, uncomfortably clarifying questions.

"I thought . . . I thought I might receive some spiritual guidance from Learned Hamo, as we both share the burden and gift of a demon, but it turned out to be more the other way around," sighed Pen. "Though I don't think he's going to bolt off in the night to try to commit murder on Learned Magal's behalf."

"Was that a risk?"

"Mm . . . not now."

Her lips twitched. "Then your counsel must have been good enough."

He turned his hands out, smiling ruefully. He really wanted to lie across her silk-slippered feet like a tired dog. "But who will counsel me?"

"Your own Temple superior, of course. That's her job."

"Ah." His head tipped over, and he found himself resting it upon her knee. Her beringed hand petted his hair. Dog indeed.

"Anyone who wishes to question my court sorcerer on his actions today must go through me," she stated. *And good luck to them* stood implied, he thought. Heartening, but . . .

"So much for the realm, and the law. But what about my god? And my demon. My soul stands more naked in that court. Violence, it appears, grows easier with practice. Or so Halber demonstrates. I've seen it in the ruined mercenary soldiers come back to the cantons, too, sometimes. The pitfall of their trade. I don't want it to become the pitfall of mine. And . . . and I see how it could. So very, very easily. Hamo was almost ready to slip tonight, and he's had decades more experience than me."

"And thus you seek my counsel?"

"Aye. Archdivine."

Her slow strokes turned into more perfunctory pats, as she sat up and took thought, and then breath. "So. My counsel to you tonight—as your Temple superior, my oh-so-learned divine and demon-burdened boy—is to go downstairs to the guesthouse bathing chamber, wake the attendant, get a bath—wash your *hair*"—her fingers paused to rub together in mild revulsion—"get something to eat, and go to bed." She added after a moment, "Desdemona shall like that, too."

Pen glowered at her slippers. "That's not my Temple superior, that's my *mother.*"

"And if she were here, I have no doubt she would tell you the same thing," she said briskly, pushing him upright off her knee despite himself. "Shoo."

"That's *all*?"

"Clean your teeth, I suppose. Though you usually do that without being told. Your soul will keep for one night, I promise you, and your body and mind will be better tomorrow."

He and Des snorted in unison, this time: he at Llewen, Des at him. "Agh." He stretched, and clambered up; he had to balance on his hands and knees before he could rise to his feet. Des had made no interrupting comment throughout this interview. There weren't many people his demon much respected, but Princess-Archdivine Llewen kin Stagthorne was high on that short list. It seemed the feeling was growing mutual.

He commanded over his shoulder as he made for the door, "You go to sleep, too, Your Grace."

She smiled wryly at him. "Oh, I shall be able to now."

Pen heaved himself out of bed the next morning thinking the princess-archdivine might have been overly optimistic about how much recovery one night's sleep would provide him. He contemplated the walk all the way down across town and out to the Fellowship, not to mention back up again, and ordered a horse brought around from the Temple mews, instead. It proved another slug, suiting his mood perfectly as he sat atop it in a daze while it ferried him to his destination. By the time he arrived at the palisade and gate of the shamanic menagerie, he had come awake, helped by a cool, moist wind up the valley of the Stork that promised rain.

He handed off his mount to a helpful groom, then found his way to the fox family's stall in the shorter stable block that overlooked the menagerie yard. Lunet was in attendance, he was pleased to discover, sitting on a stool under the broad eaves and looking none the worse for yesterday's wear. She greeted him with good cheer.

Pen asked anxiously, "Does the family seem well, after their forcible relocation?"

"Quite well; take a look."

They both leaned on the lower door and peered into the straw-lined stall. The vixen was laid out looking placid enough, nursing two cubs while three slept curled in a furry mound, and the last tried to stir up trouble by gnawing on what parts of its siblings it could reach. The vixen lifted her head warily at Pen, but laid it back down with a tired maternal sigh. The shamaness, it seemed, worried her not at all.

"The cubs are happy enough, if rambunctious," Lunet told him. "We'll need to let them out for exercise, when we're sure, ah, their mother is settled."

Meaning the vixen, or the demon? The demon was ascendant, there could be no doubt, rider not ridden, if letting the vixen have her way with her family. It wasn't the fox who was dealing so smoothly with their human captors.

Des, thought Pen, *can you discern any change since yesterday in the demon?*

The vixen—no, the demon lifted the vixen's head again as she felt her fellow-demon's uncanny regard, but she tolerated the inspection. That much of her Temple tameness lingered, at least. A hopeful sign?

No new loss since yesterday, Desdemona allowed, *in her density. Calmer, which is good.*

It could be too early to tell. Pen wanted to be able to declare her stabilized, and Des knew why, but he also needed the claim to be true.

Hamo and his lad will be able to judge for themselves, if he gives it some time.

His lad? Oh, Hamo's own demon. *Younger than you, is he?*

Most demons are. Hamo is only his second human rider; he was a mere elemental not long before that. She added a bit grudgingly, *Hamo seems to have been good for him. He has developed quite well. That one could be ready for a physician in one more well-chosen lifetime.*

Always the golden prize, much the way a Great Beast suitable to make a shaman was the goal of the shamans' own carefully reiterated sacrifices. That might make a career for the cubs. The shamans preferred long-lived beasts, to build up spiritual strength and wisdom, so they would certainly prosper better in such care than in the wild, where half the litter would not survive their first year.

Voices carrying through the damp air pulled Pen from his meditations, and he turned to discover Learned Hamo rounding the stable block, accompanied, a bit to his surprise, by Oswyl and his shadow Thala. Oswyl must have gone to exchange reports as promised with Hamo this morning, though Pen rather thought it was curiosity, not duty, that brought him along here.

Oswyl nodded at the shamaness Lunet, who waved back in her usual friendly manner, and punctiliously introduced her to the bailiff of sorcerers.

"I thank you for your hard work yesterday," said Hamo to Lunet, trying to return the civility, but his gaze was drawn inexorably to the stall. "Can I . . . may I go in?"

Lunet pursed her lips. "Of course, Learned, though we are trying not to disturb the mother fox too much." The hint being that Hamo should withdraw promptly if he did. He nodded understanding, and Lunet drew open the lower door, closing it after him.

The vixen looked up abruptly, then rose and shook off her cubs, who complained and retreated from the human. But her posture did not speak of defense. Hamo fell to his knees before her, then sat cross-legged in the straw. She came to him without fear. Hamo was, Pen realized belatedly, the first person the demon-vixen *could* recognize.

They stared at each other for a long moment. Without speech, but not without understanding, because Hamo placed his hand out flat to the floor and whispered, "I am so sorry for your loss."

Oh. Of course. Of course. Because Learned Magal had lost her demon, but the demon had also lost her Mags. Did demons mourn?

Oh, yes, breathed Des. *It is not something we come into the world knowing, as elementals. But we learn. Oh, how we learn.*

Pen's stomach fluttered in a flash of formless, unanchored grief. Not his own. He had to inhale and exhale carefully.

The vixen placed one black paw atop the man's outstretched hand. Pen needed neither hearing nor Sight to interpret this language: *I am sorry for your loss as well.*

Hamo turned his head to his watchers only long enough to murmur, "She's in there. Something of her is definitely still in there." Then all his attention returned to the animal.

Lunet jerked her chin, and muttered, "They'll be all right. Let's leave them for a little." She, too, felt the sense of intrusion on some painfully private communion, Pen fancied.

In the gray morning light, the four of them went over to the mounting blocks where Pen had first seen the shamans . . . only yesterday? He, for one, sat with a grunt of relief.

Oswyl looked down at his hands clasped between his knees, and asked, "Do you think he loved her? Hamo and Magal."

Pen made a releasing gesture. "Clearly so, but if you mean a love of the bedchamber, likely not. It would be vanishingly rare for two sorcerers to be so physically intimate. But there are other loves just as profound. Delighting in her as a protégée, hoping for her bright future, all of that. And the future of her demon. Think of two rival artists, perhaps, admiring each other's work. The survivor mourning not just what was, but what could have been."

"Hm."

Thala listened with a thoughtful frown, but for once jotted no notes.

"How of yourselves?" asked Pen. "Did all go well last night, delivering Halber to his fate?" Now doubly earned, and Pen was not above hoping it would prove doubly ill.

Oswyl nodded. "He's in a cell, and in the hands of the justiciars. I doubt he'll be escaping on a fast horse this time around."

"Reports to your superiors go smoothly?" asked Pen, thinking of his own fraught night.

Oswyl actually grinned. Slyly, but still. Pen's brows rose in question.

"I arrived to find them anxious to tell me that my case was to be taken from me and given to a much more senior inquirer, on account of the kin Pikepool connections cropping up. I had to tell them they were too late off the mark."

"Alas," murmured Thala, in the most unrepentant lilt imaginable. She shared the smirk with her senior.

Pen had enough experience with bureaucratic hierarchies by now to have no trouble reading that one, either. "Congratulations."

"Thank you," said Oswyl. "Thank you several times over. Not least that I don't have poor Baron Wegae's corpse on my plate today. That would not have proved nearly so palatable a dish to present." Oswyl's grin turned to grimace with the vision. "He wants to see you again, by the by."

Pen nodded. "I'm sure I can make a chance, before I have to leave Easthome."

Thala asked the air generally, "So, are shamans like sorcerers? Not able to live or work together much?"

"Not at all," said Lunet. "We work together all the time. I have a group singing-practice this afternoon, in fact."

Thala didn't look entirely elated at this news, but asked, "Like a Temple choir?"

Lunet's smile was suddenly all fox. "Not exactly, no."

Combining weirding voices? *Oh my*, as the princess-archdivine might say. Or even, *My, my, my*. Pen *really* wanted to see that.

Lunet stared off at some point over Oswyl's shoulder, and remarked, "Although shamans share some of the problems I suspect sorcerers may have. Ordinary people are afraid to get close to us, afraid of the powers in our blood that they do not understand. As if because we possess strange beasts, we are them."

"That sounds . . . foolish," said Oswyl in a tentative tone. "If you don't understand something, you should just try to learn more, that's all."

Lunet's gray eyes glinted at him from under her ruddy lashes. Pen could not parse her expression, although Des murmured, *Heh. Not too hopelessly thick, that boy.*

Thala looked curiously at Pen, and said, "Then it would seem sorcerers have a doubly lonely time of it. If ordinary people fear them, and other sorcerers cannot be too near them."

That girl saw too much, and said too little, but when she did . . . ouch. "We always have our demons," Pen offered. He thought Des would have patted his head in approval if she could.

"Ah, you're all here!" came a voice, and Pen turned in some relief to wave at Inglis.

He strolled near and looked them over, almost smiling. "All well this morning with our new foxes?" he asked Lunet.

"Aye. Penric's Learned Hamo came to see them. He's in there now." She gestured toward the stall. "Private conclave."

Inglis paused, extending what shamanic perception Pen did not know, but he nodded. "Right." He looked at Pen. "Will it be all right?"

A comprehensive question, that. "I'll know in a little."

Inglis tapped his fingers on his trouser seam, nodded again at the Grayjays. No, at Thala. "Would you like to look around the menagerie while we wait? I could show you our wolves."

"I'd be quite interested in that," said Thala, rising at once to her feet and almost-smiling back at him.

Lunet's eyes narrowed in merriment, watching this play. She leaned over and said to Oswyl, "And I could show you our other foxes."

"Oh! Ah, you have more?"

"And the lynxes. They're really fine."

Oswyl mustered an actual smile at her, and rose as well, suddenly all amiable cooperation. On Oswyl, it looked very odd.

Rather than departing as a group, the two shamans started to draw the two Grayjays off in opposite directions, though Lunet paused to politely ask over her shoulder, in a most unpressing tone, "And you, Learned Penric?"

He waved her off. "Inglis showed me around the other day. I'll wait here for Hamo."

"Oh, all right."

How very tactful of you, Pen.

As they rounded the corner, Pen could hear Oswyl asking, in an almost-convincing simulation of his habitual inquirer's style, "And how long have you been a member of the Royal Fellowship, Shaman Lunet? How did you become interested in the calling . . . ?"

Hah, murmured Des. *Shamans really do work together.*

Pen watched them out of sight, then sighed, "Don't mind me. I'll just sit here and talk to myself."

Now, now, boy.

Pen's lips twitched.

His smile faded as he studied the silent stall door. This must be what it was like waiting for a judge to return from his chambers and deliver a verdict. He considered extending his Sight, but thought it might be felt as intrusive; it would certainly be felt. Going over and leaning on the stall door would scarcely be better, putting three chaos demons in such close proximity.

At length, his careful patience was rewarded when Hamo emerged, brushing a few straws off his trousers and closing the lower door behind him. He looked around a trifle blindly, then walked over and sat on the mounting block farthest from Pen.

"So?" said Pen quietly. "What do you think?"

"Stable," said Hamo slowly, "for an ascendant demon. Magal's and Svedra's influences lingering, I think. Safe enough for the moment. But I must be careful not to thoughtlessly take this fox for the same thing as a new elemental, ignorant of the uses of its powers. The same marred imprints that make it tamer make it more dangerous. It will require much more shrewd and mindful care."

Pen rubbed his booted toe across the cobblestones. "I was thinking about how the Order sometimes pairs a trained aspirant with an aged sorcerer, to acquaint the demon with its proposed new home in advance." A gruesome deathwatch Pen had been spared by Ruchia's sudden roadside accident, or at any rate, the experience had been compressed to minutes and not weeks or months. "What if, once the vixen has weaned her cubs, she might be given into the care of such an aspirant? It might make for a more gentle transition. And a kinder surveillance."

Hamo tilted his head. "She would make an extraordinary pet," he allowed.

Pen could not only picture it, he envied it. The vixen and her young sorceress-to-be, going about together. If he didn't have a demon already . . .

You just think it would be madly stylish to have a clever pet fox, Des mocked him. He didn't deny it.

"It would take some careful matchmaking," said Hamo.

This man, Pen was reminded, *made* sorcerers for the Temple. "I expect you're up to that."

"Maybe," said Hamo, his eyes narrowing as he considered Pen knew-not-what pertinent factors. "Maybe. I so want to salvage . . . I must take some thought who might . . . hm. Hm."

Pen liked the tone of those *hms*. Very hopeful. By the time the cubs were weaned, Hamo would have had some weeks to scour, really, the whole Weald for suitable candidates, among all the aspirant-divines scattered across the Hallow King's realm. The task, he had no doubt, would be done well, and shrewdly. Somewhere out there was a very lucky aspirant indeed.

Are you regretting the haste and disorder of our own pairing? Des's query was soft, the faintest tint of hurt coloring her doubt. Not that it could be undone now. Save by a few arrows to his back or some like mischance.

Pen returned ruefully, *Oh, I have for a while suspected we had a better Matchmaker than Hamo, conscientious though he is.*

. . . That thought would be more flattering if it were more comforting.

Aye, Pen sighed.

The Easthome royal magistrates hanged Halber kin Pikepool a week after the Grayjays had returned him to their custody.

Penric did not attend. Hamo did, he heard.

Three days before they were to depart for Martensbridge, Penric made a formal request to call upon the princess-archdivine.

She received him in her private chambers, waving out the servants attempting to pack all that she had brought, topped by all that she had acquired in the royal capital, for the four-hundred-mile journey home. The Easthome hills were fine in their way, but they were not the austere white peaks fencing his horizon that Pen was used to. Though the mountains, he was sure, would wait for him, with the endless patience of stone. All the impatience of flesh and nerve drove him now.

He flashed his finest smile as he seated himself on blue-and-white silk, safe now against the trousers of his Order's well-laundered whites. "I have a proposal for you, Your Grace. To enhance my abilities as your court sorcerer."

"Shouldn't there be more pleasantries before you leap in?"

"Oh. Er, do you want some?"

"Not particularly." A quirk of her gray eyebrows indicated interest without commitment. "Do go on."

"I've been speaking with my friend Shaman Inglis. And with his superior, Master Firthwyth, over at the Royal Fellowship. He is supervisor of the training of the young shamans. The Fellowship being part school, part farm, part a community of historical scholarship, and part, these days, hospice for injured or sick creatures."

"It sounds a lively place," she conceded.

He nodded vigorously. "Anyway, Master Firthwyth agrees that it would be of great interest for me to study awhile with the royal shamans. Learn what I can of their magics."

"And what do my nephew's shamans gain from this?"

"Well, they get to study me back, I expect."

"How long do you imagine this study would take?"

"Hard to say. I mean, a shaman can spend a lifetime exploring his calling, but I already have a calling of my own, that, er, calls to me as well. But the Fellowship maintains a fine and growing library. I was allowed to see it, when I was over there visiting the other day." Inglis had sternly forbade him to drool on the priceless volumes.

"And how long would it take you to read every book in it? A month?"

"Oh, longer than that!" He hesitated. ". . . A year?"

"A cap of sorts, I suppose." A quizzical tilt of her elaborately braided head. "And what would my reimbursement be, for the loss of your services during all that time?"

"When I came back, I could do more kinds of things?"

"What things?"

"If I already knew—if anyone knew—I wouldn't have to go study to find out, now would I?"

"That's . . . actually a less specious argument than it sounds at first blush."

They exchanged nods, like two swordsmen saluting.

She drummed her fingers on her silk-swathed knee. "When we returned home, I was going to tell you . . . Master Riedel of the Mother's Order in Martensbridge was very impressed by your new edition of Learned Ruchia's work on sorcery as applied to the arts of medicine. He wanted to extend you an invitation to study at the hospice. Part-time, as your other duties permitted."

"*Oh.*" Pen sat up. He hadn't realized his gift of the fresh-printed volumes to the hospice's library, and his few meals at the princess-archdivine's table with Master Riedel, had borne such excellent fruit. "Oh, yes, I'd like to do that! Too."

"Not instead?"

"Too," he said, with more certainty. "Though I grant I can't do both at once. Not even with sorcery."

"Then you have a puzzle." She sat back in some fascination, as if to watch him solve it. Or, possibly, as if to watch a man trying to eat a meal twice the size of his head, Pen wasn't sure.

"Two of Des's prior riders," he said slowly, "had trained and practiced as physicians."

"Master Riedel is aware. He thinks it would make you a very quick study."

Pen nodded. "In my prior experiences with, with drawing on Des's vast knowledge, it doesn't exactly just appear on its own in my mind. I have to induce it, more or less. Like, I don't know, digging a ditch from an irrigation channel to its water source. Then it flows on its own. Well, sometimes it's more like raising it bucket by bucket, but in any case. It was so with the languages. What Master Riedel might teach me would allow me to know all Des knows, eventually."

Pen wasn't going to ask Des's opinion on this one. She'd had her own reasons for jumping to not-yet-Learned Ruchia last time, rather than the physician-aspirant that the Temple had planned for her. Besides, having transcribed every word of Ruchia's medical text for printing, not to mention translating it into two and a half languages so far, he'd gained more than a trickle of understanding already.

"The point is"—he slowly felt his way forward—"if I study the shamanic magic first, I will have a chance of bringing something new back to more formal medical studies. More than just a review of things already known."

Llewen pursed her lips. "That is an honestly compelling view." She hesitated. "And how would you plan to support yourself, during this scholarly holiday?"

"I, er, was hoping you could grant me a stipend?"

"So I am to *pay* to be deprived of your services for some undefined amount of time?"

". . . Yes?" Pen tried for a sop. "Although I am fairly sure Wegae and Yvaina kin Pikepool would feed me, from time to time. I've already enjoyed some very interesting dinners over there."

"Set a savory table, do they?"

"I don't remember the food. But Yvaina has had this terrific notion, if I can get Learned Hamo interested. She proposes to invest in a press, using the sort of printing plates I produce with sorcery. Except I had this idea, really from rusting out Treuch's knife before he gutted me, well, anyway, explaining it over dinner, it occurred to me that a sorcerer could create steel plates as well as wooden ones. Which could last for thousands of copies, not just dozens or hundreds. So students wouldn't ever have to stab each other over sharing expensive texts again. And then she asked if I couldn't do woodcuts or engravings the same way, and I said no, never thought about it because I couldn't draw, but then she said, maybe some sorcerer who could. And I said, Oh. Of course. I think I can get Hamo to let me teach the technique to some of his people. And then—"

Llewen held up a hand to stem this tide. "Remind me to have my secretary explain the concept of a percentage recompense to you. Soon. Possibly tonight."

"Er, yes, Archdivine." Pen subsided.

"Certainly before you are turned loose in Easthome to cut whatever swath seems inevitable."

Pen's heart rose in hope. In quite another tone, he said, "*Yes,* Archdivine."

"Hah." She rubbed her fine chin, regarding him thoughtfully. "There is a line from a poem that rises to my mind. I no longer remember from where, but that's the hazard of my years—oh. Do you suppose Baroness kin Pikepool's press would ever share out poetry?"

Pen sat nonplussed, then afire. "I was thinking of texts, but certainly, why not? Or maybe books of tales . . . Really, anything." He paused, wanting to ask what she would offer for a stipend, but his curiosity was caught. "What was the verse?"

"Just a fragment, really. A call-and-response song. The bard was describing an itinerant scholar. 'Joyously he learned/joyfully taught.' Went about in rags, poor man, which I thought quite unfair."

"Probably had spent all his money on copyists. One must make choices, after all."

She snorted, delicately. But then asked, "And what does Desdemona think of all this?"

Pen started to open his mouth, then said, "Des?" yielding control of his speech to her.

"I'm for the shamans," said Des without hesitation. "It will be something new. Also, Ruchia has some very fond memories of one."

Pen shut his mouth again quickly, before she could go into the more ribald details. And then wondered what (possibly horrifying) conversations Des and Llewen might get into if he wasn't around, listening in.

Surely you must test that, Des quipped. He tightened his teeth.

Llewen tapped his hand. "Just bring him back to me, Desdemona."

"As you wish, Archdivine," agreed the demon.

AUTHOR'S NOTE:
A BUJOLD READING-ORDER GUIDE

THE FANTASY NOVELS

My fantasy novels are not hard to order. Easiest of all is *The Spirit Ring*, which is a stand-alone, or aquel, as some wag once dubbed books that for some obscure reason failed to spawn a subsequent series. Next easiest are the four volumes of *The Sharing Knife*—in order, *Beguilement*, *Legacy*, *Passage*, and *Horizon*—which I broke down and actually numbered, as this was one continuous tale divided into non-wrist-breaking chunks. The novella "Knife Children" is something of a codicil-tale to the tetralogy.

What were called the Chalion books after the setting of its first two volumes, but which now that the geographic scope has widened I'm dubbing the World of the Five Gods, were written to be stand-alones as part of a larger whole, and can in theory be read in any order. Some readers think the world-building is easier to assimilate when the books are read in publication order, and the second volume certainly contains spoilers for the first (but not the third). In any case, the publication order is:

The Curse of Chalion
Paladin of Souls
The Hallowed Hunt

In terms of internal world chronology, *The Hallowed Hunt* would fall first, the Penric novellas perhaps a hundred and fifty years later, and *The Curse of Chalion* and *Paladin of Souls* would follow a century or so after that.

The internal chronology of the Penric novellas is presently

"Penric's Demon"
"Penric and the Shaman"
"Penric's Fox"
"Penric's Mission"
"Mira's Last Dance"
"The Prisoner of Limnos"
"The Orphans of Raspay"

The first three are collected in the Baen compilation *Penric's Progress*; the second three in the (currently upcoming) *Penric's Travels*.

OTHER ORIGINAL E-BOOKS

The short story collection *Proto Zoa* contains five very early tales—three (1980s) contemporary fantasy, two science fiction—all previously published but not in this handy format. The novelette "Dreamweaver's Dilemma" may be of interest to Vorkosigan completists, as it is the first story in which that proto-universe began, mentioning Beta Colony but before Barrayar was even thought of.

Sidelines: Talks and Essays is just what it says on the tin—a collection of three decades of my nonfiction writings, including convention speeches, essays, travelogues, introductions, and some less formal pieces. I hope it will prove an interesting companion piece to my fiction.

THE VORKOSIGAN STORIES

Many pixels have been expended debating the 'best' order in which to read what have come to be known as the Vorkosigan Books (or Saga), the Vorkosiverse, the Miles books, and other names. The debate mainly revolves around publication order versus internal-chronological order. I favor internal chronological, with a few adjustments.

It was always my intention to write each book as a stand-alone, so that the reader could theoretically jump in anywhere. While still somewhat true, as the series developed it acquired a number of sub-arcs, closely related tales that were richer for each other. I will list the sub-arcs, and then the books, and then the duplication warnings. (My publishing history has been complex.) And then the publication order, for those who want it.

Shards of Honor and *Barrayar*. The first two books in the series proper, they detail the adventures of Cordelia Naismith of Beta Colony and Aral Vorkosigan of Barrayar. *Shards* was my very first novel ever; *Barrayar* was actually my eighth, but continues the tale the next day after the end of *Shards*. For readers who want to be sure of beginning at the beginning, or who are very spoiler-sensitive, start with these two.

The Warrior's Apprentice and *The Vor Game* (with, perhaps, the novella "The Mountains of Mourning" tucked in between.) *The Warrior's Apprentice* introduces the character who became the series' linchpin, Miles Vorkosigan; the first book tells how he created a space mercenary fleet by accident; the second how he fixed his mistakes from the first round. Space opera and military-esque adventure (and a number of other things one can best discover for oneself), *The Warrior's Apprentice* makes another good place to jump into the series for readers who prefer a young male protagonist.

After that: *Brothers in Arms* should be read before *Mirror Dance*, and both, ideally, before *Memory*.

Komarr makes another alternate entry point for the series, picking up Miles's second career at its start. It should be read before *A Civil Campaign*.

Borders of Infinity, a collection of three of the five currently extant novellas, makes a good Miles Vorkosigan early-adventure sampler platter, I always thought, for readers who don't want to commit themselves to length. (But it may make more sense if read after *The Warrior's Apprentice*.) Take care not to confuse the collection-as-a-whole with its title story, "The Borders of Infinity".

Falling Free takes place 200 years earlier in the timeline and does not share settings or characters with the main body of the series. Most readers recommend picking up this story later. It should likely be read before *Diplomatic Immunity*, however, which revisits the "quaddies", a bioengineered race of free-fall dwellers, in Miles's time.

The novels in the internal-chronological list below appear in italics; the novellas (officially defined as a story between 17,500 words and 45,000 words) in quote marks.

Falling Free
Shards of Honor
Barrayar
The Warrior's Apprentice
"The Mountains of Mourning"
"Weatherman"
The Vor Game
Cetaganda
Ethan of Athos
Borders of Infinity
"Labyrinth"
"The Borders of Infinity"
Brothers in Arms
Mirror Dance
Memory
Komarr
A Civil Campaign
"Winterfair Gifts"
Diplomatic Immunity
Captain Vorpatril's Alliance

"The Flowers of Vashnoi"
CryoBurn
Gentleman Jole and the Red Queen

Caveats:

The novella "Weatherman" is an out-take from the beginning of the novel *The Vor Game*. If you already have *The Vor Game*, you likely don't need this.

The original "novel" *Borders of Infinity* was a fix-up collection containing the three novellas "The Mountains of Mourning", "Labyrinth", and "The Borders of Infinity", together with a frame to tie the pieces together. Again, beware duplication. The frame story does not stand alone.

Publication order:

This is also the order in which the works were written, apart from a couple of the novellas, but is not identical to the internal-chronological. It goes:

Shards of Honor (June 1986)
The Warrior's Apprentice (August 1986)
Ethan of Athos (December 1986)
Falling Free (April 1988)
Brothers in Arms (January 1989)
Borders of Infinity (October 1989)
The Vor Game (September 1990)
Barrayar (October 1991)
Mirror Dance (March 1994)
Cetaganda (January 1996)
Memory (October 1996)
Komarr (June 1998)

A Civil Campaign (September 1999)
Diplomatic Immunity (May 2002)
"Winterfair Gifts" (February 2004)
CryoBurn (November 2010)
Captain Vorpatril's Alliance (November 2012)
Gentleman Jole and the Red Queen (February 2016)
"The Flowers of Vashnoi" (May 2018)

. . . Thirty-plus years fitted on a page. Huh.

Happy reading!

—Lois McMaster Bujold